Client-Centred Dog Training

30 LESSONS FOR DOG TRAINERS TO GET MAXIMUM ENGAGEMENT FROM YOUR CLIENTS

By Emma Jane Lee

CLIENT-CENTRED DOG TRAINING
30 Lessons For Dog Trainers To Get Maximum Engagement
From Your Clients
Written by Emma Jane Lee ©2021 by Emma Jane Lee. All rights reserved.

All rights reserved. No part of this publication may be reproduced or transmitted in any form or by any means, electronic or mechanical, including photocopy, recording, or any information storage and retrieval system, without permission, in writing, from the author.

Emma Jane Lee
emma_janelee@hotmail.com
www.woofliketomeet.com

JC Studio Press
Design and Illustration by Jane Cornwell
www.janecornwell.co.uk

ISBN: 978-1-7399088-0-5

To all involved in the relentless pursuit of better lives for animals.

Emma Jane Lee

Client-Centred Dog Training

30 LESSONS FOR DOG TRAINERS TO GET MAXIMUM ENGAGEMENT FROM YOUR CLIENTS

Virtually every training organisation that helps you prepare for working with human clients and their companion animals is focused on the canine element. You can specialise in behaviour issues or training, be that obedience, rally or even just basic manners classes. Virtual training schools have popped up globally to help you learn how to train animals. Even if you arrive as a graduate with a BSc, MSc or PhD that grants you access to Certified Applied Animal

Behaviourist status, you'll most likely have spent the majority of your time focusing on training the animals. Skinner, Pavlov, Watson and Thorndike will have been your primers. You might be able to quote Ken Ramirez, Bob Bailey or Karen Pryor verbatim. But nobody trained you for the human element. Nobody told you that your human clients would bring you messy and disorganised scenarios, that they'd be all thumbs even when it comes to playing a simple game like 'Find it!', that they'd be filled with grudges and resentments, or that they'd disengage half way through a training programme for no good reason at all.

This book hopes to address all of that.

What I will share with you in this manual are all the ways I've found to coach humans better. That comes off the back of twenty five years of working with people, of leading them (or, at least, trying to) and of reading a lot of manuals about coaching - then trying to sharpen my own practice in the real world. What follows are thirty lessons from human psychology, from change management and from client-centred consultancy, adapted especially for dog trainers and behaviour consultants.

It's my strong belief that dog training courses should spend at least 50% of the time on dealing with and teaching humans. Sadly, most dog training courses don't teach this vital bit in any detail, if at all. Some leave you with a qualification in training dogs with a licence to go into the world and get a job, yet don't include a single unit on dealing with people. If you were just going to train dogs and never work with humans, you'd do well in a shelter, since these ownerless dogs don't come with the complex human attachment that makes working with dogs so challenging for so many of us. But I'm guessing you're running classes or you're working in one-to-ones and nobody prepared you for the fact that a sixty-year-old retired firefighter might start ranting at you just because they couldn't get their timing right. Or that a forty-year-old office manager would be quite so reluctant about every single proposal you suggest to help her house-train her dog. The truth is that nobody tells you working the human side will be quite so hard. This manual aims to help you with that.

If you want to know why your human clients are so messy, irrational, difficult, lazy, disengaged, contradictory, surly, stroppy, argumentative or challenging, and why you can be so stubborn, opinionated, touchy, defensive or vulnerable to their barbed comments, slights, slings and arrows, these lessons are designed to help you get the best out of them and the best out of yourself. If nothing else, you'll pick up 30 tricks that will help give you a competitive edge.

And, if you want more, the courses at The DoGenius are designed to really help you get the best out of the human side, as well as give you a certified qualification.

Emma Lee
July 2021

Contents

1.	Appreciate the virtues of client-centred coaching	10
2.	Decide who you are and specialise	16
3.	Understand the beauty of efficient systems	20
4.	Understand the shadow side of human behaviour	26
5.	Streamline your front-of-house services	32
6.	Triage	40
7.	Streamline your intake system	52
8.	Let your client tell their story	64
9.	Learn how to manage your judgey face	70
10.	Recognise and challenge your client's blind spots	85
11.	Recognise and challenge your own blind spots	94
12.	Understand and deflect the negativity bias	101
13.	Learn how to see objectively	110
14.	Stop, collaborate and listen	136
15.	Learn to match solutions to problems	148
16.	Bring hope	156
17.	Understand human habit forming	164
18.	Understand why change is difficult	176
19.	Appreciate the fallout of stress	182
20.	Learn when to take negative feedback seriously	188

21.	Learn how to let unqualified negative feedback go	196
22.	Learn how to give good feedback and be a cheerleader	205
23.	Secure commitment	213
24.	Learn how to set realistic goals	232
25.	Understand and deflect the optimism bias	240
26.	Understand how humans learn	246
27.	Get feedback	259
28.	Understand biases and the irrational ways humans think	264
29.	Reinforce boundaries	272
30.	Keep learning about people, and never stop	286
31.	Concluding Statement	290
32.	Further reading	292
33.	About me	294

1. Appreciate the virtues of client-centred coaching

There are essentially three different models of how we work with humans and their problems: the doctor-patient model, the expert model and the client-centred model.

The first is the doctor-patient model. In this scenario, the client feels that something is wrong and that they need an expert to make a diagnosis. The client may have a sense that something doesn't feel right, or that there's some kind of problem, but they don't know exactly what it is. We have this relationship with our veterinarians. We have a suspicion that something is wrong, but even if we've seen the same problem a number of times before, it's the vet who will make the diagnosis.

In this model, the vet is the one with the knowledge and we approach them for a diagnosis and a solution. All being well, even if they have to send us for specialised tests, we should get a diagnosis. If the problem is treatable, we should get a solution too. If it's not treatable, then the veterinarian should at least be able to offer some treatments that can alleviate some of the symptoms. Dog training can also work on this model, especially in one-to-ones, where clients approach us with a problem, perhaps suspecting what that problem is, and they are seeking an accurate diagnosis of the problem and a solution.

The second model is the expert model. In this scenario, the client already knows what is wrong and they need the expert to fix it. Sometimes that's not because of lack of skill, but because of lack of time or resources. Groomers are one example of an expert model. As clients, we know our dogs need grooming or clipping and we send them to people who have expertise in this area.

In this model, the expert is the one with the skills where the client has some knowledge about what the problem is. Puppy classes or obedience classes are another example of how dog trainers might work within an expert-client model, where the client knows exactly what they need; they pay the expert to deliver a very specific set of skills to address that need. To an extent, all kinds of dog classes are built around the expert-client model. The trainer is knowledgeable and skilled in agility, protection sports, obedience, rally, scentwork, detection work and so on. Clients approach them with a very specific need and they respond by delivering a very specific set of expertise.

Finally, the client-centred or person-centred approach. This is a relatively new approach as we move away from the expert and doctor-patient models. It's rooted in person-centred approaches from the therapeutic community in the 1950s, where psychologists such as Carl Rogers realised that many humans already have the skills and resources to be able to make the best choices. They may not have all the knowledge available yet, but once presented with that knowledge they are best placed to make the right choices for themselves. The role of the dog trainer when working in a client-centred way is to help our clients make the right decisions for themselves, and to help them overcome any obstacles that might stand in their way.

This model grew out of the fact that, even when clients present diagnosticians and experts with a problem, they often fail to engage with the solution. Even doctors are now moving away from a rigid adherence to the doctor-patient model as they come to realise that there are often many solutions rather than just one, particularly where psychological or psychiatric problems are present.

For instance, take the example of depression. Depression is a very common reason for people to visit their GP. A doctor or psychiatrist is the only person qualified to diagnose depression. Once they have done so, they may then offer their patients a treatment, such as Cognitive Behavioural Therapy or an anti-depressant medication. Now, we're coming to realise that a dietician or nutritionist might also help, or that physical activity or social support might be the solution, rather than a pill. Doctors may also consider developmental stages and design a solution appropriate to the needs of the patient. Ideally, anyway.

What health practitioners are coming to realise is that both physiological and psychological problems often have complex and interrelated causes. Humans are messy, illogical, irrational and complex. They come with deep-seated, sometimes subconscious or unspoken reasons that mean they fail to take their medication, even if it will cure them or prolong their life.

The internet has also turned many people into armchair experts, meaning they come already primed to refuse medications for reasons that often seem irrational to practitioners who are much more conscious of the successes of treatments compared to their very rare side-effects. Practitioners are also faced with the fact that the internet has also opened up their clients' eyes to the whole range of potential treatments, and that many patients are also arriving fully-armed with the range of solutions to their problem, or that they are actually capable of good research themselves. Clients can no longer be fobbed off with a simple pill if they realise that dietary or lifestyle changes might be more appropriate to their own unique situation, or if there are better choices available from the range of potential treatments on offer. Doctors are much more likely to offer you pathways and choices about your treatment, once you know what the problem is, because they realise only you can decide what's right for yourself. Informed consent is all about offering you all the information you need about the risks, side-effects and benefits of a treatment, intervention or procedure, and letting you make the decision. The medical world has realised that most people are able to make choices they are more likely to stick to if they can choose a treatment that best fits their unique circumstances.

What we need to be doing as dog trainers is thinking about the concept of informed consent within our own work. Informed consent, the process of both getting all the pertinent information from the client as well as making sure they understand the facts, implications and consequences involved in treatments, is ultimately about dignity and agency. That's why it's timely that dog trainers should also think about moving away from the doctor-patient model if we want to be truly respectful of our clients - both the human ones and the canine ones.

To some degree, dog trainers are stuck in the doctor-patient model. A client calls. You diagnose food guarding. You send your client a copy of Mine! by Jean Donaldson, or sign them up to any other proprietary package that has been designed to treat food guarding behaviour, and then you leave them to it. Or you might use your own individual package that you've designed yourself. After all, there is little new in the world of dog behaviour. There are a limited range of behaviour problems or training issues that guardians may present you with; if you spent a year or so, you could probably design a solution to all problems. You could create a nifty video package complete with daily step-by-step guidance, illustrated text books, and you could simply refer your clients to your neat, carefully constructed, pre-made packages.

It's the same in the training world. You could design a very slick package of in-person or virtual step-by-step instructions for agility, for protection sports, or for obedience - whatever it is you are in the business of selling - and there are many wonderfully skilled dog trainers who work in this way. You can buy an online package with varying degrees of support, coaching and feedback. You can buy graded programmes of support where you pay more for an increased level of instruction from the masters. In the modern world, the best dog trainers have the potential to solve all our dogs' problems or training needs with a carefully-priced package. World-renowned experts already sell packages like this; you've no doubt already completed courses using this approach or read How To guides from the masters.

So why aren't guardians simply signing up to a great package from someone who is probably a much better, much more experienced trainer than we are? Especially where that package has the opportunity for one-to-one feedback from the best experts on that subject in the world?

The answer is that humans are suckers for How To books. Self-help sections of libraries and bookshops are immensely profitable. It's a huge market. There are at least three really, really good books out there on separation anxiety, for example, that if a guardian were to read all three, they would be able to solve their dogs' problems with separation-related behaviours. Yet humans often need more than How To books, DVDs, or videos on YouTube, helpful as those may be. It's also when life is most stressful that following the simple step-by-step guides becomes really complex. These packages also don't respect the client as an individual, nor do they really respect the client's agency or individuality with a one-size-fits-all approach. Interaction is one of the missing ingredients from these packages, wonderful as they can be. Negotiation and bespoke tailoring are two others.

We also need more than interaction. Many of the blended learning packages - where you can access reading materials, videos and feedback from the course tutors - don't offer bespoke training that fits you, your dog, your needs and your situation. They're relatively inflexible, even if there is feedback. There's no way to deviate from the programme.

We are also human beings. We are social animals who learn from others and who learn from feedback. This is why working in ways that respect your client will help you ensure you are delivering what your client truly needs, not just what you think they need. We work better when we move away from expert-client models and move towards a clearer understanding of our client's needs.

2. Decide who you are and specialise

There is a really good reason many clients fail to truly engage: us!

It is really tempting when you start a career as a dog trainer or behaviour consultant to offer all things to every person who calls. You may find yourself offering agility and puppy socialisation classes, one-to-ones on behaviour, dog walking classes, reactive dog classes and even offering in-house support.

Even if you love dogs, being a jack of all trades means that you will inevitably come into contact with people who need you to be more than a generalist. These cases are inevitably frustrating all round. We're frustrated because we don't have the specialist knowledge to help the client, or because we don't enjoy that particular aspect of working with them. As your career unrolls, use this frustration to guide both your learning and your own specialisation. If you truly hate working with the people side of dog training, then there are certainly opportunities out there and specialisms where you won't have as much contact. If you feel this frustration is one you want to overcome, you can always do this through professional development. However, the problems of being a generalist are often more than simply running into people who frustrate us or situations we find challenging to handle.

Bringing your passion to the table is a vital aspect of client engagement, believe it or not. When we are truly passionate about the dogs we are working with and the situations they present, then we can tolerate a certain level of challenge from the people who come attached to them. But if we're already finding the situation difficult, unimportant, frustrating or unrewarding, then the person who is most likely to disengage from the client-trainer relationship is most likely to be us.

Clients disengage. They do so both formally and informally. If they find major fault with what we're doing, it's likely to end in a huge confrontation.

More often than not, however, clients simply tail off. For our behaviour cases, our clients arrive in conflict. They arrive with problems and in need of support. Often, their calls are precipitated by a worsening of the situation and the fact that they've probably reached rock bottom.

Once things inevitably start to improve and once we remove some of the straws from the proverbial camel's back, many people are happy to stick where they are. If their dogs are barking at other dogs in the street, as soon as it gets to a more manageable level, our clients are likely to stop putting the same amount of effort in.

Likewise for our puppy classes, even if we offer a package deal. We inevitably start with the most important aspects of puppy learning; as soon as people reach a point where their puppy is relatively obedient, the majority of clients will just stop there. Life gets in the way. The first time there is the slightest speed bump on the way to puppy class, then clients are likely to let puppy class slide. Be it a late finish at work, a parents' evening, a bit of snow on the road or a hard day, once clients miss a class, then we're much less likely to see them again.

Not only that, but their embarrassment at having disengaged is likely to be poisonous enough that they just aren't going to contact us again the next time something goes wrong.

Even if we're running weekly agility classes or we're running adult dog socialisation walks, once people break the habit, they're likely to disengage completely. The same thing is true of most club memberships, be it sports club, chess club or gym memberships. How many people sign up for the gym in January and never go again after the first two weeks? The first speed bump and people check out, never to check back in again.

In order to overcome this, you either need clients who are committed enough in the first place or you need commitment yourself. Ideally, you need both.

Committed clients are some of the last people to accept a mediocre trainer, however. If you've got obedience students who want to win competitions, they need you to be able to coach them to get there. That will take expertise and a degree of insider knowledge. If you've got clients who are absolutely determined to take their fearful foreign rescue and turn them into a dog who can accept most social situations, then that is going to take your very best game. If you're a generalist, you are much less likely to be able to offer that, and they're likely to leave in search of someone who can.

On the flip side, most of the people you will work with will lack motivation and commitment from time to time. Particularly if they've signed up to a package, the first time they fail to show up, you're probably going to let that slide unless you are truly invested in the dogs, the family and the situation.

Sometimes, your commitment is going to be the driving force behind your professional relationship.

If you lack the motivation or drive because you're really not that enamoured, then you can expect disengagement. If one thing is true, it's the fact that sometimes, you'll need to chase up your clients from time to time. You're only going to do that if you're invested in the situation. If you're running puppy classes and you hate every minute, you're likely to just take their money and run. If you're working fearful dog cases and you love every minute, you're likely to check in with your clients and chase them up if they skip a session.

Another reason to specialise and find your passion within the dog training world is that it is a highly populated world, particularly by amateurs who tend to offer opinions from behind a keyboard. It's a noisy world where it can be difficult to find your voice. Truly knowing your stuff is one way to make your voice stand out. It's also the very best way to be really good at what you are doing. There is simply too much to learn to be a master of all trades, no matter how much you'd like to be. When you look at the very best trainers and behaviour consultants around the world, you'll notice that they are all specialists in their field. Occasionally, they may have two specialisms, but rarely more. There is a reason for this. When you're spread so thin, it's impossible to keep up with developments. You become a dilettante rather than an expert. Unless we have a real passion for what we're doing, driven by a deep love and a profound understanding, then we're also going to be in the same position as our clients: when speed bumps occur, we're the first to find a million reasons not to keep going.

It feels good to unburden yourself of all the bits you don't like doing. Also, it's going to help you with many of the other lessons in this manual.

3. Understand the beauty of efficient systems

In his work on organisational systems, psychologist Gerard Egan talks often about what he calls the 'shadow side' of people: the messy, covert, complex and often unspoken values, ethics, ideas, prejudices, cultures and attitudes that sometimes act as a block on change or progress. It is true that most of this manual is about the human side of the client relationship. However, in a helping relationship like that of a dog trainer and client, success also depends on a healthy workflow and good systems.

People sometimes think of systems as paperwork and mechanisms, and to some degree that is true. However, the "systems" side of things cannot - and should not - be divorced from the "human" side of things. They are integrated and impact constantly on one another. Smooth systems, however, allow you to iron out the many of the "people" problems that emerge. Messy systems don't allow many people to function, especially in the business world.

Imagine, for instance, that you need to buy a new car. You go into the showroom and all the cars are housed out back in a huge lot, where there is absolutely no organisation whatsoever. Four thousand cars of different sizes, values, purposes and ages. You need a relatively new, small car for four people, within a certain budget. When you're spending your time wandering around four thousand cars trying to find the one you do want, it's frustrating and likely to bring out the worst in you. Add a lack of sales staff, a lack of any kind of reference system and a lack of any kind of logical way to get what you need, then you can understand why this particular showroom won't have very many clients. Change is uncomfortable, and if your systems are unpredictable, then this will contribute to your clients' frustration as well as their discomfort.

Having efficient systems is not just about your clients: it's about you. How many of us have a list of expectations for the social media groups and pages that we run, yet don't have these for our real-life in-person meetings? It's important at the beginning of the contracting period to set out expectations so that clients know what kind of things might warrant a phone call on a Sunday night, and which things need to wait until office hours.

Many self-employed people, as many dog trainers are, or small businesses suffer from their work life bleeding into their home life. Where in France it is a state-mandated employment law that employers cannot contact their employees at home outside of office hours, there are no provisions that stop clients contacting you at 11pm on a Friday evening. It is up to us to keep the divisions clean. We can only cope with the messiness of people if we have clear systems in place to help them understand what is urgent and what is not. Without clear systems - and this goes throughout the entire contracting period - then the person most likely to suffer from that is you, Clients can simply disengage and go elsewhere.

Many dog trainers and behaviour consultants get into dog training because they like dogs, and they accept that they are going to have to work with people. Few dog trainers get into dog training because they like people, and they accept that they are going to have to work with dogs. Fewer still are going to choose careers with canines that involve human interaction if they find humans to be terrifying. Mostly, we're "dog" people - or "animal" people. Not necessarily "people" people, let alone "systems" people. For that reason, unless we're particularly into the mechanics of life and training, we can find it hard to appreciate how important systems are. Smooth operating systems make everything that sits on top of them run smoothly too.

Without an efficient system, there are many problems that can occur.

Lack of flexibility within the system means that you are likely to be delivering one-size-fits-all training programmes and packages. These are fine, but one size certainly does not fit all. There are a lot of packages like that out there on the market, from virtual ones from master dog trainers, right through to ones running in your local village hall. There are reasons people don't want this - usually because they need something bespoke. If you don't have a flexible system and you haven't planned for flexibility, you will eventually find that, under pressure, your system fails both you and your client, as you don't have capacity to adapt. Rigid systems and lack of turning space are what lead to giant-sized tankers crashing on sandbanks. You don't want to be the same.

Too much bespoke in the system, however, means that you will forever be reinventing the wheel. Thankfully, unlike humans, there are a relatively limited number of problems that dogs present with: there are many packages that you can easily adapt for specific circumstances. If you're forever creating entirely individualised programmes for each unique client and their own idiosyncratically messy life, you will find that you are spending so much time planning and supporting that you aren't spending as much time as you'd like delivering. Entirely unique programmes aren't necessary.

Being able to deliver what the client truly wants in a way that doesn't involve completely reinventing each programme is a key feature of an efficient system.

Systems failure also means that you'll have a messy front of house, just like that example of the car showroom. If you haven't got your workflow sorted and the rough edges smoothed off, this will be evident in everything you share on social media, on your website and in your practice. This comes back to why we need to specialise. The most successful (in terms of marketing and presence) dog trainers are those who are clear in their purpose. Everything else hangs off that. Their videos, social media posts, blog posts, articles, talks, presentations and in-person work is a smooth and efficient system that presents them coherently and consistently. If they're heavily involved in agility, all their videos and posts will seamlessly show that. While there is always room for individuality, we should not confuse messiness with individuality. Messy systems aren't quirky or fun. They're just confusing for clients. Knowing who we are, what we deliver and how we deliver it underpins a professional image. When everything dovetails neatly, that's attractive to would-be clients. You can be exactly who you are without making yourself look unprofessional.

Systems give you clarity. A clean workflow and a polished, tailored approach gives your work a certainty that clients need when they come to us at times of stress or confusion in their own lives. You're not trading in state secrets to outline your puppy plan on your website, or to share your objectives. What you are doing is communicating clearly so that your clients can make the right choice for them. This saves them the disappointment later when they realise they've signed up to something that doesn't deliver what they need.

Systems underpin good measurement and formalised work. Many dog trainers are highly enthusiastic experts. A client rings to say their dog has growled over their food bowl and before they know it, we've recommended a book, a DVD and a work plan. We've signed them up to 6 hours of support for food guarding without really getting to the bottom of the behaviour. When our work is unsuccessful, when the behaviour escalates or changes, then our systems have also failed us.

When we don't have a clean workflow, we spend more time than we need. For instance, if you regularly use Lightroom or Photoshop to edit photos, you'll understand that the best photographers have a workflow. They may run through a series of well-rehearsed adjustments and processes before spending a little time on each individual image. Because their workflow is so well refined and smooth, they aren't spending time messing about clumsily like an eleven-year-old trying to choose a font for a school project. Good systems are incredibly liberating, time-wise. That leaves you more time for doing what you truly love: working with dogs.

Another reason a good system is important is that it stops overload or periods of slack. In future lessons, we will be discussing the need for a good triage or sorting systems for incoming clients. When you've put time into the system to audit your workload, to look at the kind of cases you want, and to consider how you can get more of those, you also need to be able to handle the other cases efficiently but without wasting time on them.

Many people, especially busy and talented people, work in the same way as overworked firefighters, constantly running around putting out fires without realising that their own hair is on fire and the firetruck is out of fuel. The busier you get and the more clients you have, the better systems you will need in place. Better to have those from the beginning and adapt slightly than get to a point where you are working a 70-hour week doing reactive dog classes and dealing with barking dogs when you'd really rather be coaching dog dance for the Nationals. This manual will help you get those systems in place, but you can see now why Lesson 2 was so important.

When we're working without clear systems, we're also more likely to make snap calls, rush judgements or make gut reactions. Often, these will work out just fine, especially if we're knowledgeable and experienced. However, failure to take time to really assess the problems is a fault of poor systems and planning. It might only take you 10 minutes to confirm your judgement, to spend time discussing it with your client, to ask more probing questions or to get a bit of video, but if you don't have slack in the system, you won't have time to do this.

Systems make everything run smoothly in the background. Our own sanity and income depend on us getting it right. It liberates you from spending time on tasks you hate and gives you more time to spend on the things you enjoy. Our clients depend on it too. If you're working a 70-hour week, you're the last person someone will be able to get hold of in an emergency. That's when you'll realise that fatigue is not just a term for our own tiredness and feelings of being overwhelmed: stress is also the term used in engineering to test how structures cope under pressure. When structures fail due to stress, this is also known as fatigue. The exact same principles are at work within our own workload. Because smooth and functional systems are so vital, if perhaps tedious to set up in the first place, we'll spend some time exploring ways to make yours more efficient. You'll learn more about how to create these smooth and efficient systems in Lessons 5, 6 and 8.

4. Understand the shadow side of human behaviour

As you read in the previous lesson, organisational psychologist Gerard Egan writes in his work about what he calls the 'shadow side' of organisations. While he means this term to be used about workplaces, it is also applicable to individuals. According to Egan, humans are an interwoven blend of the rational and the a-rational, where sometimes rational and logical processes will dominate and other times, more complex and covert processes are at work. He calls the 'a-rational' to signal that they are not irrational, running contrary to the rational, but they just work without a clear logic in the same way as rational things do. Just like we can think of dogs as being "amoral" or without human senses of morality and ethics, rather than immoral - running deliberately against human codes of behaviour and conduct - so these shadow-side processes should be seen as neither bad nor counterintuitive. The shadow side, then, is not something bad or nefarious. It is just something we need to understand when we engage with people to help them. We can even harness the shadow side to help fuel progress.

Shadow-side issues are covert and difficult to discuss. Later, you will read about human blind spots and dissonant ways of thinking, and in some ways, these are very much part of the shadow side. Unlike rational and logical processes, shadow-side issues are often unmentioned or difficult to describe. These can be our deep-seated attitudes or values, our culture, our ethics or our beliefs. Sometimes these might be hard to articulate or describe. Other times, they might be so entrenched in who we are that it can be very difficult to discuss them without feeling uncomfortable.

The concept of shadow sides is also rooted in other psychological perspectives. Carl Jung used the idea to talk about all the things that make up ourselves that are unknown or unconscious. Unlike earlier Freudian understanding, a Jungian approach is similar to that of Egan. Shadow sides are neither good nor bad, neither moral nor immoral, neither positive nor negative. All of these ideas help us understand what Egan meant when he talked about the shadow side of helping relationships.

Let's look at one example. As rational and empirical dog trainers, we know that punishment only suppresses behaviour temporarily. We know that positive reinforcement, by its very nature, is successful. We know that using things that dogs find valuable, like good food, is designed to succeed. We understand how these training methods function from the very great number of behavioural experiments using animals in psychology, and in behaviour science laboratories or research institutes across the world. Yet when we work with people, we would expect that they grasp these concepts too, and that they would, on the balance of evidence, be able to make a logical and rational choice about what training methods to employ with their dog.

Despite this, we can often run up against unspoken conflict that sits beneath the surface as an obstacle or block on progress. We can face petty resentments and cynicism. Our clients may be acerbic, given to complete cessation of positive training methods over the smallest hurdle. We, too, may consciously work within a least intrusive, minimally aversive framework - yet find ourselves yelling at our dog when they snatch a sandwich from the table. Why is this?

Often, it is the underlying "people" side of things. It's our view that dogs should just be obedient, that they should follow our instructions willingly and blindly because they are dogs and that is what dogs are supposed to do. Or we may feel angry for having to "pay out" when our dogs haven't "deserved it". Tied up in our relationship with dogs is a 15,000-year-old story about commensal relationships that has been subsumed in the West by a 3000-year-old narrative about mastery, dominance and loyalty. Dominance and inequality are pervasive themes in the modern world - a shadow side of our own cultures. Dog ownership can also be tied up in gender issues: a dog is supposed to be obedient to their master and if they aren't, some men may find this a challenge to their very masculinity. Our relationship with dogs can be tied up with issues about care and femininity, too. It's not rare to hear people speak of their "ungrateful" dogs in the same way they might speak about their children.

All of these beliefs and behaviours are part of what Egan called the shadow side.

We might assume that the shadow side is always negative. Frequently, these cultural or individual beliefs and behaviours about dogs in general, or our own idiosyncratic attitudes to our own dogs as individuals, are seen to be things that run counter to logic and rationale.

Our local shelter vet in France, who is also my own personal vet, often says that Anglophones make better choices about euthanasia, for example. It is true that in our shelter, both behavioural and medical euthanasia are scrupulously discussed by our staff and volunteers in ways that I don't think are as evident in British shelters. While France is a secular country, Catholic values about life run deep and influence both law and belief systems. These Catholic values mean that euthanasia can sometimes be seen as taking a decision that is God's alone. Even if you grow up in a secular household in France, you are exposed more frequently to these beliefs than in countries where Protestantism is the dominant paradigm. Both Catholicism and Protestantism have been used to justify a theocentric or anthropocentric worldview where God or Man is at the top of the ladder, and all the animals are beneath. When thinking of euthanasia in these traditions, it may be that animal life is more easily justified as expendable, especially if the animal is costly or if they are in conflict with humans. These unspoken views are the kind of issues that shape our choices and our behaviours, and those of our clients. Understanding them is important. So often, these beliefs - whether about something relatively trivial, such as whether a dog should sit when told, or whether they are about something that is literally a life-or-death matter - affect our behaviour and are stubbornly resistant to objective discussion.

At the same time, when we hear anecdotes like this, it may just be the unspoken values and beliefs held by my vet. It may have absolutely no basis in evidence. Later, when we explore storytelling and blind spots, you will understand how we construct narratives to explain our situations, but also understand how these can be tangled up in messy belief systems.

Dealing with shadow-side issues starts by our acknowledgement of them.

The final shadow-side issues may very well be our own.

Of all the conversations I have had with my vet, this comment has stuck with me. Perhaps it says more about me than it does about her or about French culture. In most likelihood, all three are likely to play a part in the tangled and messy beliefs that can alter the way we behave. When we consider shadow sides, we should always consider our own. If we do not, they can derail our own work and our own relationships with clients. If we get too stuck in our own "truths" without acknowledging them as our own unspoken and messy belief systems, it can make us too rigid to work with clients whose unspoken views and attitudes are different in turn.

These issues sit beneath the surface and, if we are not careful, they can derail our progress and cause us conflict with our clients. Indeed, working with clients from different cultural backgrounds on cases where behavioural euthanasia needs to be discussed can be one complex example of this. However, it's not always the very large issues that are affected by shadow-side tensions. It can affect even the very choices we make about what training methods to use with our dogs. The unspoken differences that have led to the proliferation of the use of punishers in some cultures compared to others provide just one example of how these issues affect our work. Understanding that they exist is the first step in understanding that we can't fight shadow-side thinking with logic. It simply does not work that way. Anyone who has tried to engage clients' shadow-side issues over punishers by using logic will have a good understanding of the fact that it fails. However, understanding shadow-side issues means that we will be better placed to work with clients when they emerge. Doing this successfully underpins the remaining lessons in this manual.

Yet cultural factors and individual belief systems can also be harnessed to make progress. When we truly understand what makes our clients tick, then we can harness this to fuel their actions. For instance, you may find that your client is incredibly logical, verging on cynical. They may find fault in whatever you suggest, finding flaws in all of your recommendations. We can see this as a shadow side, of course, and it may derail our relationship. Their troubleshooting skills may cause them to hesitate from taking action. Yet we can also harness this skill in helping them move forwards. When we ask critics to help us troubleshoot all the potential tensions and drawbacks, and then draw up a practical list of solutions with them, we may find that the training plan that they build on the back of their concerns is actually much more solid than any we might have proposed.

The rest of this manual will focus on how to work with those unspoken and sometimes unconscious shadow-side issues, but for now the main thing to understand is that these can either provide anchors that stop us taking action in the first place, or speed bumps that slow us down. They can form insurmountable obstacles if we don't at least acknowledge them. Yet when we work with the shadow side, we can truly engage our clients and get the most out of them.

5. Streamline your front-of-house services

Although shadow-side issues can profoundly impact our work and even derail it, putting smooth systems in place can help mitigate some of the damage that the "people" side of our work may do. The next three lessons focus on systems. In Lesson 3, you saw the example of a disorganised car sales showroom as an example of a frustrating and inefficient system. Many of us would walk away from such a messy workplace. The same is true with our potential clients.

Most of what our clients see of us comes via a one-way process before they even call us. Sometimes, it happens before they even think of calling us. It's easiest to think of this as a one-way process simply because even if there is a facility for clients to engage with us, most of our potential clients will not. They're making their mind up about us and the services we offer, and we have very little say in the matter.

Sometimes, we don't even realise we are haemorrhaging clients right from the get-go.

Most of the problems that emerge at this point fall into one of two categories. The first category relates to systems. The second relates to the shadow-side issues.

Shadow-side issues can cause us to lose clients right from the outset. Sometimes this is a positive filtration system. For instance, if we deliberately set out to showcase our training methods and those methods we eschew, then people who use the methods that we will not engage in are unlikely to engage with us in the first place. That can certainly save you a lot of hard work in confronting attitudes that don't conform with your own. If you present yourself with fluffy pink bunnies and rainbow unicorns, then you'll no doubt get clients who believe madly in fluffy pink bunnies and rainbow unicorns, and you won't ever really have to deal with the kind of clients who don't believe in magic. Even if you are the only trainer in a one-hundred-mile radius, if you wear your heart on your sleeve when it comes to sharing your own ethos, it's a solid way to ensure that you won't ever have to deal with people who don't think like you do. There are some people who'd rather live with their complicated canines than approach someone who seems so very different from themselves.

That's a choice you can make.

On the other hand, when you don't set out your stall and you don't wear your heart on your sleeve, ethically speaking, you can pick up a good number of clients who are yet to place their own bets and haven't really got an opinion.

Whichever way you go should be your own, personal, conscious, rational decision.

Social media and business entrepreneur Leonie Dawson is one such example. She consciously and deliberately chooses to market her shimmering, turquoise, magical mermaid sweary self. Nobody would sign up to Leonie's masterclasses without engaging in her truly authentic self. You wouldn't get past her landing page without having made a decision that your own shadow side is in tune with her very overt, very smart, highly educated, wonderfully creative and very authentic self.

Many people sign up for exactly that. We are our brand. We can choose to be our full-frontal, love-it-or-leave-it self and if we do, then we should do so consciously and know the fallout of doing so.

On the other hand, many people want to present an image of themselves as blank and professional. No turquoise (unless it's been chosen for its corporate values and meanings). No glitter. No sweary mermaids. No unicorns. No rainbows. No impromptu 3am podcasts. But the risks of this approach are that you never stand out. Worse still, because none of your potential clients know what you stand for, they fail to find any rapport with you whatsoever and fail to engage. Like it or not, most of what attracts people to our business in the first place is likely to be rapport and trust. If they can't see us because we're hidden behind the grey frosting of a professional image, we're likely to spend much of our time either in conflict with clients whose ethics are not aligned with our own, or having to downplay our own ethics.

There is, of course, a middle ground. This is one reason Lesson 2 was about working out who you are, what you stand for and specialising.

Finding your own balance for front-of-house materials is something to do in the infancy of your business. It's also something to consider in terms of what you want to say about yourself.

Coming back to the car salesroom image, do you go with sleek chrome and anonymous, robotic salespeople? Do you go with your own authentic self, be that messy, quirky, whimsical or wise? Plenty of people prefer the personal experience and are happy to buy a car from a one-person business, especially if they feel like they can trust the person they're buying from. You can, of course, find a middle ground that is neither too much of one nor too much of the other.

From a psychological perspective, these things matter. They communicate a message. They're also one-way. This means the information is passive rather than transactional or dynamic. Your website, your social media pages, even your adverts in local papers or your posters outside the local church hall are all things that don't involve much of an exchange of communication. This is why we first need to decide who we are.

The next thing we should do is make sure that all of our public faces are dovetailed. Your YouTube channel should say the same things as your website. These should say the same things as your social media presence.

Since these are a one-way process, make sure they communicate exactly what you want to your clients.

To make these a first, efficient cog in your efficient work machine, make sure they're acting as the filter you intend them to be. If you want to attract a wider range of clients, then make sure you don't pin your heart too obviously to your sleeve. That way, you won't put off prospective clients who might still be sitting on the fence. If you don't want to attract clients who expect you to train their dogs with shock collars and prong collars, make sure you say so. You don't want to be three lessons into a contract and only then realise that you're not truly invested because you think your client is a knuckle-dragging, unevolved bully and your client thinks you're an inefficient trainer who doesn't command respect.

Set out your services.

If your social media channels, your adverts and your website don't let people know exactly what you do (or at least what you'd like to do!) then you could potentially spend all day fending off phone calls from people asking for services that you absolutely do not provide. Although that's tempting at first as you find your business feet, it's a recipe for disillusionment and disappointment. If you're spending even

10 minutes a day telling people that you don't do puppy classes and you don't do agility, then that's over an hour a week. That's 50 hours a year. Ten minutes a day might not seem like much, but what else could you do with those 3000 precious minutes of time? 50 hours a week is almost a two-week holiday, thinking of work hours alone. Wouldn't it be better to have two weeks off than spend two weeks of your year telling people what you don't do?

In the next lesson, we come to triage processes. Triage is the system in hospitals of deciding who needs urgent treatment and who can wait a little. It's a sorting system, not only in terms of priority, but also in terms of where you send them next. Accident and emergency departments handle most triage in hospitals. But most patients don't get treated in A&E beds. This is going to be the same for you. However, what is a nightmare for hospitals and leads to them becoming quickly overwhelmed and unable to cope is if nobody has any idea what they offer or what they do, or under what circumstances they should go to A&E. Your front-of-house materials - be they your website, your YouTube channel, even your Amazon author page - should always say precisely what you do offer, and also how much those services cost. If you don't, like your local A&E, you'll end up swamped with people who've got colds, who've got mumps, who've got a sprained wrist, who've got a mole they want checked and people who need immediate treatment right now.

On the other hand, if your front-of-house filter systems are inefficient or unclear, you may end up turning almost everyone away.

It's all a balance.

There is so much to know about how social media functions that it is worth specifically investing in social media training. However, if there are any simple principles to remember, it is that social media streams on Facebook, Twitter, Instagram or any other platform, are temporary and are very quickly old news. Engagement with them can be great, but it doesn't mean that people will engage with your services. I see so many people throwing hours and hours a day into Facebook marketing without realising how temporary it is. On average, your posts will have been seen and forgotten about within hours, if not days.

I also see a lot of dog trainers investing a huge amount of time trying to attract people to their Facebook pages with competitions or 'share your dog' type posts. Again, these are time consuming and they don't really show you in a professional light. Not that this means putting on a suit and tie to do them, but what your potential clients want to see is you working with dogs. Tempting as it is to run 'share if you agree' type posts, it reveals a real lack of understanding of marketing and an unprofessional edge.

The most important thing will always be your evergreen content. That means content that is not time-sensitive. Websites, blogs and YouTube are good examples of this. Many people overlook the importance of a good website, and yet it is one of the cornerstones of business marketing for the small business. Ranking highly on search engines because you've got a great website is more valuable than 50,000 fans on Facebook when it comes to return on investment.

Because your front-of-house services are so important, don't skimp. Decide what you want them to say and, if you can't produce something professional yourself, pay someone else to do it. Though you lose a lot of control when you outsource rather than doing it yourself, nothing says "unprofessional" other than a cheap-looking website. In this day and age, where anyone can set up a website, if you can't produce something that looks professional and keeps to a theme so that it's most notably "yours", then it will show a mile away. Graphic design, website layout and website content can be challenging, so don't feel like you have to do it all if it's not your forté.

Cheap-as-chips productions will attract cheap-as-chips clients.

You have a choice over that and it's a difficult one to put right later, so it's worth starting with something polished and crisp, even if it is filled with diamonds, unicorns and rainbows. There are many, many great books and courses if you want to go it alone, but if you don't have time, hire a professional and make sure you look slick. Also hire a proof-reader and have someone check your site out in terms of written content. It's always worth it.

Remember too that being too polished can be counterproductive. Gimmicks may sell for a while, but without the personal touch, most are just a flash in the pan unless they are very good. Quality is vital. If you're all about the image and your front-of-house materials are immaculate but slick and soulless, then you'll also find many people put off by that too.

In all, don't overlook your front-of-house materials, be they your website, your social media or your printed materials. Either learn about them or pay someone else to do it. Make sure you are making a very conscious decision about how much of yourself you include in them and why. It's okay to be a turquoise mermaid with your heart on your sleeve if that is your very conscious decision to be so, knowing all the costs and the benefits. It's also okay to be cool and professional without any unicorns if that is your very conscious decision to be so, knowing all the costs and the benefits. And it's okay to be cool and professional with the occasional mermaid and unicorn too. But choose. And be 100% that choice. Authenticity comes through consistency in image presentation that is 100% rooted in your own self-awareness and self-governance.

6. Triage

Assuming that clients are filtered successfully through your front-of-house services, that they arrive for a service that you are happy to deliver, and that you've passed their value test about whether or not they think you are suitable, capable and compatible, the next thing you will need to do is triage.

As you learned briefly in the last lesson, triage is the process by which you sort cases by severity and urgency. Some cases may be severe but not urgent. Others may be urgent but not severe. Triage sorts your cases.

First, though, you need to know what kind of people are calling over a month or so by conducting an audit. It doesn't matter if these contacts become clients or not. Getting data about your typical contact and client caseload so that you can audit your intake is vital. Say for instance you decide to look at November. You write down how many people contact you and the various means by which they do so. You might note that you have ten contacts directly by your landline number, which is available on your website, and through your Google business account. You count fifteen mobile phone calls, which only ever arrive by referral. You count how many emails you get, noting that twenty people contacted you by email. Then you note how many Facebook, Skype or WhatsApp messages you get, seeing that thirty people contacted you this way. You also run a couple of daytime events at a local park and twenty-five people ask for further information or chat with you about their dogs' problems. You ask every client where they heard about you and how they found your contact details. From the hundred contacts, you have seventy-five responses and you now know how most people are finding you.

From this audit, you can then work out how many conversions you have.

You might notice that your conversion rate for landline calls is poor, giving you some feedback on the effectiveness of your website and Google business account. You may notice that most referrals turn to clients, perhaps indicating how useful other people are as a filter.

All these conversion rates give you important data that can tell you where to focus and where not to. For instance, you might then link up the landline number and email address to a virtual secretarial service to filter out all the people who haven't really done their homework about the services you offer, or you might give commission (or gifts!) to those who are referring work to you. Their filter services are as useful as a secretary, if not more so.

This data about how people find you is not necessarily the important bit. You need to know how many stick with you. Of the hundred contacts, who went on to become a paying client? If all your clients come from events and face-to-face conversations, you now know a little more about your own market. You have your conversion rate and a bit of knowledge about your market that would need confirming by running another month-long audit another time.

But for now, you have your average kind of intake. Marketing aside, you should be able to create a ratio of those cases which needed dealing with immediately - even if they didn't go on to become a paying client. For instance, one person rang because their dogs were in the middle of an injurious fight right there and then and she needed help to split them up safely over the phone. These kind of cases need dealing with in the moment even if you aren't paid for them. They're truly urgent. Make a note of how many truly urgent cases you get in the month that need dealing with right there and then, even if they end up with a referral to someone else. Hopefully it won't be hundreds unless you are manning some kind of hotline for dog emergencies. You might also want to include your own paying clients who suddenly move up to an immediate urgent status. Unless you have lots of flexibility and you can always answer your mobile phone, no matter where you are, these kind of immediately urgent cases are not ideal because they require you to drop whatever you are doing.

In your model, describe the kind of typical situations in which you get 'must deal with right now' emergency clients. One example might be a dog who is in the middle of doing something dangerous right in the moment, and the client needs help to stop the dog without causing injury to themselves and without traumatising the dog. These types of situations are usually either dangerous to the dog themselves, dangerous to the guardian or the family, or dangerous to another resident animal. Usually, you will not be able to get there to help before it is too late, but you might need to direct them to a vet, trainer, police officer or municipal worker who can help them. For instance, a former client called at 10pm one night to say a strange dog had broken into their yard and when he had tried to trap the dog, the dog had bitten him. Being able to call emergency services as well as that of animal control is the only real option to be taken. You may also be engaged in describing defensive handling over the phone, such as how to make an emergency muzzle or how to break up a dog fight without risk of injury. With the advent of video calls and conferencing, you will even be able to see the fight and differentiate between a repeated slash-and-dash type of fight compared to a brawl where both dogs have locked jaws. Being able to see the fight will allow you the ability to make better judgement calls about how best to advise the dogs are separated.

You may never get any calls of this nature, but if you do, it's always useful to have a document stored on your phone with the numbers of local animal control officers, emergency services or local vets. If you deal with aggressive or overaroused dogs, then you may need to be able to offer defensive handling services over the phone in order to help the guardian out in the moment. Again, these tend to be rare. One case involved a lady who was a dog walker for a very rambunctious dog. One day, the dog started jumping up at her and grabbing her on the walk. By calling a colleague, the colleague was able to advise her to wrap the lead around a tree to secure the dog and to make some space, and advised her on how to create a temporary muzzle with a spare lead or even the cord from the hood of her coat. If you are going to deal with this kind of emergency call, a defensive handling protocol is a necessity. If you are trained in canine first aid, you also may get emergency calls where you will need to offer immediate advice over the phone in lieu of getting the dog to a vet, assuming, of course, that the guardian cannot get hold of the vet at that moment in time.

Most day-to-day dog behaviour and dog training courses are not emergencies, however, and if you never get this kind of call, then you might not want to include it on your triage plan.

Fearful dogs are the other types of dogs who may need urgent intervention if they have escaped or if the guardian is unable to move the dog who has frozen in place and is growling if anyone approaches, especially if the dog is in a dangerous position. Sometimes, you are going to be the emergency number for a client or former client, whether you advertise that as part of your services or not. On the other hand, if you just teach puppy class or basic obedience, it's much less likely that anybody will ring you with a true emergency. That's not to say you shouldn't prepare for them. Not only that, people may think that their situation is truly urgent, when in fact it doesn't merit immediate attention at all.

Once you have identified your procedures for your emergency calls, you can then work out high risk calls, where the behaviour has finished but is very likely to recur unless management is put into place immediately. An example of this kind of case might be two resident dogs who have had an injurious fight that the guardian managed to separate for the moment, but the home is not secure and the guardian cannot keep the dogs separated indefinitely.

Again, having emergency contacts can help here.

It's also really useful in situations like this to know a number of kennels who are happy to take dogs in emergencies. For instance, one client's grandchildren had come to visit, but her new dog had taken exception and had spent the afternoon growling. She had no way of keeping the dog separate from the children other than tethering the dog, so it was more sensible to move the dog into kennels that afternoon so that the dog and the children were safe. Some kennels might be happy for you to use them as long as you put the dog in and get the dog out, or if you can offer a free defensive handling course for staff. It is not ideal for a dangerous dog to be in kennels if inexperienced and unfamiliar staff are the only people who could get the dog out in the event of a fire, for example. But temporary kennelling in an emergency can be ideal. Sometimes, there may also be municipal services who also have kennels for strays and who might be able to at least house a dog in an emergency for a few hours.

You never know when such urgent cases or high risk cases might occur. Another client called to say her dog had just bitten her husband. He had gone to the hospital by ambulance and she had followed in the car. The husband was suffering from dementia and had kicked the dog who had got in the way when he was shouting at his wife. Although the wife wanted very much to keep the dog, she needed someone to go and pick up the dog, check the dog was okay and remove the dog from the premises before she returned home with her husband. This kind of high-risk situation often involves vulnerable humans who are often targets for bites, but they may also involve vulnerable animals, including fearful or aggressive dogs.

If you're only offering classes or reactive rover one-to-ones, you may find that your only course of action when someone rings in a situation like this is to pass them over to a trusted colleague. Knowing that you have someone's number is vital. Several dog trainers local to me know they can ring at any time if anyone contacts them in such circumstances and that I will return the favour when people ring me asking for puppy classes or preparing their dog for confirmation shows.

You may find from your audit that most of your clients have chronic problems or needs rather than anything vital, and so your timeframe will certainly adapt accordingly. That said, if you are dealing with young dogs whose socialisation needs are important and time-sensitive, you may also need a triage system to help deal with emergencies. Just because you don't envisage emergencies in your business model doesn't mean they won't happen. One new puppy guardian had inadvertently tripped over her ten-week-old puppy and the next day, the puppy had got tangled up in the lead. The puppy screamed on both occasions and had been very reactive to handling where previously she had been happy to be touched. Just because you run puppy classes, don't think that there won't be emergencies of this nature from time to time, where clients will need immediate intervention to nip a problem in the bud. The next 48 hours were critical to that puppy's recovery and resilience, and as the result of immediate intervention, the guardian was able to help the puppy get over what could have been a major mishap.

In all cases, a flowchart for your cases is not just useful, it is vital. Audit the six most common reasons for calls, and then decide how you can most quickly direct the client away from the phone (or messaging) and into a more formalised setting. Coming back to how much time we waste, if you're spending 30 minutes a couple of times a week chatting with potential puppy guardians who want to know which classes to sign their dog up for, over the year, that tots up to almost a couple of weeks of time off. What you want to be able to do is direct them quickly and efficiently to signing up. Never let anyone absorb too much of your time without payment.

Say, for instance, you offer a range of dog training classes. You have ten contacts in the week via various different means. Some come by phone, some by email, some by social media messaging services. Work out your most efficient route to getting them signed up to a class. That is probably to direct them back to the website and to fill in an online questionnaire that helps them pick which class is suitable for them. With a variety of mobile apps and electronic services, you can direct them to the right class, book them in and take payment without spending more than the time it takes to set these services up.

If you offer one-to-ones for individual behaviour problems, you do not want your client pouring their heart out over the phone for ninety minutes without ever committing to a behaviour modification package and paying you. This is again where triage helps. If the problem is urgent, you can decide how much time to take to offer advice about securing the dog, but less urgent and less severe problems can be directed to a behavioural questionnaire.
Since one-to-ones are generally more expensive than puppy classes,

future clients can be more reluctant to sign up without a clear plan of action. You may also be hesitant to sign a contract without knowing if you can help. An online booking service and payment service is counterproductive if you need to either refer clients to someone with more specific expertise or if you are unable to commit at this time to services. Payment for one-to-one contracts are usually different, therefore, and may come when you sign a much more official contract. Classes will not need the same level of contracting: something more akin to signed terms and conditions may well be enough, as well as any appropriate waivers.

Specific contracts for behaviour modification can be more complicated. They may be more open in terms of likely duration, or they may be more flexible in timetabling and services offered. Thus, directing them to an intake form can be helpful. The information required on intake forms will vary: these are discussed in the next lesson. Intake forms act as a way to filter out people who are not committed. It costs you little by way of time to send them to prospective clients. If they don't complete them and fail to follow up, then it is no great financial loss for you. Intake forms also help you get a very quick overview and take the burden off you in terms of note-taking during the first interviews. You may glean important information from your intake form as to the likely genesis, motivating operations, context, antecedents and consequences of your new canine client's problems that you would not necessarily pick up during the interview. Intake forms may be lengthy documents and may take some time to complete, but including these as part of your triage process is an incredibly useful way to filter out clients you can't help and to begin your helping relationship with those who need it. You can also use online questionnaires and forms to streamline your work.

Fig 1: triage model

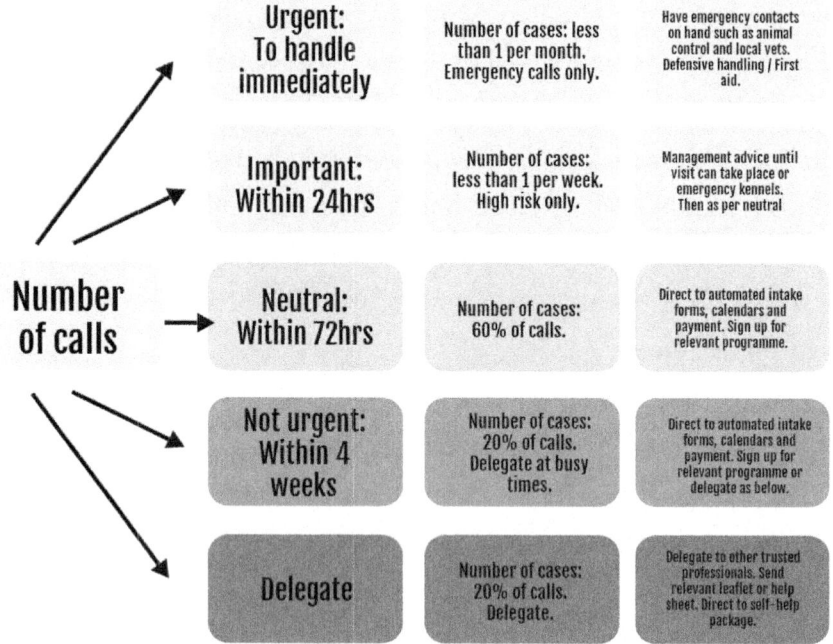

Once you have completed an audit of your cases, you can work out which ones you are going to take on and how you are going to get them signed up with the minimum time commitment from you. That is usually directing them to an automated service to gather information, such as an online behaviour consultation form or a class booking form. You can also take payment virtually and ask clients to complete an online calendar if you don't have timetabled events. The more new clients you have, the more important this is. At some point, you may need to think about outsourcing this to admin services if you have more than 10 or so new clients a week, since if you are spending even 5 minutes with new clients either in messages or on the phone, you are losing an hour a week. Again, that's a week and a half of your time over the year. If you have many classes of a fairly short duration and you are dealing with over a hundred clients a week, it will be more important to automate your services and outsource administration, otherwise you are going to spend all your time doing this.

On the other hand, if you do mostly one-to-ones and you have a slow-burn business, then you are going to have a deeper relationship with your clients from the beginning. Even so, spending 15 minutes a week with 4 new clients all adds up. It doesn't even mean spending 15 minutes speaking to them or in direct messaging. If you spend a minute emailing them but 10 minutes finding links and sending them course information, or even spend 10 minutes thinking about their situation, then that is all unpaid time you need to account for.

This is especially important if you have any disengagement from initial contact messages or calls through to signing up. Let your website, automated booking, scheduling and payment services take the weight. Your time is too valuable to spend on clients who don't end up paying you.

That said, just because you don't offer the service the client is in need of doesn't mean that you can't point them in the right direction. Having trusted colleagues upon whom you can rely is essential. If you don't offer behavioural consultations, find like-minded colleagues who do and work with them. If you don't offer puppy classes, be able to point your contacts in the right direction. If you don't run agility classes, find those who do and direct clients to them. Ideally, if you are working in your own niche, you'll find your trusted colleagues contacting you with would-be clients in the same way. Think beyond your own niche as well. It's useful to have contacts with local kennels, with groomers, with local shelters, with veterinarians and even with professionals like pet photographers. When you know and can trust their way of working, then you will find a collaborative approach opens more doors than it closes. We can be very guarded over our clientele, seeing all others in our field as competition or rivals. While you may very well have other professionals in your area who do not work in a way that is in harmony with your way of thinking, building a strong team of those who do is invaluable. After all, if a new contact asks if you provide a particular service and you offer them a polite, 'No, sorry. Good luck though!' message, then their next call could very well be to a trainer who uses methods that are going to cause more damage than good. A simple, 'No, sorry. Here are the websites and contact details for a number of other trainers in the area. Good luck!' need not take much longer if you have them already prepared in a pdf to send.

For contacts who get in touch and want services that you don't deliver, you may also want to think about offering these as stand-alone packages. You might send them a link to a worksheet or paid self-study course, to a prepared YouTube channel with a series of videos to work through, or even to a book that you have written. Instead of spending your spare minutes of each week fending off contacts who want to know whether you can train their multicoloured chimera-doodle to jump through hoops when that is not a service you offer, clear website information should filter out a number of these and quick triage should minimise the amount of time you spend in contact with them. It's then easy to use that freed-up time to develop your passive income through books, DVDs, stand-alone courses and subscription channels to meet the needs of clients who are easy, non-urgent and whose problems can be solved easily without interaction. If you are considering offering support for those who need it but aren't able to pay, you can always spend that time designing pro bono materials. They work well for your image, as well. If four or five people ring you per week to ask if you can give loose leash lessons to their dog, but you'd really rather not do that even if you could, you're potentially losing income that you could easily profit from via non-interactive methods. If those same people don't have the means to pay what you'd cost and you could easily provide simple How To videos free of charge, then you'll reach more people who could benefit spending that precious time on sharing free content that's available to all. If you're going to give away your time and knowledge, at least do so to the biggest audience you can and make sure you choose evergreen content, not transient social media.

Don't forget, for the kind of clients who like a bit more interaction, you can also offer blended learning packages that are a mix of reading, watching video tutorials, access to dedicated Facebook or WhatsApp groups and a quick 15-minute online meeting every two weeks. Blended learning can often meet the needs of clients who are happy to study by themselves but appreciate support from a community or from you.

Understanding who is calling you and for what is your first step in designing a triage process and workflow that can maximise the time you spend on cases you enjoy and with clients you can help. It can also help you profit from a number of other people who call you but you would rather not spend time with, even though you are capable of helping them. And it also means that you are building links within your community which can be a powerful source of income if you have other professionals in the area who will reciprocate when people call them for help that they can't or don't offer.

Streamlining your client filtration system with a clear triage workflow process will mean that you're helping the maximum number of clients in the most efficient ways rather than tying up your time listening to people chatting for 90 minutes about a problem with their dogs that would be easily resolved. The small profit from contacts like this will never outweigh the value of your time. Being helpful and being profitable don't need to be mutually exclusive, and an effective triage system ensures you get to the people you can truly help.

7. Streamline your intake system

Via a clear vision about who you are and what you deliver, and then via clean front-of-house services, efficient triage system and delegation to either passive training materials or other colleagues, you should get the clients that you really want. That in itself is an absolute bonus. By the way, if you are getting here and you haven't got any clients but you've been in business a while, that is usually for one of two reasons: inefficient marketing or offering a niche skill in a low-density market. Both come from inefficient systems: either nobody knows you and what you offer, or people in your area don't need what you offer and you haven't understood the limitations of your market.

Among my other roles, as part of my work in the shelter, I take photos of the animals available for adoption. From time to time, amateur photographers get in touch. It's clear that a number of these people are hoping to open a pet photography business and piggyback on the shelter's reputation as part of their marketing strategy. They think that their business is not taking off because they haven't marketed properly yet. Some of these photographers are really great photographers. One would no doubt kill it if he lived in an area where a niche luxury service like pet photography was in demand. Unfortunately, he lives in a rural area where poverty is higher than average, there are fewer people than average and people have different values about what luxuries are and the value of pet portraiture. He, sadly, failed to understand both the overt and covert tensions in his intended market. If you reach this point and you've not got the clients you want, then it's worthwhile taking a detour to either skill up, to market better with a better product or to understand your market and adapt. As most marketers will tell you, it's not a case of 'if you build it, they will come' anymore.

Marketing aside, managing your intake effectively is also a systems thing.

Information gathering is crucial. Many dog trainers and behaviourists are able to immediately spot what they think the problem is, and we're eager to dive in and get straight to work.

Not only that, we're faced with clients who want us to do exactly that.

They may not see the value in spending an hour completing an online survey and then an hour in discussion with you before you even consider coming up with an action plan. That's going to be especially true when the problem seems relatively superficial or straightforward. Here, the problem seems superficially simple but the solutions are complex. Let's take loose-lead walking as an example.

You've got a streamlined system. Your client contacted you because they saw on your website that you offer a loose-lead walking class. They phone you to check and you direct them to your loose-lead walking package. They sign up via your app, pay there and then for your ten-week loose-lead walking classes on Wednesday nights. Then they bring their dog to class and you realise that the reason the dog is pulling on lead is because they hate other dogs and they're extremely aggressive to other dogs. Plus, they're a six-month-old cane corso that hasn't been socialised. The only way they can manage the dog at all is with a prong collar. And now you've got to spend your first class with them telling them they need a different class, probably one-to-ones, and that you're ethically opposed to prong collars when it's only tool they've been able to manage the dog with at all and they've already tried harnesses, flat neck collars and a choke chain.

If you regularly face inappropriate people getting into your classes

- "puppies" who are twenty-four weeks old in with ten-week-old puppies, "reactive" dogs who are not reactive at all but just object to being told to 'say hello!' in with dogs with extreme dog-dog aggression issues, people bringing their extremely fearful adult foreign rescue dog to classes for "socialisation" because a guy in the park told them that's what their dog needs - then these are systems failures. You may have set out who the class was targeted at and what it involved, but your clients have failed to understand what you said, failed to communicate key information about their dog and they've also failed to understand the nature of their dogs' problems. Going back to Lesson 1, they needed a doctor-patient relationship or even a client-centred one, but they assumed they knew what the problem was as it was superficially simple. As a result, they went for the expert model.

On the other hand, you can find some problems that seem highly complex to the client, yet require a simple solution. Let's take the client who calls with a destructive dog who is inadequately house-trained, can't be left alone for a minute, digs in the garden, chews incessantly, counter-surfs and gets in fights with other dogs. It may take your client twenty minutes to tell you all the problems they need solving. Such problems may have relatively simple solutions. Better management, a little enrichment and teaching the dog to settle would be straightforward solutions to all of the problems the client presents in this case.

Both complex problems and complex solutions can be eased through good intake systems.

Good intake systems can avoid flaws in the expert model, if that's what you're offering. And plenty of dog trainers do offer expert-client models which are perfectly valid business models. Puppy classes, loose-lead classes, reactive rover classes, puppy obedience classes, agility classes, they're all based on self-diagnosed needs by the client; the client then comes to you because you're the expert. It goes without saying that many, many dogs and their guardians get turned away from class because their dog is a bad match for the group. If they're lucky, the trainer will steer them in the right direction, refund them and help them out. But many trainers - and that will certainly include us if we offer group classes without thoroughly vetting clients first - end up angry at the client for not reading all the information they put out there, for wasting their time or for derailing the class and upsetting the other class members. It can be difficult to be kind when someone brings a barky, unsocialised maniac Malinois to beginners' agility when the dog then gets in a fight with several other members of the class.

For each of your groups of clients - be they puppy clients, adult dog clients, agility clients or any other service that you offer - it's a good idea to make a tailored intake form for guardians to complete and to be scrutinised by you before you let them set foot in your door. Some information will form a core, such as contact details, age and breed of dog, medical history, insurance details and veterinary contact details. Other information may be specialised and tailored to the service.

Don't be afraid to ask all the things you want to know in an online survey or questionnaire. Your time is too valuable to sit there asking every single client what food their dog eats, at what time their dog eats and if the dog has any allergies. There is a lot of information we need that can be given in writing before we start the contract officially - information that will stop our classes or one-to-one sessions being disrupted or derailed.

Later, you will learn about blind spots. You've already learned a little about the shadow side. A good intake questionnaire can help you work out people's underlying values before you even speak to them or meet them. You can see what training methods they've tried in the past, what they want out of the sessions, whether their dog has a problem with other dogs... the information you can glean by setting up an intake proforma is up to you but it can be a massive time-saver so that you can have a cursory look through, red flag any potential issues and direct clients to a service that suits them best.

Start by making a list of the common things you want to know the answer to. You can include owner-reported personality surveys like James Serpell's CBARQ questionnaire, or the Monash scale of canine personality, too. That gives you an opportunity to get to know the dog better. Some clients may find it pointless to fill in such a questionnaire, but it is far better that they disengage with you here before they have trouble committing further down the line. If you can't spend the amount of time needed to complete this information, it doesn't bode well for being able to dedicate time to your dog training. Be mindful of disabilities, too. It's useful to have a dyslexia-friendly form, those in foreign languages frequently spoken in your area or to run these orally for people with dyslexia or literacy problems. It's also useful to have a spoken version available for blind clients. Outlining on your website that you provide services for guardians with disabilities is a good way to access a niche market, and to do something that is of benefit to groups who are often overlooked. In this day and age, especially with the ability to outsource tasks to translators, scribes or readers, you shouldn't be neglecting companion animal guardians who are so often excluded anyway. Having mixed learning methods such as video, audio transcripts or even just the flexibility to offer other forms of appropriate interview for deaf clients, blind clients or dyslexic clients is a good way to make sure your systems aren't so rigid as to be exclusionary.

Make it your rule, however, to collect as much information as you can without your own involvement. That allows you to save time for more important things. It also stops your initial contracting interview from being derailed so that you end up missing something, or being so structured that they fail to create rapport. You sitting there reading out a list of pre-prepared questions that you absolutely need answers to does not create a great bond. On the other hand, you can get so lost in the initial problem that you fail to pick up information that is relevant.

One example of this was a client who filled in the questionnaire. Their two-year-old labrador had recently started guarding items and was incredibly sensitive to touch. He had bitten his guardian a number of times when his guardian tried to remove things from him. Because the interview was very emotional, without the questionnaire, the behaviour consultant would have missed out on a crucial factor: the dog had recently returned from kennels a week before. In the kennels, the kennel owners had used a head halter without prior habituation or training. The dog had run into the halter whilst wearing a long flat lead and had a neck injury as a result. His aversive experiences in the kennels in other ways had been a trigger for the behaviour in the home which had not appeared immediately. This kind of information may seem irrelevant and trivial, but the guardian often travelled and the good work that she did on resource guarding protocols was derailed by his stay in the kennels.

The information that you glean from intake interview forms and questionnaires can be essential in helping you effectively triage. It can also help you with risk analysis. Finally, it can help you decide whether you will take the case or not. You can, of course, pass on your intake assessment forms to other professionals.

In another situation, a client's intake form revealed she had had the dog for ten years having taken the dog as a rescue puppy that she had failed to socialise at all. The dog lived outside in a run and had done so for at least nine years. He had killed cats. He was antisocial with everyone other than his female guardian. He had attacked other dogs and had bitten a neighbour. The guardian wanted to start a rehabilitation programme. This potentially time-consuming case had such a negative prognosis other than management that to engage the guardian as a client would have been verging on fraud. Sad as cases like these may be, being able to dedicate 30 minutes, send a muzzle training video and a leaflet about keeping dogs secure in the garden and the home was a much more appropriate response under the circumstances. Without an intake form, few of these details would have come to light and even the initial interview could have taken over an hour, only to arrive at the same conclusions.

There are no good reasons not to add an intake form or pre-class questionnaire to your intake system so that you don't end up with the wrong clients in the wrong classes. So before you go any further, devise a questionnaire for each service you offer and trial it with a few clients before taking it live, so that you can pick up on any duplications or errors. If you find yourself in the first interview with a number of clients and you are repeatedly asking questions that you could easily add to the intake form, adapt it as you go.

By the time you get to face-to-face, video or phone meetings, you should either be ready to run a class that you've already tailored to the needs of your client group, or you should be conducting one-to-one interviews and contracting sessions that are entirely individualised from this point in.

Good intake systems mean either that you find out everything you need to know to set up the perfect classes for your clients, or that you can hone in on the most essential bits when you are dealing with clients in one-to-one situations.

Part of your intake will also be your initial face-to-face meeting if you are doing behaviour cases or one-to-one work. There are several aspects to think of when we set up those interviews, not least the location, the duration and who should be present.

The first aspect about your interview should be to consider the length of time you tell clients it should take. Always be realistic. The more complex the case and the greater number of moving parts, the more time you will need. There is no real reason why you should not split these over two sessions if necessary. In general, even a simple problem may take around 30 minutes to hear out in detail. More complex cases where there are a number of other dogs involved, or where there are a number of humans involved, may also take a longer time. Anything longer than 90 minutes, however, is likely to be too long for both you and the client. Make sure you share the expected duration with the client. There is nothing worse than a client who has to break the meeting in order to go and do something else. You may ask them to schedule a 90-minute slot so that you can have a little time before and after as a cushion should something go wrong.

You may also wish to consider how you will conduct your interviews. Face-to-face is always useful, but as we learned in 2020, not always possible or necessary. If, for instance, you are dealing with a dog who ceaselessly tries to attract their guardian's attention, then having the dog present may not be helpful. At one meeting with a client relating to their anxious dog who barked all the time when visitors were present, it became impossible to conduct the interview at all. Other trainers talk of turning up for the initial meeting with their client and finding the dog unsecured, unmuzzled and ready to bite. For dogs with separation-related issues, it may not be possible to conduct your interviews off-site, but if the dog also has attention-seeking behaviours or is aggressive around unfamiliar humans, it may not always be easy to conduct the interview in the home with the dog present. The client may feel they need you to see the problem in order to validate their concerns, but don't forget, there are a large number of problems that won't happen with you there or where you will need video footage to get to the root cause.

First, consider whether you can conduct the initial meeting virtually. There are benefits and tensions of doing so. The benefits are that you are able to see how the dog is without you being physically present. That is invaluable. Our presence will often have an impact on the dog, whether that is good, bad or indifferent. Video conferencing means we can see the client in the home and see their environment, their dog and their relationship with their dog. We can also record it very easily and play it back later. Another benefit is being able to conduct interviews during anti-social hours if necessary. If you normally see dogs in a clinic space, in your training facility or in your own home, it also gives you the option to see the dog in their own milieu. You can also make notes and make reference to parts of the interview you'd like to go back to later if necessary, if you have recorded it. Video conferencing is much easier with dogs who are fearful, reactive or aggressive around strangers.

But there are many tensions. First is that you can't see the entire home environment and you may miss subtleties of the dog's relationship with the humans. The second is that it can be very impersonal. You may also think about doing your initial consultation without the dog. Sometimes this can allow you to deal with the human side first, especially if the dog is dangerous or distracting. It may seem counterintuitive, but it may be necessary in order to allow the client the room to think carefully. Changing environment, especially using a professional space, can mean that the relationship has a professional feel from the start. You have zero need to worry that you won't get the real picture if you have good interview skills. It's hard to let go of the notion that your clients are untrustworthy when describing their dog's problems, but as you will learn, asking the right questions in the right way can help both you and the client understand the problem. Mismatches will happen. Of course they will. You will certainly get clients who exaggerate their dog as 'severely aggressive' because they growled at the vet taking their temperature, and you will get clients who make light of their dog's serious and repeated bites. These clients are usually the exception, not the rule. If you're stuck in thinking clients are untrustworthy, the lessons later in this manual will help.

Once you have decided how to conduct the interview, you can then choose your location. When choosing your location, make sure you have already weighed up the pros and cons of a video meeting, a face-to-face meeting in the home, a meeting in a neutral space or a meeting in your own workspace or home, and be flexible about where this should take place. Perhaps it is not a decision that you will make yourself, but something that can be agreed with the client.

The final aspect to consider is who should be present. Sometimes, you will be lucky and you will be working with one human and one dog. Other times, there may be a cast of thousands. There may be other dogs in the home and you may choose, or not, whether to have the other dogs present. There may be children in the home and you may wish to understand how they interact with the dog. There may be other individuals who visit the home, such as babysitters, grandparents or neighbours, who are regular fixtures or may be involved in the dog's care. Again, be flexible about who should be present, but try to gather as much information as you can.

Aside from informing the client about the length of the first meeting, it's also useful to inform them about what will happen and what will not. We should not be expected to attend a meeting, listen to the client's problem situation with their dog and offer solutions on the spot. You need time to reflect and make good choices. That won't happen if you're making suggestions on the spot.

For that reason, it's useful to say that the first meeting is to gather more information and that it will conclude by agreeing the nature of the contract. The first meeting will not be the end of the information-gathering process, and you may wish to say that between the first meeting and the second, you will expect your clients to be engaged in gathering more information themselves. Other than environmental management, you may make very few suggestions about how the client should attempt to resolve the problem. It is useful to say that the second meeting will begin action planning and decision making so that your clients do not expect to finish the first meeting with an action plan or expect you to dive straight into training mode.

For example, having received the intake form for a dog who has been growling, barking and biting visitors in the home, you may have scheduled an hour-long interview via video conferencing or social media. You can hear the clients tell their story (Lesson 8), identify any blind spots or potential obstacles that will get in the way (Lesson 10) and then suggest interim management strategies so that visitors are safe and so that the dog does not have the opportunity to further practise dangerous or obnoxious behaviours. You may also suggest interim reading materials, books, courses, DVDs, YouTube videos or additional information so that the client can better understand the nature of their problem as you devise a contract for support and develop materials that will be used to train the dog. If these are your expectations, make them clear as you take clients on, so that they are clear about the process.

Once you have made all your decisions, your first meeting can then focus on letting the client tell their story and on identifying potential pitfalls or tensions. We move at this point to the more client-centred aspects of your work.

8. Let your client tell their story

If we specialise in helping clients whose dogs' behaviours are causing stress or tension, our clients are often going to arrive in a state of need or chaos. If our triage process works efficiently and we're keeping initial contacts to fifteen minutes, clients are going to arrive in need to tell their story. Although they may have completed intake forms that help filter their experiences and help them be objective about their companion animal, they haven't yet had an opportunity to really talk about what has happened.

We will not get all of the story at the beginning of our relationship with our clients, however. Usually, we learn more and more as our relationship develops. For instance, many clients may feel comfortable talking about their dog, the dog's behaviour, their perceptions of the dog, their relationship with the dog, they may not open up about themselves or their behaviour within the relationship until much later. Telling the story is therefore not restricted to a set timetable or an opening gambit in our contracting.

Facilitating the telling of the story allows us to find out what is wrong. We might also hear of opportunities and resources a client has that they are perhaps unaware of. Questions that we may need responses to may naturally be answered. This is the client's opportunity to make sense of the messiness and for us to help them find a clear path through.

There are many benefits to allowing clients to tell us what happened, especially at the beginning of the contract.

The first benefit is that it provides enormous relief. Our clients have been living in an unpleasant situation, sometimes for many months or years. It may have been deeply stressful or awkward. Opening up can be an incredibly cathartic experience. It's not uncommon to have tears as clients relive the worst moments of their lives with their dogs. Being able to explain what has been happening allows our clients to lighten the load. Sometimes, we will be the first people to whom they have really explained how difficult things are. They may feel ashamed of how they treated their dog at the time, or they may be embarrassed about how bad things have become. It's not unusual to see the worst of emotions related to companion animals, from disappointment, anger and frustration to abject misery. Allowing our clients the opportunity to safely share their stories without judgement can be hugely useful in itself.

Telling our stories also provides insight into what has happened, albeit in a subjective way. Here, we can ask for concrete details to flesh out any specific incidents. It also allows us to move away from judgemental language a little, and away from generalisations, into specifics. Simply by asking what happened just before, what happened just after, who was present, what had happened earlier in the day, we can be pinpointing useful diagnostics for the behaviour analysis that will inevitably follow. Careful and investigative questioning can help us get a clear picture of what has happened without resorting to having to replay the situation to see if the dog responds in the same way. Often, our client's companion animals have been living in stress themselves, and to ask the client to put the animal back into the situation to test again is deeply unethical, despite any concerns on behalf of the client that we may not understand what happened unless we see it with our own eyes. Explaining that this is an opportunity for you to unpick and interpret what happened through their eyes is sometimes helpful in order to see the practical value of describing what happened. It implies a trust in their version of events.

When clients are reluctant to say what happened exactly, there are often many reasons for this. For instance, in taking a statement for a surrendered dog at our shelter, the dog's former guardian had to describe the incident in which a bite had occurred. He had wounds to his hands and wrists and the placement of these wounds in itself told a story. When asked how the bite had happened, he simply said, 'The dog went mad. That was all. Can't you see?' The gaps in our stories are often telling in themselves. Where clients are unwilling to provide clarity or detail, often this is a sign that there are tensions or blind spots at work. These are covered in the next lesson, but it's important to bear in mind that a lack of detail or clarity is often important. Clarity at this point will also help us with practical aspects of treatment, such as rearranging the environment or removing antecedent stimuli that prompt behaviour. Vagueness is unhelpful and careful questioning can avoid this.

A third benefit of storytelling is that it builds our relationship with the client. Although clients may be embarrassed by what they share during this time, it usually creates a trusting bond to have been able to share without fear of judgement or reprisal. When we have established rapport in this way, it allows us enormous flexibility and leverage later on. Respect, empathy, compassion and a genuine atmosphere of care are incredibly powerful in establishing a positive working relationship. For some clients, they may be trusting us with information that nobody else has been party to. That places us in trusted privilege.

There can be many tensions which block good storytelling, not least issues of gender, class and race that may hinder open dialogue. Cultures are also very different and may impact on what we are told. Many dog trainers are women. Much of the care for dogs may also fall to women, but it's important to remember that there may be other reasons a client may not wish to reveal everything straight away. Reflect on how uncomfortable it might be for an older man of some status to confess that he cannot handle his dog when the trainer is a much younger woman, for example. We should remember that relationships with companion animals may reflect on complex and unspoken shadow side beliefs about power and mastery, or even relationships about care and nurturing. Clients may be embarrassed because they can't "master" a "dumb animal", when society around is filled with images and narratives of Man's Dominion over Animals. They may be concerned that we may judge them for failing to provide sufficient nurturing, that they're a "bad pet parent". During story telling, many factors may float to the surface of the narrative without ever being directly aired, but without which, may threaten to derail the whole process. We should be conscious of the gaps in narratives, as well as hesitations.

Often what our clients' stories reveal is their ability to see possibilities or limitations. One client said that she 'just wanted a dog to curl up on the couch with in the evenings'. She wanted companionship and her dog was often frustrated, engaging in thwarted attempts to play that ended in repeated and injurious bites. What she was saying is that she wanted to relax. What was clear was the clash in what she wanted compared to what the dog wanted. Her speech was filled with limitations and frustration, as well as a lack of understanding about canine needs. The storytelling process is such a good time to be able to pick up on our client's real goals and the hidden ethos that underpins their desires for the future with their companion.

Sometimes, the storytelling can be simple and the problems are clear. At other times, we get a messy narrative and a cast of thousands that perhaps reflects a little of the disorganised life the client leads.

At times, emotions and feelings are aired without restriction. One client said, 'I hate my dog when this happens, and I hate myself even more.' Conversely, clients may choose their language or backtrack, correcting themselves as they go, editing their story. 'No, that's not right… that's not what happened…' suggesting a thoughtfulness and the ability to reflect. At other times, it may be the partner or a family member who does the editing.

If you are conducting these meetings by phone, in person or through online software, you should find that you are engrossed in the story rather than spending a lot of time making notes or jumping to conclusions. You will learn about active listening in another lesson, but the best example of genuine storytelling is the client checking in with you. If possible, recording the sessions should always be an option so that you can listen to the story again. Avoid taking lengthy notes, other than for jotting down things you want to pick up on late. Lengthy note-taking during the story-telling session interferes with the process.

Good listening when our clients tell their stories is not just about clarifying the situation or providing initial stress relief. Nor is it just about listening for possibilities and limitations, or using the story to flesh out details for a functional behaviour analysis. It also allows us to assess the severity of the situation and to assess the client's current capacity to change. What we learn at this point allows us to develop the foundations of a respectful and supportive working relationship with our client. We get to see their blind spots, hesitations and tensions that may become speed bumps to progress in the future.

Think of this opportunity as one to fill in the details around events that have happened with the client and their companion, but also as a primary way to allow your client to take a breath as they move towards a less stressful future. In the shelter, many dogs shake off just outside the shelter gates when they go for a walk. Whether the "walk of shame" past the other kennels and the cattery is exciting or distressing, that shake-off signals a release of emotional tension following a challenge. If our clients were dogs, at this point, we'd be expecting that shake-off after storytelling. You are not truly ready to move on to exploring emergent tensions and blind spots if you can't see that your client has visibly relaxed at least a little. However, if you find your clients are just as tense, you may want to sideline the tensions for another day and move onto something more practical.

By the end of the story-telling process, we should have an open and honest history of dialogue as well as a good understanding of the process and the client. The client should have a trusted ally and we may expect to see visible relief as they finally put the problem into words.

9 Learn how to manage your judgey face

Active listening requires a clean and objective approach. Despite how we feel about our clients and the ways in which they have previously tried to deal with their problems, we will lose any rapport with them if we lose our objectivity. No matter what, it is not our place to say, 'What the hell were you thinking?'. Of course we know this. Yet, at the same time, words that don't come out of our mouths may be written all over our faces. Managing to stay impartial can be particularly challenging.

On the first level, it can be challenging because animals are involved. To some degree, dog trainers are generally united because they love dogs. At least, we'd like to hope so. Nevertheless, many dog training methods are cruel, unscientific and even barbaric. French animal welfare charity One Voice conducted an investigation into France's many ringsports and protection sports clubs in 2017. What they found was extensive use of whips, "helicoptering" dogs (suspending them by a choke chain until they almost pass out) and much worse. We hope that our clients will arrive with us eschewing cruelty towards animals - after all, they have come to us because they want to change their relationship for the better, surely? Still, many clients will have done things that we cannot reconcile with our own standards of welfare. What they tell us may also contravene national welfare laws. Clients may tell us unemotionally of the time they tasered their dog, or the time they tapped them on the nose. As you will learn in Lesson 10, some of these blind spots are very natural ways of talking. Before we are ready to tackle blind spots, we need to be able to manage ourselves.

Writer Daniel Goleman in his books on emotional intelligence writes about how the first two strands of emotional intelligence relate to ourselves. The first is recognition of our own emotions. The second is management of them. Only when we recognise and manage our emotions are we able to hear what other people are saying and remain in dialogue with them. Like it or not, if we don't remain in dialogue with our clients, the situation is likely to get worse for the dog, not better. We need to be able to manage our judgey face, for better or worse, no matter what the client tells us. Under every story, we need to hear only that the client (and their companion) have a problem and they are looking to us to help them find a solution. We're not there to pass moral judgement on their immortal soul.

In order to maintain our objectivity, we need to be able to start with the basics. Recognising our own feelings, emotions, attitudes, cultural values, our own shadow side, is vital to an open dialogue with clients.

When clients admit - sometimes without any apparent shame or sense of embarrassment - that they have infringed the welfare of their animal, this can be a challenge for us to manage. Even if laws have not been broken, sometimes our clients will have made choices that we find impossible to understand. Finding empathy, maintaining positive regard and being genuine can be tough tasks when a client tells their story. Our own thoughts and feelings are likely to stray into the helping relationship.

Goleman says that one of the first steps to emotional intelligence and emotional mastery is to be aware of our feelings as they occur. Eckhart Tolle discusses this in more depth in his own writing, and you will find many of these practices underpin mindfulness training.

As our clients talk, then, the trainer should be self-aware. It's unhelpful when this is at the forefront of our thinking. We can't engage in active listening if we're consciously and regularly involved in a self-assessment and an internal dialogue asking ourselves, 'What do I feel right now?'

Rather, it should be a form of operating software, running in the background, enabling the effective functioning of your interview process. Goleman says that it is a 'neutral mode' we enter into, even among turbulent emotions. It involves something of a stepping back from the moment. He says that being self-aware means knowing what our moods are and what our thoughts about that mood are. If you find yourself getting angry when clients bring up theories which you disagree with, be it something simple such as believing the dog has to sit and wait for food until the rest of the family has eaten, or whether it is something more serious such as a clear infraction of the dog's legally-protected welfare, it's really important to start by working on your own emotional intelligence. It is one thing to be angry internally and another altogether to allow these emotions to interfere with the helping process. It's as simple as recognising that your hackles are rising when the client tells you they were bitten trying to take the dog's food away to 'prove they were the boss', recognising your anger is about a much larger narrative than simply thinking that the client is incapable or cruel, taking a breath and leaving that anger to deal with outside of the dialogue.

Recognising your own emotions can be something as simple as journaling them afterwards and starting with less complex cases or clients whose thinking is more akin to your own. If you're unable to un-grit your teeth when people mention how much they like a certain television presenter on a dog show, then the first step towards managing these emotions is to recognise that you are having them. You may decide that you aren't ready to listen to people who have used aversives or who aren't prepared to give up their neck collar and extendable lead combination. That is fine too. As your cases become more complex, the more you will need to be able to accept, to acknowledge and to regard your own emotions dispassionately in order to manage them. For instance, it can be very hard to work on cases where behavioural euthanasia may need to be considered. Equally, though, you may find your hackles rising on relatively trivial things, like a client who messages you at 9pm or uses a 'xx' after their message. Recognising your own reaction is the first step to managing it.

For instance, in one case, a client presents with a dog who had fairly purposely been deprived of socialisation as a puppy. The guardian admits that she did not have time and she thought she would be able to rehome her, a dog whom she'd only taken on for a friend. Over the years, the woman had failed to address these issues, and recently the dog bit a neighbour who the guardian encouraged her dog to 'go say hello' to. Ten years of neglect of socialisation and a misunderstanding of canine codes led to a mistake that cost the neighbour two fingers. Recognising that you are angry at the client's negligence and angry they put both the dog and the neighbour in this position are the first steps to being able to work with the client.

Later, as she tells you her hopes of rehabilitating the dog, 'socialising' him as she calls it, you recognise you feel disgust at her ignorance of canine behaviour and anger at her naivety. You also recognise your own feelings of anger that you are the one who is going to have to break it to her that this is not possible. When you discuss this, she asks if you could run a bootcamp for the dog as a 'last chance'. You feel yourself gritting your teeth as she tries to pass over responsibility once again. Eventually, the conversation turns to whether you think the dog could be rehomed. Not only do you think it would be a liability to rehome this dog, who is mistrustful of all strangers, but you also acknowledge your anger once again that this client has failed to understand her dog and the potential danger the dog poses. You sense once more that the client is trying to pass the buck and refusing to take responsibility.

Knowing that you are having these thoughts is the best way to bring them into your conscious awareness, so that you don't blurt out unhelpful or unproductive comments. Goleman tells us that these unconscious emotions that simmer beneath the surface of consciousness have a powerful impact on our work and our relationships. Being able to manage our emotions and our emotional reactions depends on accurate awareness and recognition of them in the first place.

This is where taping conversations can be helpful. If you don't already practise mindful and conscious internal processes by which you periodically take stock of what you are thinking and feeling, being able to do so in retrospect is one way forward. Journaling and professional discussion with a trusted colleague can really help. It's not offloading or "bitchy" to discuss how you felt with a trusted colleague in confidentiality: it is recognising your emotions and being aware of your thoughts so that you can have better relationships with your clients. I suggest you don't do this in a large forum with people you don't know, even if they are all dog trainers, simply because if you do it frequently, other professionals will jump to conclusions about you. Not everyone is able to see your spleen-venting as a necessary part of your life, and may see you less as engaging in discussing and managing your emotions and see you more as someone who is often in conflict with their clients. You'll look at this more in Lesson 14. For the moment, suffice to say it is useful to review client conversations and to have a trusted colleague you can also discuss your responses with. All this should be done within the boundaries of client confidentiality, of course.

You can also move to doing this in the moment. Social media is a good place to practise this skill, as when we read or see something that triggers an emotion, we have the ability to stop and take stock.

Given the number of people who react emotionally in the moment and whose comments reflect this, you can see how hard this is to do.

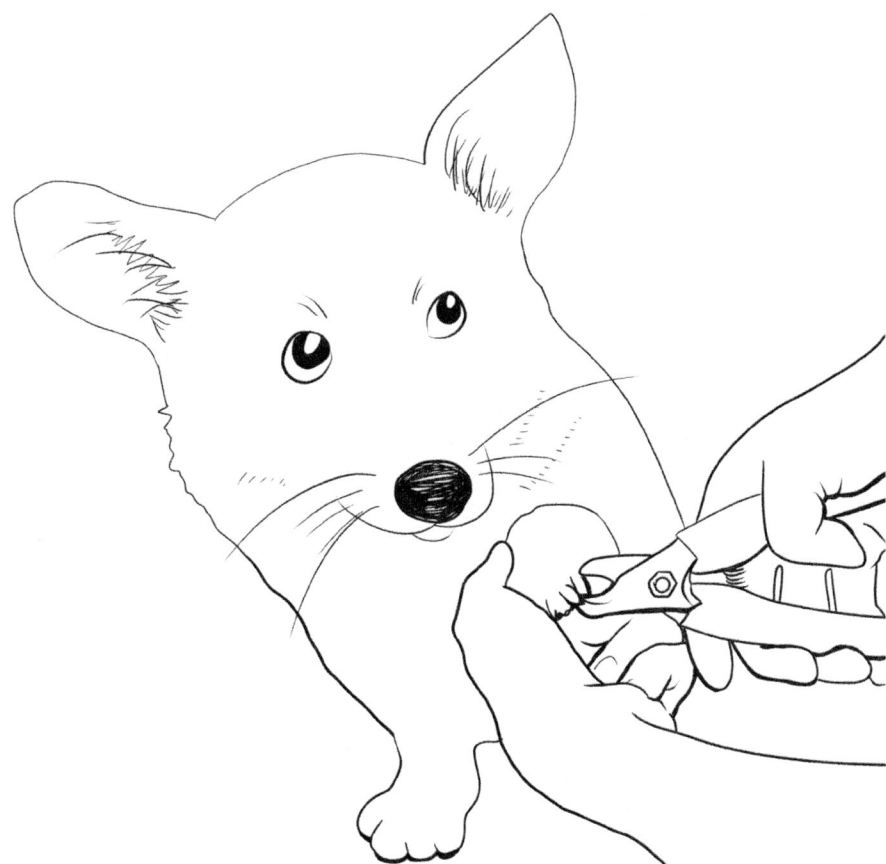

For instance, in one large dog-owner group, a would-be trainer reported a video to the admin. The video had a number of laugh emojis and positive comments about a dog who fainted when their guardian clipped their nails. The trainer was angry and had lashed out at people who did not understand the dog was flooded and this was learned helplessness. In fact, not only was the trainer wrong about this, since the dog was most likely suffering vasovagal syncope relating to stress or even narcolepsy where a vet would be much better placed to make a decision, but they were unable to explain this kindly and gently to people who really would have benefited from learning the dog's behaviour was neither funny nor frivolous. No doubt the trainer spent a few minutes at least angry at humanity, angry at admin and angry on behalf of the dog. If you want to build self-restraint muscles, spending a short amount of time in dog groups on social media will certainly help you strengthen your ability not to respond. It's not a good idea to do this if your willpower is lacking, however. Don't do it on a Friday night after a few glasses of wine! But if nothing else, observing, taking stock of your feelings and choosing not to respond is a skill you can practise liberally with access to social media groups.

We have a choice when our own emotions are triggered. We can choose to let those emotions control us, in which case we are likely to cause the client to disengage, or we can control our emotions and continue a dialogue. We have a choice and we have to ask ourselves what is more important. Later, you will read about biases and human patterns of dysfunctional thinking, where you will see that challenging other people's views in confrontational ways actually does not lead to them revising their opinion, no matter how much you firehose them with evidence or argument. We can choose to confront people or we can choose to manage our emotions and steer them through to different thoughts and clearer understanding. When we have powerful emotions, we have that choice, but only if we acknowledge our own emotions in the first place.

You may find that it is not wrong to sometimes share your thoughts and tell people exactly what is on your mind. Sometimes, when dealing with shelter dogs, I am in this very position. When people's demands are unreasonable or irrational, or if I suspect their methodology and approaches will harm the dog, then I will start by acknowledging my own thoughts and feelings. Then I might hope to open a discussion with the would-be adopter about the situation in order to change their behaviour and their thinking. But if this does not work, I am left with the decision about how to share honestly, openly and professionally, my own feelings that they will not be able to adopt a dog from us, and to face the inevitable emotional fallout and anger that will follow as a consequence. Managing your emotions doesn't mean suppressing them.

Acknowledging and managing your emotions need not lead to blurred lines, ethically speaking. Sometimes, it just means knowing that you are about to enter a minefield if you voice your emotions; the inevitable consequence of that will be recriminations, anger and hostility. What we shouldn't be doing is repeatedly and accidentally finding ourselves in minefields and wondering why.

Once we have acknowledged our own emotions, thoughts and feelings, we are in a better position to manage them. Appropriate expression of these is what works: choosing the right moment, the right words and the right approach. This is particularly challenging when that feeling is anger. Anger is energising and motivating: it can be one of the hardest feelings to manage. After all, there are very few "happiness-management" classes compared to "anger-management" classes. Once we get past the unbridled joy of childhood, we're long past the point of wetting ourselves with excitement, on the whole. Yet managing anger is a completely different game and one that social media often shows us can be very tough for a surprisingly large number of people.

Goleman calls these moments an 'emotional hijacking' which often happens when we feel endangered. Anger often comes when we feel threatened or where we are defending others from threat. That may be physical or it may be a threat to our ethics and values. Recognising our own anger, indignation, outrage and knowing our own values will be explored later in Lesson 11, but for now it's enough to say that we need to be able to appraise our emotions, recognising them as they germinate and catch fire, rather than trying to put out a huge emotional conflagration later. What we can also do is de-escalate our emotions by taking on board all the mitigating factors and information that help us deal more compassionately with the things that other people say that trigger negative emotions within us.

For instance, it mitigates things to know that the guardian whose dog bit the neighbour already had a number of other dogs that she'd taken on. All of them had been dumped on her by friends and family who'd taken advantage of her generous nature. She'd also not been able to socialise him as a puppy because, despite her meeting his physiological needs with a warm home, good food, a comfy bed, companionship and clean water, despite making sure he had vaccinations and wormers, she herself had been dumped on by a friend who knew that the client was undergoing chemotherapy. Instead of supporting her friend and finding a more appropriate home for the puppy, a fairly egregious wrong had been perpetrated on a vulnerable and sick woman who was too kind to say no, but who was also not kind enough to the puppy and to herself to say no, either. Mitigating information and understanding people's motivations can often lead us to cool off without triggering our further rage. Another way to mitigate building anger is to take a break: another reason that it is not a good idea to let sessions spin on and on until you've sorted the problem. Hearing what people have to say and listening to their stories can mean that we're overwhelmed with hearing things that can have a powerful emotional effect on us. Taking a break before action planning is a good way to help you digest those thoughts and process them before moving forwards.

These are not excuses: we are all doing the best we can in the best way we know how. Remembering that is crucial.

Besides anger, another factor that can impact our relationship with our client is our inability to empathise with them. This too can bring out the worst in us. Understanding that clients come to us because they are out of options, because they have tried everything they know how to do, because they have failed is the first step in remembering they are in a place of vulnerability. It's likely they've been living in chronic stress for many months. Later, you will read about how stress affects our thought processes, but suffice to say right now that we may only see differences. It can be hard to focus on the things we want that are the same. For instance, remembering that your client probably likes dogs just as you do - even if they've been perpetrating harms against them. Personally, I find it very hard to accept the need of certain individuals to take smart, purpose-bred dogs and weaponise them. To remember that they want a dog that looks at them with adoration, a loyal companion in whom they can take pride, reminds me that my clients who've used choke chains or prong collars are often in search of a dog who looks like they're completely loyal - but that they have chosen a dog who deliberately looks like an equal, not a small toy poodle or a cocker spaniel who might dote on them equally. They want a bonded relationship, they want a dog they can be proud of and they want a dog who trusts them instinctively, loyally and blindly. And why do we want these things? Because we are afraid? Because our human relationships don't fulfil those needs?

Once we start to unpick superficial differences, we can see our clients' vulnerabilities. Stress makes us selfish, as you will learn more about in future lessons. It makes us unable to empathise. It makes us less altruistic. Recognising that what you are seeing is the very ugliest, the very worst, of your client's relationship with their companion is essential to our ability to empathise with them. I find it ironic that trainers and behaviour consultants spend time investigating the underlying motivations and contexts of animal behaviour without ever stopping to consider what the underlying motivations and contexts are for human behaviour.

Sociologist Brené Brown recounts in Rising Strong an encounter that left her feeling anger and disgust, a time that brought out her niggly little judgements about another person. One of the events she discusses is how, if we recognise that people are doing the best they can in the best way they know how, and that they've come to us for help, then it carries with it the subconscious knowledge that in judging them, feeling angry, frustrated, disappointed or disgusted, then we are forced to acknowledge how unhelpful and how unkind we are when we recognise what we've been doing.

She also writes about something she calls the 'hypothesis of generosity'. This is the process of making the most generous assumption we can about our client's intentions and what they say. Going back to the client at the beginning of this lesson - what if we generously assume that she introduced her dog to a neighbour and she wants to socialise her dog because she recognises the dog's life is very limited and she wants him to get the most out of life? What if we generously assume she has seen photos of dogs running freely and joyously on beaches and she wishes her dog could access that same joy, too? What if we assume that she has not had access to the privileges we have in learning about dogs? After all, she is here because she was trying to introduce her dog to people, because she wanted to 'socialise' him and because, in calling, she is tacitly acknowledging she doesn't have the answers and she is with us for our expertise. What if we generously assume that before, she did not have the capacity for improving the dog's life, and now she does?

And here we are scoffing at those intentions and her hopefulness, at her decision to do the best for the dog. Inside, we are scornful and derisive of her lack of knowledge and her attempts to improve her dog's life.

Pretty ugly, right?

Accepting others' actions under the hypothesis of generosity does not mean losing your ethics and integrity. It means being able to honestly ask the client about their intentions in the open and non-judgemental workspace we should have been able to create in allowing our clients to tell their story. It means actively listening to what they are saying. Sometimes, that also means being clear about what behaviours are acceptable and what are not. This comes back to knowing yourself and your own motivations. Lesson 2 is a valuable lesson so that we know who we are and so we clearly express our intentions, but equally, when we come to Lesson 11, we're going to have to think carefully about our own shadow side values, ethics, feelings, emotions and issues. The better we understand them, the more likely we are to be able to regulate them and use them purposefully.

Does accepting people's good intentions and being generous about why they have ended up in this situation with their companion mean that we shouldn't be concerned about illegal behaviour, about welfare standards and about the human situations that can lead to animal neglect or abuse?

No.

Just because someone is doing their best in the best way they know how does not mean that is legal or that it is not harmful. Equally, being empathic, compassionate and kind does not take anything away from us.

To take one example, a guardian of a dog was forced to go to the police following her dog biting her husband. The husband had briefly been hospitalised and such hospitalisation following a bite required the legal owner of the dog to follow a legal protocol including a police statement and possible prosecution. What transpired was that the dog had bitten the husband because the husband was in the early stages of dementia and was extremely violent towards his wife. Does this mean it was acceptable for the man to lash out at his wife or for him to kick at the dog? Absolutely not. Does it mean it's reasonable or acceptable to leave both the wife or the dog in the home when the husband returns? Not in the way that they were, no. Not least because the dog was likely to cause significant damage should the husband lash out again. It costs us nothing to be compassionate in such circumstances, even if that means we are going to be making a recommendation that the dog is rehomed, at least temporarily, to prevent further abuse. It costs us nothing to understand that this will be hard for the wife, who will no doubt be facing the imminent institutionalisation of her husband as well as losing her dog, who has been her only comfort in the preceding months. It costs us nothing to be kind, even if egregious wrongs have been committed that make us sick to our stomach. Does our being kind mean these things aren't wrong? Absolutely not. That is an immovable, unwavering, hard 'no'.

At least, though, when we are confronted by our clients' stories, we should spend some time recognising and managing our own emotional response. Our clients' stories are not about us. If they are opening up, it is because they trust us to see them at their worst. If we are truly authentic to our own views and values, then these are not shaken when other people do things differently from us. We can acknowledge that our own feelings of superiority and judgement are pretty ugly and that, whilst our head might well be saying, 'What were you thinking? What got into you? Why the hell would you do that? What kind of person are you?', to air these thoughts and reduce our clients to tears of shame and guilt would actually achieve nothing apart from ugly self-satisfaction for ourselves. They're already in a dialogue with themselves that they can't do this without our help. They're already in a dialogue acknowledging that the way they've been doing things isn't working. To reduce them to rubble simply because they didn't make the choices we would make is not helpful. Ironically, they're at the beginning of asking us for the choices we would make. It's why they're here. They're here because they're brave enough to realise they aren't doing things right. Keeping our judgements to ourselves and managing our own reactions will be vital if we intend to move forwards.

All that said, this is not to say that our clients will come to us knowing that they need help. As far as they're concerned, it might simply be that they only need help because they don't understand why what they've done for the last forty years isn't working and they have no idea what's wrong with their solution. Some will have arrived because of the threat of police intervention or legal repercussions. Others will arrive as a referral from the vet without truly understanding why. As we move on to help clients tackle their blind spots, we need to be incredibly adept at remaining clear-headed and objective. That means recognising our emotions and managing them appropriately.

10. Recognise and challenge your client's blind spots

In the eye, there is a part where the optic nerve joins the retina which is insensitive to light. It's known as the blind spot. Similarly, in driving, we talk of blind spots where rear view mirrors fail to pick up other cars, bikes or pedestrians. For Gerard Egan, the blind spot is a perfect metaphor for those unintentional, dysfunctional ways of thinking and behaving where we fail to see, to understand or to appreciate things that we should have taken into consideration. These blind spots are the things we can't see for ourselves.

Everybody has blind spots. When we work in discussion with others, they're able to bring these blind spots to the fore. Sometimes they are driven by inexperience or lack of knowledge. Other times, they are things that we have just overlooked. As trainers and behaviour consultants, there are many areas where we confront a client's lack of awareness about what their dog is doing or trying to communicate.

For instance, we might run into this where a client's dog has laid on their back and exposed their belly, and the client has interpreted this as a desire for contact and stroking, only to be bitten by their dog. Canine body language and human understanding of it has developed so much in the last thirty years, but that knowledge is far from widespread in the dog-owning community, especially where there have been contrasting paradigms in the past that still dominate popular media.

Blind spots can also be a result of self-deception. Often, this comes from a place of cognitive dissonance where choosing to accept reality would mean having to face up to things that we might find ethically questionable in other circumstances. We see this often in the language of people who have used punishers or aversives with their dog and yet would consider themselves kind and loving guardians. When we face up to these blind spots and areas of dissonance, it makes us feel uncomfortable and it challenges our way of thinking. Even where we rationalise our blind spots where challenged, this can also be a form of self-deception.

In the 1970s, Richard Nisbett and his colleague Tim Wilson conducted a now-famous social psychology experiment to assess people's ability to report on their own thought processes. They set out four identical pairs of hosiery and asked women to make a choice about which they liked best. Where we might expect there to be an even ratio, the majority picked hosiery to the right, with the final pair being the most commonly chosen. When they repeated the experiment, this time explaining that the items were exactly the same, people still made the same choices and justified them in the same way. When confronted by their irrational lines of reasoning, that in fact, product placement was the only difference between the four items, Nisbett and Wilson found that most people denied that this was a factor and justified even more strongly their preference based on perceptions about difference in quality or in texture. Psychologist Dan Ariely writes about this experiment in his book The (Honest) Truth About Dishonesty: How We Lie to Everybody - Especially Ourselves. What he draws from this is that we may not know why we do what we do, but we're very good at justifying our choices and creating logical stories about why we behaved as we did. The point is not that we make gut choices or even choices governed by factors we don't understand, but that when we are challenged, we're likely to construct very plausible explanations for why we did so. These explanations may have absolutely no basis in reality. However, the more strongly we believe them, the more firm we will become in our defense of them - even in spite of being faced with information that should make us change our mind. Ariely concludes that we are storytellers by nature and we're very good at creating plausible narratives, especially if those narratives present us in a positive light.

This should resonate with us in two ways.

The first is that when confronted by their illogical thinking, clients will often seek to justify it and strengthen their belief in the irrational even further. It may also make them angry to be confronted by their irrational behaviour.

The second is that it is human nature to do so, especially if those reasons paint us in a better light.

Thus, if you plan on facing down your clients who continue to use aversives by firehosing them with rational evidence, do not be surprised if it actually hardens their position, or even makes them angry, instead of making them see sense.

Moreover, if your client is creating a narrative in which the dog seems to be a super villain, intent on ruling the household, don't expect them to want to face up to the fact that a) they're ignorant about real dog behaviour, b) they're probably wrong and c) it might be their fault their dog is counter-surfing and hogging the bed, not the dog's. Nobody wants to face up to the fact that they are, at best, uneducated. Unquestionably, nobody likes to hear that they are categorically wrong, that they are uneducated and that they are probably responsible for the problems they are having with their dog as a result of being uneducated and doing the wrong thing. After all, if they'd been doing the "right" thing, whatever that might be, they probably wouldn't have the problem with the dog.

These things are especially pertinent because nobody wants to hear these things when they are in a moment of crisis or when their relationship with their dog, whom they may love very much, has deteriorated to such a degree that they've been driven to seek help. They definitely don't want to hear this from someone they've only just met.

Clients may also choose to be evasive and want to avoid addressing the real causes behind behaviour. It is not only embarrassing to admit that our own lack of knowledge or skill has led us to have to consult an expert in something that is so fundamental to the human experience as keeping a dog, but it can also be a source of deep shame.

Other clients, despite being faced with the fact that what they have done is likely to continue to cause problems or even cause escalations in their dog's behaviour, continue to do it anyway - despite danger to themselves. It's vaguely reminiscent of that old 'Doctor, Doctor' joke… 'Doctor, Doctor, it hurts when I do this!' and the Doctor replies, 'Well, stop doing that then.'

There can be blind spots when we continue to behave in ways that we know cause tension, challenge or difficulty in our relationships, but we can't seem to stop doing it even if we know the potential risks. For example, one client had forcefully handled her dog in removing a burr from his coat. The burr tore some of the dog's skin and it became slightly infected. The veterinarian pointed out that the dog had very sensitive skin that was easily torn and that the dog was very sensitive to handling. The dog had bitten her a number of times when she tried to administer antiseptic cream. The trainer had advised cooperative care and muzzle training. Despite working on cooperative care protocols and knowing the potential risks of continuing to handle the dog without consent, the client pulled a thin bramble from her unmuzzled dog when out on a walk and the dog bit her hand resulting in a hospitalisation. It's easy to be judgemental about clients who have been clearly told what the consequences of their actions will be and yet do it anyway, but we need to remember that this is human nature and understand how human habits are dismantled and reconstructed. This is especially true when shadow-side issues put the brakes on behaviour change. In this case, those issues related to our relationships with dogs and our feelings about certain tools such as muzzles. We also need to remember how stress, cognitive load and instinct affect newly-learned habits.

These forms of blind spots are very common. We will explore ways to address them in other parts of this manual, but for now it's just important to know that they exist and to recognise them when they occur.

Blind spots aren't always just what we say, or what we don't. Blind spots can also be discrepancies in the way that we act that is incongruous with the things that we say. There are many examples of clients who say, for instance, that they have clear rules and routines for their dogs, yet the chaos and messiness of their lives is the reason behind problem behaviours in a home where this is leading to conflict with the dogs or between the dogs. It's not uncommon to see guardians who have been bitten by their dog as a result of a long history of coercive handling, claiming that they are not handsy with their dogs and yet seeing the exact opposite. It's also not uncommon to see guardians who say their dogs are never allowed on the couch or bed… with dogs on the couch or bed. These aren't reasons not to trust the client, by the way. The stories they have told us don't suddenly become completely untrustworthy because a client has a blind spot. Don't use blind spots to invalidate the rest of the client's narrative.

Blind spots can also be a result of the client suspecting that we might judge their choices, especially if their choices run contrary to what they think the perceived wisdom is. Of course, that perceived wisdom might not be what we believe, but these kinds of discrepancies and blind spots can be more purposeful than they might seem. Remember, stories are not just constructed by our clients to make sense of their situations, but also for an audience: us.

There may also be blind spots simply in the way we behave. For instance, a client may not be aware that what they are doing is reinforcing their dog's barking, or that their behaviour is encouraging the dog to pull. We might observe such actions and notice that the client is unaware of what they are doing and how it is contributing to the problem situation.

Blind spots may also be much bigger than simply our occasional thoughts or actions: it may include our inability to see our own cultural beliefs, our own emotions, belief systems, attitudes and so much more. This is the shadow side at work. One of the most common places a client might clash with a trainer might be over the use of food. So many of us have ingrained beliefs about the place of a dog or how dogs should be fed that it makes it hard for us to accept that a trainer might want to use food. It feels like bribery or a free ride that goes against the grain of many unspoken and unaired beliefs about the role of the dog in the family and our relationships with animals on the whole. We may face cynicism and even mistrust of training methods simply because the client has long-standing historical attitudes that date back to preconceptions formed in their childhood. Our attitudes and perceptions can seriously impact our ability to think clearly about our own problems.

These blind spots can also include flawed ways of thinking. That might relate to ourselves or to others. Clients may overlook the importance of having a positive mindset, or the need to be able to be objective about their dog's behaviour. Their blind spots might include judgements about the dog, including thoughts about the morality of their dog, judging them as if they were humans and taking their actions personally, as if the dog is out to spite them or as if the dog is wilfully disobedient. One client's terrier was in the regular habit of running off with her shoes just before she went out. 'He's just doing it to spite me and make me late!' she said. Sometimes we can be deeply unable or unwilling to empathise with our companions, despite the fact that we are assigning motivations to their actions. Blind spots and logical flaws like this - where we are simultaneously making assumptions about our dog's motivations whilst at the same time unable to think about what the dog might really want - are commonplace.

Finally, our clients' blind spots might also relate to their inability to see others, to understand others and being blind to their needs. This is also commonplace when working with humans and their canine companions. Trainers and behaviour consultants are often involved in explaining on behalf of the dog and in putting the dog's experiences across to their guardian. What we are often engaged in doing is translating for the dog and helping the client reframe their understanding of canine behaviour. This may be at a species level, a breed or mix level or at an individual level. That may also involve explaining what it means to lack socialisation or how hard it may be for a dog to cope with the experiences that the clients regularly find problems with.

For instance, one client called with a problem with her reactive terrier who was aggressive to other dogs on the street, particularly if they put their face into her space. The client wanted to be able to take her dog with her to social events such as markets, but the dog was regularly lunging on lead and barking at passing dogs, or biting any who approached. Unfortunately, the dog had spent 18 months before this home in a garden with very little experience of others, and what the client was expecting was very stressful for the dog. Veterinary behaviourist Dr Karen Overall calls these 'negotiated settlements', where we discuss common ground and what scenarios their dog would reasonably be expected to cope with. We act as the voice of the dog. That necessarily involves a degree not only of understanding canine behaviour but also understanding how to communicate this to humans who have been living with a species they don't truly understand. This often involves bringing these blind spots to the surface and it is little wonder people feel defensive about their own lack of understanding. When we hear statements such as, 'I've had dogs all my life!' or 'I've had this breed for forty years!', we are hearing blind spots being aired. As you will read when we discuss the effects of stress on humans, it's not unpredictable that we become less empathic and less compassionate when we are under stress.

Teaching clients about their dogs is part and parcel of helping them understand the behaviour of their dog. Helping them find empathy for the dog's experiences need not rely on anthropomorphic explanations along the lines of, 'how would you like it if…', but may involve analogy or comparison. Instead of asking the client to imagine they are a dog, it can be most helpful to explain the dog's behaviour and then explain the equivalent of this in human terms. For example, one client expressed concern that her off-lead dog would always get into fights. She saw her dog as a victim. The dog was running up to on-lead and off-lead dogs in the park. Within two or three seconds, the dog would either invasively attempt to smell the other dog, stand with his head over the other dog's back, attempt to mount the other dog or engage in very high energy and insistent attempts to play. Whilst it's unhelpful to tackle this kind of blind spot by saying, 'Imagine if…' or 'How would you like it if… ?', it can be very helpful to say that what her dog is doing is the equivalent of a fully-grown man going into a restaurant, sitting down at other people's tables, attempting to hug strangers, touching people inappropriately and asking to arm wrestle anyone he feels threatened by. Explaining things as the human equivalent is more helpful than asking clients to imagine themselves as a dog. Anthropomorphic analogies are not something to steer clear of when dealing with people's blind spots about their dog's behaviour, but they are something to be used judiciously.

Dealing with your client's blind spots is both the most challenging, yet the most productive aspect of client-centred dog training. To do so prevents further damage occurring, and also opens up our eyes to the reality of the situations in which we find ourselves. However, we should always proceed knowing that to do so requires rapport, skill and careful timing. Nobody needs to hear how ignorant they are, how their behaviour is at odds with reality, or to be firehosed with logical evidence and scientific reports in an attempt to get them to change their mind. You can hopefully see now why the storytelling part of the contract is vital and why we need to have managed our emotional reactions. When we have trust and we've established rapport, we have more scope to tackle blind spots.

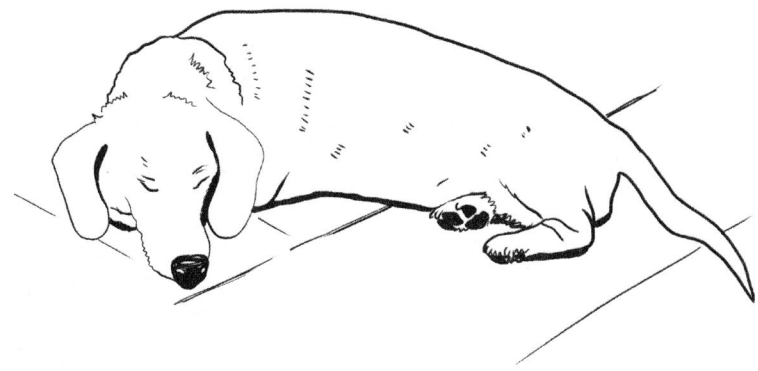

11. Recognise and challenge your own blind spots

Much of this manual is about the client, and rightly so. When trainers say they worry about their own skill when clients are angry or frustrated, or when they ask how to be more resilient, it's often helpful to remember that it isn't about you.

This is largely true. What clients do is rarely about us. If they're rude, if they're cruel, if they're angry or frustrated, it can be very hard to look at their behaviour from an objective point of view and say that it isn't about us: it's about what they are going through themselves.

Yet, where our clients are living with stressful situations or unpredictable behaviour from their dog, if they are dealing with destructive behaviours, separation-related behaviour, aggressive behaviour, unruly behaviour or complex combinations of all four, when we enter into a training contract with them, we need to remember that we have now become a part of the situation, for better or worse. We bring with us our own shadow side and blind spots.

One way to recognise our own blind spots is to truly understand who we are, what we love about animals, what we love about working with people and to make sure we are clear and authentic in the services we offer. You saw this in Lesson 2. Another way we can be aware of potential tensions, obstructions, barriers and conflicts is to remember that all people and all relationships have a shadow side, as we explored in Lesson 4. We also know that shadows can grow or shrink, that they can be pale or strong, depending on the angle of the spotlight under which things are illuminated. In letting clients tell their stories and in listening genuinely and compassionately, we can often build a trusting relationship in which these shadow side issues can come to the surface and into the light, as you saw in Lesson 8. In the last two lessons, you have been looking at how we can help ourselves remain objective or refrain from judgement by recognising and managing our own feelings, and how you can recognise your client's blind spots - those sticky, messy and sometimes stubbornly resistant beliefs and values that run the risk of derailing both your working relationship and their progress.

As we revisit our lessons learned from Lesson 2, we now begin to consider our own shadow side and our own blind spots in more detail.

What we enter into when we engage in one-to-one consultations with clients, or we engage in helping them with problem situations, is a working alliance. First discussed in the late 1960s, this concept means that our contracts are collaborations. These collaborations are based on mutually-agreed goals. You would not sign up to train your client to do anything you found unethical, for instance. But training one-on-one is not something we do to clients. Insisting on "my way or the highway" is a system fraught with problems, not least the fact that it causes minimal engagement from the client and creates a dependent relationship of dominance and submission that may be a long way from our values about working kindly and with consent when it comes to animals. What we do is just one of many routes to success. Of course, the client has responsibilities. They are responsible for choosing solutions that will work for them, and they are also responsible for implementing action plans. But this also depends on our own skills as a trainer or consultant. It depends on our competence - not only in training dogs, but also in helping their humans.

Dog training is a team effort. If any member of the human side of the team refuses to collaborate or does so incompetently, the whole working alliance is likely to fall apart.

Humans are social learners and if psychology has taught us anything in the last 70 years, from Millgram's electric shock experiments to Zimbardo's Stanford Prison experiments, humans are easily led by "experts". When we enter into a training alliance with a client, we need to understand that what we do and how we act is going to influence our clients. We may feel like our clients don't respect us or don't believe in what we are saying, but if they are still with us, they believe in us. They wouldn't stick around if they didn't, no matter what their words and actions might say to the contrary. We're their white coated experts and what we do and say is incredibly influential. That's true even if it feels like the client is in confrontation with us.

We are their guides. That needn't be an accidental or subconscious process. Good trainers deliberately model attitudes and behaviour, as well as training methods. In turn, these affect how our clients work with their own animals. The more our clients cherish and trust that relationship, the more likely it is that they will emulate what we do with our dogs, from the treats we use to the food we feed to the leads we use and the harnesses we select. That means that what we get out of our clients is often a reflection of ourselves. If we are meticulous and diligent in planning carefully constructed training plans, then we will find our clients often subconsciously mimic the way that we work. We get back what we have given.

However, this is not without consequence. It means we have to understand our own values, attitudes and beliefs and we also need to make sure that what we do is robust. No blind spots that we don't know about.

Some of our blind spots will undoubtedly be related to culture. In our work, we are often confronted by the type of dog guardian that we have deep-rooted feelings about, even the types of dog we have strong feelings about. These are shaped by our own personal histories. For instance, when I was 13, I visited a friend whose mother bred working labradors. The dogs jumped all over me when I went in through the door. Rather than my very gentle family dogs who had great door manners and who would never rush guests, this early experience with three very exuberant and very large dogs shaped how I felt about both labradors and their guardians for many years. Other trainers confess they don't like to work with this breed of dog or that breed of dog after a negative experience with the breed early on either in their life or in their nascent training career. It's not uncommon to hear trainers say they 'don't work with rescues', as if rescue dogs are some kind of despicable underclass. You may hear many frustrated comments in dog trainer forums related to 'irresponsible rescues' and 'naive rescuers' and 'rommies' or 'streeties', as if such dogs are some kind of terrible disease. We carry these prejudices with us when we enter into relationships with clients. It works the other way too. I have a deep love of red cocker spaniels and American cocker spaniels stemming from my youth, and an empathy for the plight of the much-maligned Malinois, many of whom passing through our shelter have arrived with horrendous stories of abuse and who go on to suffer the most extreme kennel stress. These blind spots interfere with my feelings towards these dogs. We have to acknowledge our own blind spots, be they positive or negative.

We need to recognise and challenge these blind spots within us, not just about dogs but about people too. Accepting that we find clients challenging if they have unruly dogs who jump all over us may be part of that process, or that we find it challenging if clients have taken on a breed beyond their capability and skill, without having thought deeply about the kind of dog they are getting, may be another challenge. Again, that works both ways. We can be inclined to consider people more capable than they are if we have an affinity with them. That might mean we go on to overestimate their skills and capacity, and underestimate their need for support.

We may also have blind spots related to diversity. How many of us instinctively address the man or the woman in the relationship, rather than both? How many of us unconsciously bring subtle race or class values to the table? Whenever we think to ourselves that 'certain people shouldn't have dogs', we run the risk of stereotyping and also of not challenging blind spots that can interfere with a genuine, warm and open relationship with our clients.

If we are very dog-centred, interested both in rights and in welfare, we may find it hard to stomach clients who use dogs differently than we do. If we're asked to work with gundogs on gundog training and we're staunch vegans, can we think cleanly about how our values and feelings might interrupt the working process? Sure, we might decide that if we are anti-hunting that we won't work with gundog training and we can decide that this is a hill on which we are prepared to die. That's our line in the sand. But what if a potential client contacts us with his self-mutilating short-haired pointer, and we learn that the guardian works his dog, do we step back from the contract because the client engages in something with which we disagree, even if we're not working directly with them on gundog training? There is a reason we have lines in the sand: sands shift and tides wash them away.

Just as with our transient feelings, emotions and reactions to our clients' stories that may necessitate recognition of our reactions in order to better manage them, the same is true for our own shadow side, our own ethics, our own values, our own beliefs and drivers. Whenever you feel them rising in you, acknowledge those tensions for what they are and be mindful of them.

As we move forward having identified our own blind spots in the working alliance, we can then manage them. We need to make sure our own values do not adversely affect the client or their dog. Their best interests should be the only focus of our work. We also need to be aware of our tendency to stereotype. By acknowledging our tendency to do this, we can remove it as a blind spot. Listening to one expert talk on a local radio show recently about dog ownership in the UK, I was struck by her rather large, middle-class white female blind spot that I see often in dog training - a profession dominated by middle-class white women. What I heard was her view that some humans don't give dogs good lives - in her opinion, of course. But her view of a good dog life was based very much on a white middle-class Anglo-Saxon construct of what a good dog life involves: daily walks, a mother who is home and does not work, a family, a large garden. When we hold views like this that inadvertently outlaw other forms of relationship with dogs in such an exclusionary way, these are bound to affect how we interact with our clients. We start to hold views about how dogs should live and what we think should constitute a high level of welfare.

All this is not to say that all dog lives with humans are created equal, but that we need to make sure our stereotypes about what a "good" dog life is don't interfere with how we relate to the client or the recommendations we make. The only way we can do this is by recognising that we hold these stereotypes in the first place. After all, a stay-at-home, middle-class mum who engages only with the dog on the daily circuit of the local park or when she is outside in the large suburban garden needs to be considered exactly in her own relationship with her dog. And a working-class couple who work long hours, who own a terraced house and a small yard need to be considered exactly in their own relationship with their dog. These are not comparable. We cannot rank one life over another. We can't have expectations that we bring to one situation but not to the other.

Every one of our clients deserves us to bring our best game. That means recognising and managing our own deep-seated beliefs and values. What we can do as trainers is work with the cases we see in front of us and remember that each and every single human-canine relationship is as unique as a fingerprint. Our own blind spots about unruly labradors, grumpy westies, the delights of American cocker spaniels, the plight of the Malinois, what "good" homes for dogs look like and what "bad" homes for dogs are - these should not interfere with our work. Only when we recognise them, unpick them, explore them and manage them do we truly bring our best self to the working alliance.

12. Understand and deflect the negativity bias

In the 1960s and 70s, psychologist Martin Seligman and his colleagues undertook a series of experiments using dogs to explore a concept he later came to name 'learned helplessness'. What Seligman wanted to understand was why people who are offered a lifeline or offered help, be it of an emotional or physical nature, are sometimes unable to take it. His work explored the reasons we might stay in unhappy and unfulfilling relationships, difficult environments, in jobs we can't stand or even stay with a violent and abusive partner. His work on the concept of learned helplessness suggests that, in the past, if we have been unable to escape aversive situations, when we finally have a way out, we are unable to take it.

His work, and the work of other psychologists such as Alfred Adler and Aaron Beck, helps us understand how humans think and talk when faced by stressful situations or when feeling helpless. What work in the field of depression and mood disorders tells us is that many humans are involved in negative self-talk and a pattern of negative beliefs. We are likely to both talk and think in self-defeating ways when faced with challenges, and this can often be evident in our first meeting with clients. For a long time, they may have been trapped in a situation that they feel they cannot change, where every attempt they have made to address the problem has been stymied so that they feel there is no point trying anymore. They may have previously tried all of the things that we are about to offer them. Clients also call us in times of crisis when they are unable to cope any more with the life that they have been living with their dog. Our clients often present us with situations that are complex and messy, but also come armed with a wall of negative self-talk. When clients tell us that we are the dog's last chance, what they are saying is that they have no hope that anything is worth trying anymore.

One example of negative self-talk is our tendency to talk in absolutes and to generalise pessimistically when we discuss our problem situations. Clients might tell us that their dog barks 'constantly', that he 'always' lunges towards strange dogs, that he 'never' behaves himself. It's not unusual for clients to tell us that their dog 'always' behaves in this way or that way even when we are right there watching the dog and they are patently not in the process of 'always' doing what the client describes. Even if our clients don't say these things out loud to us, they may be involved in thinking them, adding to their generally pessimistic view of their relationship with their dog and their pessimistic view of potential success.

Despite the fact this is undoubtedly the worst moment for the client when they initially contact us, they may think that things are likely to get worse in the future or that there is no hope for success. We hear this when our clients tell us they are worried their dog will go from attacking cats to attacking children, or that growling will almost certainly end in horrific attacks and severe bites. We catastrophise when we are stressed or unhappy, and we imagine all the worst things that could happen. Our growling dog suddenly becomes Cujo and we end up envisioning the neighbourhood children in hospital as a result of our dog. Or we think that our dog's fears will increase and increase until we have no choice but to euthanise them as a welfare issue. We can't imagine it can improve. We use words like 'never' when we say 'it's never going to improve' as we literally can't envision things getting any better. It's this kind of negative self-talk and thought processes that can be bigger sticking points than lack of knowledge or capability with a clicker.

We also minimise our coping skills and our own inner reserves to get through, and we do so with our dog, too. We imagine our dogs being completely incapable of change, despite the fact that, on the whole, our dogs might actually be pretty great, bar that one big problem. We see their separation anxiety as their defining quality, forgetting that they are sociable, friendly, well-behaved and joyful outside their condition. We see our dog who barks at the neighbours as being aggressive, forgetting that they get the zoomies and they're silly and giddy in the home. We see our destructive dog and forget how much he likes swimming and how much joy he brings us when he romps through the fields, that he's great with strangers and his recall is perfect. Not only do we overlook our own skills, inner reserves and talents, we also overlook those of our dogs. And we think that when set-backs occur, we're right back at square one. Negative thought patterns or negative thinking are likely to pop up every time there is a minor set-back.

When we think negatively, we also start to mind-read. And worse, we do this with our dogs! It's amazing that in conversations with most clients, the ugly myth about dogs trying to take over the household does not come up, yet, faced with a bit of counter-surfing or a dog who doesn't like being disturbed on the sofa, we fall immediately into mind-reading. We only have to hear certain popular television celebrities who work with dogs to realise that they encourage vulnerable 'clients' to engage in the same processes. 'The dog's intention is to…'

And, truth be told, we do it too.

The trouble with mind-reading is that we often make inaccurate assumptions and think the worst of our dogs, so if we hear this, we need to be ready to challenge this.

Theories about our bias towards negativity also tie into this work. On the whole, humans tend to think negatively about the future, thinking that things are unlikely to get better. Unpleasant thoughts and experiences dominate. When clients discuss their dog and the problems they face, bad times are more salient and more easily remembered than the good ones. Times when bad things happened are more vivid when we recall them than the more transient feelings we experience when it worked out. We pay more attention to the negative. Negative experiences also affect our ability to form impressions differently. Thinking back to the previous lesson and my example about bouncy labradors, that negative experience is more powerfully recalled than any of my other experiences with the family pets of my childhood friends - to the point where friends tell me they had dogs and I can't even remember them if they didn't have at least one offensive quality. The negativity bias also affects our ability to take risks and make choices in the future: we stick to safe waters because of the negativity bias; this is why it can be really hard for clients to let go of habits, even if those habits are unproductive, unhelpful or even dangerous to them. When we ask, 'How long has the dog been doing this?', it is not so much to learn about how much experience and practice the dog has had, but how long the guardian has practised their own unsuccessful habits. It's going to be much harder to get the guardian to stop doing what they do than it is for the dog, in many cases. When we're stressed, we're more likely to rely on those ingrained habits than we are likely to try anything new. The negativity bias affects both how we look back - our memory and our impressions - but also how we look forwards - our ability to plan and to change our behaviour. We look back and see failure and challenge; we look forward and see failure and challenge.

The first step in dealing with negativity is to recognise it. Look out for that language that reflects clients' generalisation or black-and-white thinking. Learn to spot where they're catastrophising about the future. Identify those "could have" moments where they reflect on how things could have gone very badly wrong. Recognise those "should have" moments of self-critical behaviour. This is another good reason why it can be useful to record sessions so you can really unpick how clients talk about themselves and their dogs in the past. Look out for those moments of self-defeating talk where the client is already convinced that the future is going to bring them little other than failure. Active listening skills can really help you tune in on moments where clients talk in excessively negative ways or unrealistically pessimistic ways. For instance, if you have just engaged with a client who has a dog suffering from separation-related behaviours, if you hear them say 'nobody helps them out' or 'nobody cares', 'everybody is too busy to help', then this kind of extreme generalisation can derail your treatment plans right from the start if a support network will be needed. So it's really important to pick up on words like 'always' or 'never', 'everybody' and 'nobody' so that you can identify where this self-defeating talk and negativity bias is happening.

Once you have recognised it, then you're in a position to slow things down and unpick this a little. One of the most useful ways to do this is to review. Ask your client, 'When you said that, can you just tell me a little more about…' or, 'I'd just like to go back to something you said there about…'. You can see how this works with the client who says 'nobody is able to help'. When you start to unpick 'nobody', it becomes clear that there is a support network there, just that objective talk might be more fruitful than saying there is literally nobody who could dog-sit for an hour or two as the treatment plan progresses. The negative way that we talk can really become an obstacle in future if we don't tackle it. Slowing down, unpicking it when it emerges and tackling the least fruitful examples that harm how our clients view their dogs and how they view potential treatments is going to be important when we tackle the blind spots that they have.

Slowing down and exploring negative self-talk objectively gives you the opportunity to explore what your clients say in more detail.

You are then in a position to challenge what they say in a kind and respectful way. For instance, 'I know you said that your dog constantly barks, but they're not barking right now. Can you tell me more precisely when they don't bark? And when they do?'.

You have the opportunity to bring objectivity into the situation. In fact, the next steps will be very much about the usefulness of objectivity, as clinical observation and analysis is a powerful antidote to catastrophising and rumination.

When you've slowed down the interview to go back over negative statements and blind spots, teasing these out a little, it's also helpful to acknowledge what clients are thinking or feeling, or even help them clarify how they think about their dog. Remember how the first steps of managing ourselves and our emotions relates to identifying and acknowledging what we think and feel? The same is true here. You don't need to be a qualified therapist to say, 'That must be very frustrating…' or 'I can only imagine how challenging this must be for you right now.'

What you are doing here is not telling clients how they think or feel, nor are you getting them on to some kind of Freudian couch to ask them to outline their emotions, but it can really help both sides to have these shadow-side feelings and emotions out in the open.

Just as we do with blind spots, we can choose to note them and leave negative biases for later if now is really not the time to challenge clients, or if we think that it is just harmless offloading. We can also choose to tackle them if we feel that to do so will help clients in the future. We can choose to do that now or later in the process.

For instance, it's helpful when you get to the planning stage to say something along the lines of: 'Now I know you said earlier that you felt nobody was in a position to help and that you felt you were very much facing this on your own, but I just wanted to see if there's anyone at all who might possibly be able to help out for half an hour or so as you build up to leaving Benji home without you?'

Occasionally, when we do this some time after the moment when the thought arose, we can then think more clearly, finding solutions that we couldn't before. At other times, it's useful to challenge it in the moment. There is a wonderful moment in The Royle Family sitcom where the grandmother of the family states that she doesn't ever drink, and all the other family members take it in turn to remind her that she has champagne at weddings, whiskey at New Year, sherry at Christmas and a bottle of stout every evening. By the time they finish, it's clear that the grandmother enjoys a drink as much as anybody else, if not more so. It's not always appropriate to unpick our client's negative statements in this way, and we may need to do so gently and with kindness, but it's unhelpful for clients to continue in the belief that they've genuinely 'tried everything' when in fact there are lots of ways they could better deal with their problem in future.

This is also true of clients who catastrophise or who revert to "could have" descriptions about events that brought them to work with us. One client recounted how her off-lead dog had run up to a family who were eating a picnic in the park. The dog, a particularly large one, had jumped into the food, began eating it and growled at everyone who tried to pull him away. When his guardian managed to catch up with him, he had devoured half the picnic and bit her when she grabbed his collar to pull him away. Not only was the client ashamed of her dog and embarrassed about what had happened, but she worried that he 'could have' bitten a child or that he 'might' bite a child in the future. These lines of reasoning, where we speculate about things that "could have" happened in the past (but didn't) or "might" happen in the future (but won't, if we pay careful attention to managing and retraining the dog) are often likely to derail discussions. It's essential to acknowledge the underlying fears, shame and guilt that underpin these moments, but it's unhelpful for clients to speculate wildly and catastrophically about the future.

In cases like this, it's helpful to acknowledge feelings but then to put an end to excessive ruminations about hypotheticals: 'I'm sure that must have been absolutely mortifying. But luckily, Barney didn't bite a child and we'll start putting things into place to make sure he never can. Let's start by…'

In this way, you can steer conversations into the practical and the immediate future rather than dealing with unlikely or impossible scenarios either in the past or in some dim and distant future.

This is also true when clients are being unnecessarily hard on themselves about how they reacted in the past. After all, there's nothing they could have done about it. When clients are ashamed of how they responded - or how they failed to respond - it's always useful to consider what they can do in future to move things forward.

Ultimately, if we don't deal with innately pessimistic talk, however, it runs the risk of derailing us. Note it and decide on how best to challenge it.

13. Understand how to see objectively

Once you have understood your own blind spots and biases as well as being able to identify those of your client, you'll be better placed to be objective about what you see. There are two important aspects to this. First, you have to be able to truly "see" your client and their situation. Second, you need to be able to consider the dog's behaviour in a clear and objective way.

In reality, being objective with our human clients involves listening more than it involves seeing. This involves a lot of active listening. We'd think that listening is easy, but it is one of the hardest skills for humans to truly master.

Effective listening is an acquired skill for most people. For instance, take the situation where a client tells you that they've tried everything to be a good leader to their dog, and their speech is full of comments about being the master and the alpha. It can be very easy to switch off and disengage with everything else that's said, particularly the subtext. It means we might tune out, for example, if our client is telling us how hard they are finding it to deal with their dog's separation anxiety and not listen adequately to their concerns about finding someone to help at the beginning of the plan if they need to suspend absences. If we listen and dismiss our clients' concerns, we run the risk of losing them to someone else who will listen more empathetically or give them immediate solutions. Likewise, if we only listen to part of what is said, missing out on the important parts of what our clients are saying. Not only that, but we get involved with our own internal monologue, considering the things we want to say and devising plans before our client has even finished speaking. For instance, if our client is in mid-flow and they raise a point about needing to be the alpha, we might be constructing an internal discussion about this, missing out on everything else the client says afterwards. If you find yourself frequently engaging in thinking about your own responses or mulling over what the client has said rather than listening to what they are currently saying, this can also cause us to listen ineffectively.

We also need to pay attention to our clients' body language. Sometimes, their nonverbal behaviour can "speak" much more loudly than their words. Their body language might show they're engaged with us if they lean forward, offer eye contact or if they begin to speak more energetically. Likewise, our body language can do the same, and we can inadvertently give off nonverbal cues that shape what the client tells us, so that we don't get the whole truth. For instance, one trainer whose eye contact was particularly penetrating found that this was in fact acting as an aversive at times, shaping what clients chose to tell her. One look and their clients would stop talking. When she asked them how they'd dealt with the dog's behaviour in the past, they clammed up and she felt that she was missing out on opportunities to engage with methods they'd already used, or found that her eye contact was obtrusive and judgemental. By leaning forward, smiling slightly and nodding, it took a lot of weight off her rather intimidating gaze, which although neutral, was often interpreted by clients as hostile.

Clients' body language may also deny or contradict what their verbal language said. For instance, one client expressed a rather scornful response to the use of food, saying 'It's just bribery and tricks, isn't it?', yet he smiled at his dog and stroked his dog's head as he said it. It's not always that body language will catch us in a lie. Body language and vocal pitch, volume and intonation can also strengthen, emphasise or add intensity to the message, and we may find that our clients become louder at some points or that they soften in others. Again, it's something we also need to be conscious of when working with clients - that we're not constantly shaping them with what it is we want to hear by enthusiastic delivery of certain utterances compared to a more neutral tone for others.

One thing that many enthusiastic and passionate speakers do is to rush in when the client has paused. Silences and gaps or hesitations can feel very awkward and we may rush to fill them, literally putting words in our clients' mouths. Sometimes, it's really important to leave a longer gap before responding than you would otherwise. At other times, we may still be working on rapport and fill the gap as a way of doing so. This is where video or audio recordings of your own sessions can be painfully enlightening. Using a transcription service to write down what was said can give you the ability to manually count your ratio of dialogue compared to your clients. It can be very embarrassing to think that we are client-centred and that we are giving the centre stage to our clients when in fact, we are shaping, controlling and dominating the dialogue. What's the ratio for how much you speak compared to how much your client does? Are you truly listening as much as you think you are?

A simple transcript can also help you identify the main points from your client's utterances, to be able to consider more objectively what they find to be most important. We can also look back to pick up themes that might be emerging. For instance, in one rather tense discussion with a client, where the client wanted her epileptic and disabled dog to be hyper-obedient and had engaged the trainer to stop chewing and to teach the dog a perfect walk to heel over several kilometres, listening back, it was clear that there were many tensions around the theme of freedom, and that the client was very determined to control every movement her dog made. Digging deeper into this at the next session, discussing canine behaviour, agency and freedom, it became apparent that the guardian was very anxious about the dog, particularly those aspects of the dog's behaviour, such as her ataxia and seizures, that were completely beyond the guardian's control. A narrative about control emerged where the client's attempts to control what she could because the seizures and ataxia were so unpredictable became clear through revisiting the interview.

If nothing else, it's useful to periodically review your own interview style when working with clients, just as you would if you were reviewing your performance in entering an agility competition or a heelwork-to-music competition. If we're afraid of self-assessment in our work with humans, we will find ourselves stumbling at the same hurdles every time and making the same mistakes. It is impossible to listen to clients in a truly objective and unfiltered way: our own experiences interfere with that process. Our own cultures and blind spots interfere with that listening, too. These biases distort our view of our clients.

When we listen, we may also find ourselves listening evaluatively and even judgementally. We are sometimes trapped in subconscious processes, deciding if our client is good or bad, capable or incapable, likeable or not. When we listen judgementally, this gives way to advice giving and 'well, I think you should....'

The same is true, of course, in written dialogue. Following a particularly fraught euthanasia case in which a client had first engaged a trainer because the dog was responding to restraint and grooming by biting her, the client had then disengaged when there had been a very slight improvement, but had failed to really make as much progress as the trainer would have liked regarding cooperative handling and husbandry. Some 18 months later, the client re-contacted the trainer to say that the programme had failed and the dog had started biting again. From the get-go, the trainer felt hostile because 18 months had passed with no recurrence of the behaviour, and in fact, the behaviour had been recovered because the guardian had once again grabbed the dog. Unable to take the dog into kennels and rehome them as the guardian requested, the guardian then had the dog euthanised. Her final message to the trainer was that the veterinarian had said the dog was dominant, unreceptive, stubborn and uncooperative and had recommended euthanasia. In fact, whether or not the veterinarian had indeed said these things was moot: they reflected what the guardian needed to believe in supporting the choice she had made. Instead of listening judgementally and thinking that the client was making a sly dig at the failure of the trainer, what the trainer heard was the guardian needing to justify a very hard choice and sent her a kind message in response and a personalised card. Six months later, the client bought a new puppy and enlisted the trainer from the start. The trainer was able to show the client how to help the dog habituate to the client's rather handsy approach from the start. Instead of blurting out recriminations in response to what was undoubtedly the client expressing her guilt and shame, trying to justify her choice, the trainer stepped back from taking it personally.

Stereotyping also affects our ability to listen and see without bias. We may be very adamant that labels are unproductive when describing behaviour, only then to refer to our clients and their dogs by their condition: 'the resource guarding spaniel', 'the Pomeranian with stereotypies'. We might find ourselves making judgements about this or that type of man or woman, age groups or ethnic groups as well as personality types. Our views about our clients and their dogs should remain background thoughts, not in the forefront of our thinking.

We can also go the other way and become hugely sympathetic. This is especially true if the client is affected by similar experiences to those with which we have had to cope. Some of our clients will come to us with heartbreaking situations. Going back to the client in Lesson 6, where human situations mean a dog's welfare is compromised, we can become very involved and sympathetic rather than being able to remain rational and objective.

One such example involved a dog in a foster home for a local rescue. The dog needed surgery to amputate a digit and prevent the spread of necrosis in the bone. Despite setting up the appointment with a local clinic which was entirely paid for by the rescue, the client failed to show up on a number of occasions. The investigator for the rescue, a retired police sergeant, went round on numerous occasions to the home and finished by spending over an hour with the fosterer, whom the investigator described as clearly drunk. The investigator listened sympathetically to the fosterer's story: his wife had left, she'd taken him to the cleaners and he'd lost his business during the coronavirus pandemic. He could see that the dog was not afraid of the fosterer despite the fact there was a lot of drunken shouting between the fosterer and his friend. On talking to the neighbours, the investigator learned that the dog was relatively well-treated but that the man was a well-known rowdy drunk who spent most of his days with a group of friends. The investigator felt a deep sympathy for the fosterer that was at odds with the chair of the rescue, who was able to see more objectively. Despite the sadness of the situation, it was not an environment conducive to the good welfare of the dog, particularly when the fosterer had repeatedly failed to follow up on appointments – even if an animal taxi had been provided and he needed to do nothing more than be home and open the door. It's important to realise that our objectivity is affected by being with clients, and this can also cloud our judgement.

What is enormously helpful in cases like this is to work with a colleague, as you will explore in Lesson 14. They can act as a useful compass to help us see if we've slipped into subjectivity. It's also useful to take audio or video footage so that you can look back over it with a cool eye later on. This is not just for your own development of active and objective listening skills, but also so that you can review any points where either you or the client were involved in steering discussions unhelpfully.

It is also helpful to engage your client in objectivity. This is especially true if they've been using all-or-nothing language or if they are involved in black-and-white thinking. You also need to be involved in objective analysis of the client and their dog.

Functional analysis is one way that you can do this. A functional analysis starts with an objective description of what the dog is doing. It's unhelpful at this point to use emotive adjectives, adverbs or labels. For instance, take the client who describes their dog behaving 'incredibly aggressively' towards other dogs. This subjective statement is unhelpful. What does 'incredibly' look like to them? What is aggression to them? Clients are sometimes involved in misdiagnosing their dog's behaviour. Whether they decide that their dog was 'protecting them' or they diagnose their dog with separation anxiety, it's vital to unpick this. A good intake form can help. For instance, if you use a document that is partly a questionnaire to be completed and uses a tick box survey for other parts, you can quickly pick up any anomalies. One example would be the client who reported that their dog was suffering from separation anxiety as the major problem that they wanted to work on with their intake form. Yet, when ticking symptoms and describing symptoms on a Likert scale of 1 - 5, with 1 being 'never' and 5 being 'always', the client had either ticked N/A, 1 or added a ? in the 'Not Applicable' column for every single symptom of separation anxiety other than destroying doors. There were none of the symptoms we'd expect with separation-related behaviour. This is worth further probing.

What is helpful is to describe the exact behaviour carefully, and encourage or shape the client to do the same. For instance, you may not wish to use the term separation anxiety at all if you feel it is an unhelpful label. For the example above, what would be a more objective description of the behaviour is 'chewing and scratching at the external door during guardian absence'. Avoid value-laden words like 'excessively' or 'compulsively'. Avoid mind-reading the purpose or function of the behaviour. It's unhelpful to add phrases like 'trying to get out', since we don't know yet if that is indeed what the dog is doing.

Instead of 'playing aggressively', we might use phrases like 'infrequent role-reversal and repeated attempts to chase other dogs'. Instead of 'aggressive towards other dogs', we might say 'barks and lunges' or 'growls when strangers pet his head'. It's really important you brush up on your objective description of behaviour and that you shape your clients' choices too. Remember also that things like anxiety, depression and compulsions are disorders diagnosed by vets: this is not language that is helpful to the trainer or behaviourist.

Let's take anxiety. How could we describe this more objectively? We might say 'low posture, tail between legs, ears pinned back against head, showing sideways glances' or we might say 'increased motor activity, pacing, panting and circling.' It's much more useful to be objective. Where it's most useful is in monitoring change. What does decreased anxiety look like to you and the client? It's much more useful to measure and assess progress in terms of amount of pacing.

Behaviour may also be linked in terms of what we might refer to as a 'response class'. This simply means behaviours that are superficially different but are designed to access the same reinforcers or escape the same aversives. Barking, lunging, air snapping, inhibited bites, growling, snarling and biting are examples of behaviour within a response class. We might call that class 'aggressive behaviours' as a shortcut. Barking, spinning, pawing, pushing a nose under the guardian's hand, swiping the guardian with their hind quarters and jumping up may also be different behaviours designed to evoke attention from the guardian. This is another example of a response class. Clean description of behaviour is vital as we move to objectivity. It's very useful to practise this with colleagues and to use video as well to help you.

You may notice different forms of behaviour that are designed to do the same thing. Other ways you might record objective data about the dog's behaviour would be through describing the frequency and rate of behaviour. Clients might be tempted to say things like 'they paw me all the time', or they're 'always aggressive towards other dogs'. What is helpful is to know how frequently. What does 'all the time' look like? How often is 'always'? It may be that you are simply counting the frequency that the dog does the behaviour. You might ask the guardian to make a tally of how many times the dog paws them during a 24-hour period. You could ask them to survey the next ten encounters with dogs and note what the 'aggressive' behaviour is and how frequently it happens in relation to how many dogs they see.

When you engage clients in this kind of assessment, you are also helping them to be more objective. When we see our dog paws us 17 times during the day, and we're focused on their behaviour, we stop thinking of them being 'attention-seeking' or 'annoying' and it builds objectivity.

Documenting behaviour may be something that you will need to rely on your client to do, especially if the behaviour happens infrequently throughout the day. Many clients feel that it's important for you to see the behaviour. Indeed, some clients find it hard to engage if you don't want to see their dog being aggressive to other dogs at the daycare centre, or the dog jumping all over people at greetings. It's important to remind clients whose dogs have problem behaviours that from this point forward, it's important that the dog isn't practising behaviours any more. This also requires you to have good interview skills in order to clearly document behaviour historically. Getting a good description out of clients can be helpful.

Take this interview as an example:

Client: I don't know. Can't you come and visit? How are you going to know how aggressive he is if you haven't seen him doing it?

Trainer: Well, in the same way the insurance investigators don't need to see car crashes in action or burn your house down again just to know how it happened. I trust your description. It's also really important that he doesn't get to practise the behaviour at all if possible. After all, all they're doing is getting better at it each time they do it. We're building a habit. So we'll talk through the last few incidents and you can tell me what you remember. Okay?

Client: I guess so. I'd still prefer for you to see it though. I don't understand how you can work with him if you don't understand what he's doing.

Trainer: Well, I'll help you tell me clearly what happened and if there's still anything I don't understand, maybe then we can go and see it in action. The trouble is that it's stressful for everyone involved, so I'd rather not have to do that if possible.

Client: Ok. I get that.

Trainer: So, let's just start by telling me exactly what happened.

Client: Well, we were walking into the park and Micky saw another dog and started going nuts. He was extremely aggressive.

Trainer: Can you help me understand what 'going nuts' looks like? Was he pulling on the lead? Growling? Barking?

Client: Yes. He started pulling towards the other dog. I tried to pull him away and told him 'no!' but he still kept doing it. He was barking but I don't think he growled.

Trainer: Ok. That's great. Can you tell me where you were and where the other dog was? Maybe you could show me on Google Maps?

Client: Sure. I had turned the corner just here when we saw the other dog coming out of the park gates.

Trainer: So 100 metres or so?

Client: Yes, I think so.

Trainer: And what kind of dog was it? Big? Small? Could you see if they were male or female?

Client: It was a big German shepherd. He stopped right in the gate and started staring at us. That's when Micky started going nuts.

Trainer: And what did the other guardian do?

Client: He just called his dog to move and they started walking towards us. Micky was going absolutely mental by this point. I was so embarrassed. He was barking and pulling around on the end of the lead.

Trainer: I can imagine that was horrifying for you.

Client: It was. The man started coming towards us.

Trainer: And he was on the same side of the pavement as you or on the other side of the road?

Client: The same side. Micky hates that dog. He's always running up to us when we're walking in the park. Micky hates big dogs. It's hard because he's so little and they don't understand he's afraid. He hates other dogs trying to dominate him.

Trainer: So you'd met this dog before?

Client: Yes, lots of times.

Trainer: And Micky's never done this to him before?

Client: No. Usually, when he runs up to us in the park, Micky just stands his ground. All his hackles go up and he starts trembling.

Trainer: And he's on lead or off lead at this point?

Client: Off the lead in the park. But we have to have them on lead outside the park because there's a lot of traffic.

What happens when you spend time interviewing clients is that you build up a picture and can help clients describe more accurately. You can see here how the trainer helps the guardian pinpoint what 'going nuts' means, but also picks up a lot of other pertinent information that is helpful to understand why the dog behaved as they did as well as ignoring the unhelpful talk. Not involving your client in the information gathering process also invalidates their opinion, as if you are the only one qualified to see what is happening. It ignores their lived experience with the dog. It also means you are missing an opportunity to allow them to become objective and also to engage them in the training. When we take on all the responsibility for deciding what the dog is doing, it is not empowering for the client, nor is it helpful to us.

What you need first is simply information about the behaviour. Clients will naturally want to tell you all kinds of other information, but what you need is to focus on behaviour.

What did the dog do in the moment? What did the guardian do in the moment (if they were there)? What did the target do in the moment?

You can also take a hypothetical situation, asking your client to imagine scenarios and predict what would happen. Ask your client to describe what would happen if…

Let's take the case of a dog who has been jumping up:

We need information about the topography of the behaviour. What does it look like? What shape does it take? Is the dog jumping up with all four feet off the floor? Are they jumping with two feet and jumping at people? For instance, one dog jumps up by leaping with all four feet and usually pushes off the guardian with two feet in a kind of circle, like a swimmer might do if they swim up to the edge of a pool and use the pool edge to propel themselves forward, or like they are using the target as a parkour prop. Another dog jumps up with all four feet off the ground but never makes contact with the target, like they have an invisible pogo stick. One dog jumps up on two legs and puts the other two legs on the target, often scratching legs or snagging tights. Another dog jumps up on all four feet and often makes contact with noses or chins, muzzle punching other humans.

As behaviour consultants or trainers, we can alter the topography or shape of the behaviour, so knowing what the dog is doing is helpful. It might also provide solutions for management. A dog who muzzle-punches people in the nose, face or chin is a dog who will need more initial management than a dog who is not making contact, for example, or who's just jumping once and balancing their paws on the person. Knowing what the behaviour looks like is not meaningless.

The dog may also be doing other behaviours in the same response class. That's to say, behaviours that are designed to get the same outcome. For example, one might bark and jump at an owner to get attention. One dog might dance around in circles and sometimes jump up on two legs and scrabble on the legs of the target.

Later, we will unpick the potential function of the behaviour, but for now, just describing what the behaviour looks like is important. However, dogs may often do the same behaviour in different circumstances and for different functions. So, you may need to explore the same behaviour in different contexts. For instance, dogs may jump up on greeting, before walks, at mealtimes or even at the fence when other dogs go past. If clients want you to work with their dog jumping up, it's important that you get all the relevant information.

After topography and shape, we also need to consider the count: how many times does this happen. You may be asking your clients to do this when recording future occurrences of the behaviour when you are not present. When you do this, make sure you ask the client to specify the time period. For instance, you may ask your client at the end of your first interview session to take the next five visitors who arrive and count how many times the dog jumps on the visitor. This may seem trivial, but there is a big difference between a dog who does it once and a dog who does it forty times. It may also seem like a fairly pointless exercise: there are plenty of trainers who proceed to treat such behaviours without cataloguing them. Imagine if, however, your client has failed to disclose the intensity of some jumping up with particular guests, where the dog is unable to be stopped and where the jumping up happens for fifteen minutes. You, as an unfamiliar guest and a seasoned dog professional might have had one or two on entrance and not consider how serious the problem is. Not only that, you simply can't say, 'Please can I see twenty people coming in,' just to test your hypothesis.

Counting the incidence of behaviour may not be useful in aggression cases or anxiety cases but it may be helpful with some problem behaviours such as barking at stimuli outside the house, jumping on visitors or eliminating in the home. It's a useful baseline that will allow you to look back and see how much progress has been made. Looking back at the initial count can be helpful later especially with pernicious or persistent problems that take a long time to solve. Being able to say: 'your dog used to bark 50 times when the delivery vans pulled up next door, now they only bark 5 times' is useful later in the process when clients become demotivated. Counts help us see progress, particularly when involved in long-term training projects. You can also use these to help you set appropriate goals with your clients, as you'll see in Lesson 24.

Besides topography and counts, you may also want to involve your client in looking at the behavioural rate or frequency. This is how many responses there are in a given period of time. Again, this can be useful with persistent problems like barking or jumping up. This can be really helpful as well to counter the 'always' and 'never' view. It helps clients reframe their problems objectively. For instance, one client was despairing about her dog's inability to come back when called. It helped her to understand that, in the home, her dog responded to all ten recalls with a solid and immediate recall. That's not 'never'. In the garden, that was 8 out of 10 trials. Off-lead, it was also not 'never', although the dog did only return once in ten trials.

This also helps with goal setting. As a rule, setting micro-goals of more than 10% is unhelpful. So to expect the dog to do more than 2 solid recalls when outside off lead is too challenging. Equally, anything less than 5% is not a sufficient micro-goal at all. Say for instance you are working with a separation behaviours case and the dog stays lying down if the guardian goes out for 60 seconds. However, after 60 seconds, the dog starts to become anxious and starts to alert to the absence or stand up and start to look for their guardian. To expect more than 10% progress as you increase trials (so more than an additional 6 seconds) is a lot of progress - possibly too challenging. But to expect less than 5% means you won't be able to increase goals sufficiently quickly. So less than 3 seconds would be an insufficient challenge.

Just to put that in perspective, a 10% absence increase every day would mean being able to leave for 20 minutes at the end of the first month and 6 hours by the end of the second month - assuming progress in separation cases was linear, which it isn't. However, a 5% absence increase every day would mean only being able to leave for 5 minutes by the end of the first month and just 25 minutes by the end of the second month. You can see that is a huge difference, and if we expect dogs to make more progress than 10% at each micro-goal, then we are setting our clients up for a very unrealistic goal which they will no doubt be disappointed not to achieve.

On the other hand, as you will see in later lessons, to not set enough challenge means that our clients will languish in hopelessness with very little progress, which is frustrating and disappointing too.

Great measurement in terms of rate and frequency can really help you set goals accurately and be realistic with your clients.

Likewise with lead pulling. A dog that can manage 10 metres of loose-lead on day one will be able to do 200 metres by day 30 on a 10% challenge. By month 2, that would be almost 4km. On the same scale at a 5% challenge, the guardians should only be expecting 45m or so at the end of the first month and will only be at 200m by the end of the second month, all things being equal.

Of course, training is not maths, and progress is not linear, but knowing the rate and frequency of behaviour will help you set realistic targets. If the dog can't walk more than 10 metres without pulling on Day 1, there is no point asking them to do 50m by the end of the first week: it's too much of a challenge.

Alongside topography, count, rate and frequency, you can also explore duration. How long does a behaviour last? This also works to help you set appropriate goals in the same way as previously. If a dog barks for 30 seconds after the doorbell rings, that's useful information. You can ask your clients to time how long behaviour goes on for before the dog stops. For instance, how long do they jump up on guests? How long are they mounting and humping the stuffed cushion? How long are they barking for when the telephone rings? They can also add this up over the entire day. Again, looking back on this will help them later understand how far they have come as well as helping you set realistic yet challenging goals for progress, extinction protocols or behavioural reduction.

Another measurable aspect of behaviour is latency. High latency means there is a long delay between the trigger and the behaviour or the request and the response. Low latency means there is a short delay. Imagine, for instance, a dog who has low latency recall in the home - it's a short time gap from the guardian calling the dog to the dog responding, but a high latency recall outside - a long time gap between the guardian calling the dog to the dog responding, if they respond at all. You might work on latency of behaviours as one of your targets. As with all other behaviours, a lot of this will depend on how challenging the environment is to the dog, but it's helpful, all things being equal, to know that you can work on this. For instance, if a dog has a very short fuse when seeing another dog at 100m, you could work on latency, so that their fuse gets longer, all things being equal. Instead of barking immediately when they see another dog at 100m, you might be working on helping them bark only after a few seconds have elapsed. This can be useful if you can't escape environmental triggers, too. What latency helps you do is measure the rate of desensitisation. You can work to increase latency, like increasing the time between a trigger and an aggressive response, or to decrease latency like you might do if you're using 'Leave it!' or 'Let's go!', wanting a much quicker or almost automatic response rather than the dog fighting with you for 10 seconds before following instruction.

We can also measure the intensity of behaviour, although that might involve making a scale to start with. For example, if we are measuring the intensity of a dog who pulls on lead, we might start by imagining the situation when they would pull most, such as when following a herd of deer. This then becomes 10 on the scale of intensity or magnitude, with 1 being 'walking nicely to heel'. These can be useful criteria for describing behaviour and help catalogue behaviour with the guardian. Intensity might include the volume of vocalisations. It might also include the pitch, whether high pitched or not.

Locus is the final measure of behaviour that can help us understand where it is likely to happen, should it happen only in one place. Although this might rightly be called an antecedent, it can also help the guardian describe the behaviour.

Some ways we can encourage the guardians to describe the behaviour might include asking them to keep a diary of the behaviour over 48 hours. You can then help them be more precise.

- What did it look like?
- Did the dog do any other behaviours that have a similar purpose?
- How many times did it happen over 48 hours?
- When it happens, how many times did the dog do the behaviour from start to finish?
- How long did each occurrence last?
- How quickly did it happen from seeing or hearing the trigger?
- How intense was the behaviour?

For example: problem barking.

The behaviour happened 4 times over 48 hours. The dog also growled twice. The first time, the dog barked 14 times in 30 seconds. The second, they barked 10 times and it lasted 24 seconds. The third, they barked 12 times and it lasted 30 seconds. The fourth, they barked 15 times and it lasted 30 seconds. It usually happens the minute the dog hears someone pulling up outside the house. The first incident was 8 out of 10; the second was 6 out of 10; the third was 7 out of 10 and the last was 8 out of 10. Every time, the dog goes towards the window or door.

You'll notice at this point we are yet to add antecedents and consequences. Here, we're just thinking about the behaviour itself and nothing more. Having samples to show your clients can also help them understand how to document the data. You may also ask them to set up wildlife cameras inside or to video the behaviour if they can. However, be mindful that this might not always be possible and guardians may change their behaviour because they realise that they are later going to have to show it to you.

By encouraging your clients to think in this way, you can also help them decide if something is truly a problem and if they really need to change the dog's behaviour or simply manage the situation better. It also helps you, as it ensures that you aren't going to put into place a treatment that is likely to fail if the behaviour is too severe, or that you aren't trying to change something that doesn't need changing. The baseline is not just so that the client can see how much progress they've made or think more objectively about behaviour rather than getting hung up on causes, it's also for you. The risk of not documenting behaviour to start with comes at the cost that we may put into place an intervention that is going to be ineffective, or that we carry on with an ineffective intervention thinking that it is working. We might also take client feedback about the treatment not working and discontinue it without realising in actual fact, behavioural change is happening after all.

Take for example a client whose dog is suffering from extreme anxiety when the log fire is lit. The guardian describes the behaviour as severe, but you do not know what that means. A 48-hour behaviour diary reveals that the dog starts to pace, whine and tremble at 11am, at least 2 hours before the fire is lit. The dog paces for 45 minutes despite the guardian asking the dog 27 times to go and lie down. The guardian had also tried to distract the dog with food treats, but the dog did not eat them. By the end of the day, the dog is trembling and shaking without stopping. She paces and attempts to hide under tables. She vomited five times. She also starts drooling and this lasts for three hours.

Realising the severity of the behaviour, you are then able to see that this situation is probably in need of pharmaceutical support. The dog is spending almost 12 hours a day showing signs of stress that mount during the day, and at least 3 hours a day, she is in a state of acute stress.

The veterinarian is also able to use your diary. A diary is not just a useful tool for the guardians, but also for other professionals. It helps them see how severe the behaviour is. Of course, for the average dog guardian, they have little against which to compare the behaviour. Perhaps you deal with back-to-back fear cases during the week and you have a very fine-tuned gauge as to how much tension the dog is showing. Objective description will help you clearly communicate that to a veterinarian. Of course, you are not in a position to say that the dog is suffering from anxiety: that is a medical diagnosis. But it is helpful to be able to say that the dog starts with visible panting at 11am and that she is more clingy. This builds up to pacing, where the dog spends 45 minutes without settling. The dog also begins to whine and vocalise, and this often continues for 10 minutes or more. You could add that the dog tried to scratch 14 times between 11am - 12pm, and that she made 7 attempts to hide under the table or escape the room. You can see how this would help a veterinarian understand how serious a problem is if by the end of the diary you say the dog has not sat down, laid down or rested from 11am - 11pm, and that by 11pm, she has been salivating for 3 hours. Trainers are not the only professionals who can't see the true picture because of client subjectivity.

On the other hand, a client who says her dog has severe anxiety relating to separation is able to video the dog for 3 hours during her absence. She reports that her neighbour says the dog barks all the time the guardian is out. Video shows that the dog turns in circles for 30 seconds after the guardian leaves, watches the guardian leave and spends 2 minutes pacing. Then the dog settles down and goes to sleep. Occasionally, when prompted by noises from next door, the dog barks. The dog settles down within two minutes. When the guardian approaches the door, the dog wakes up and goes to jump at the door as the guardian unlocks it. The dog also barks. Seeing the video makes it clear that the neighbour's complaints are biased, based on the fact that the dog only barks when there are noises next door or when the neighbour goes in and out of her home. For that reason, of course it's more likely that she has heard barking, but that's not to say it's 'all the time'. What guardians think is happening isn't always what is actually happening. Baseline assessments are as good for confirming problem behaviours and defining them as they are for ruling them out.

At this point, you may also want to do other diagnostic rule-outs. For instance, one client reports that her reactive dog is 'protecting' her. While the trainer thinks this is unlikely, since the only time the dog is reactive is when they are being handled by the guardian, it's difficult to say for sure whether this is true or not. Part of the diagnostic might be to rule out protective behaviour by videoing the dog being walked by the guardian at a distance from the trigger, but near enough to see any low level stress signs, and then walking at the same distance with a familiar human or dog walker without the guardian present. That's not to say the dog is not 'protecting' the guardian if they are calm and quiet when walked by other people. It may also be very much about the dynamic with the guardian. But performing rule-outs may very much be a part of your work. For instance, if you notice that a jumping dog never jumps on you at greeting, then it may be as much about retraining the humans in the dog's life if the dog jumps up excessively on them. It's important not just to seek out evidence to confirm our theories but also to rule out other things as well. As a rule, if the behaviour involves more than just the dog on their own, you may need to rule out human influences too.

Of course, once you have undertaken a really good data collection, you're better placed to choose the right problem to work on, to make the right diagnosis and to find solutions that work. The data collection helps your clients remove their subjective view of the dog and the dog's behaviour which can be remarkably therapeutic in itself.

To that end, then, we need to be conscious of the data we gather about the client and also about the way we interpret it. Remember, collection and evidence gathering comes first and interpretation comes second. We should never jump the gun on going out to seek information just to confirm what we already think. Finally, remember that there are many laws relating to the keeping and sharing of personal data: make sure you consult a legal expert with experience in data protection in order to make sure your business is secure. We're not talking about the need to use end-to-end encryption when your client sends you a video of their dog, but at the same time, if you are gathering information and personal data, you need to respect your local laws about how long you need to keep it, under what circumstances, and when and how you should purge your data. This is especially true if you intend to ever use client footage, case studies, videos or photos in your own work.

Make sure your contract with your client explains explicitly that this may happen, and make sure that if you do so, you have the right to do so. That includes your own photos or video footage with their dogs or with them in it. Even if you are working within a shelter milieu, it's tempting to think we can use footage taken of the dogs we're working with, but if the shelter owns the animals from a legal standpoint, then they may rightly take issue with you using these images. It's not simply a matter of making clients sign a waiver: that waiver may not be worth the paper that it's written on if your actions do not comply with legislation in your specific setting.

Gathering information is a crucial antidote to partiality and subjectivity. It's not just a useful measure by which to assess progress: it also functions as a way to counter some of the negative biases we have when thinking about the animals in our care.

14. Stop, Collaborate and Listen

As we move into interpreting the data our clients send us, or the information we pick up, there will be times that it's important to consult with our colleagues.

Of course, that may not be necessary if you're dealing with something relatively straightforward, but dog training is usually an isolated profession, even if you work in a facility and share your training plans. Shadowing colleagues seems to be something we only choose to do when learning new skills, despite the fact that it is always of use and we are all always learning, even if we have been doing it for thirty years.

When you look around, the best trainers and behaviourists will be those who you regularly see on training courses but you also see sharing their knowledge, practice and case studies, too. Likewise, mentorship is again something we tend to only look for when we are new to the profession, despite the fact that it is rewarding for both the mentor and the mentee. There can be nothing like working with a young, enthusiastic, freshly-trained colleague who comes to you with all the new, shiny techniques that remind you why you fell in love with training animals and their humans in the first place. Ask yourself honestly: how often do you share, and how often do you ask for advice or feedback?

Also, we tend to only share our problem cases or tricky cases, forgetting that what would be most useful to scrutinise would be our everyday cases. This works in two ways. The first is that we can benefit from others asking us why we do things in particular ways. Even if it only leads to you justifying and confirming your choice, having someone ask why you teach this in such a way, or why you do that can lead to some revolutionary improvements in your own practice. Similarly, if we are truly good with certain types of cases, it's often useful to share these and explain our rationale: when we achieve mastery, we can sometimes be unconsciously competent. That's to say, we are so good that we are just doing it without reflection or thought. It's become a polished motor pattern. Having to explain these processes to others brings us back into the realm of consciously competent, so that we are actively thinking about our process.

Educational theorist David Kolb designed something he called the 'Experiential Learning Cycle' in 1984. He said that humans have a four-stage learning cycle and also that we have preferred parts of this, our 'learning style'. It's not that we don't do all parts of the learning cycle - of course we do. It's more that we favour certain aspects and spend less time on other aspects.

The Experiential Learning Cycle is, of course, cyclical. Though there is no starting point as such and we can come in at any point, we could say the learning cycle begins with 'concrete experience'. We do something new or encounter new ways of doing it. Then we move on to 'reflective observation' where we review what happened and, if we are smart, tailor our performance for the future: the evolution of behaviour at work. This leads us on to 'abstract conceptualisation', where we learn from what we did and create new ideas or theories. Finally, we plan and implement the changes having refined our learning through reflection and adaptation. The cycle then repeats. Kolb's Learning Styles tie into this, as well as those of Alan Mumford and Peter Honey. You can always find these online to test yourself and find out where you sit in terms of learning styles. Be conscious that these will change and evolve too.

Someone who starts life as an enthusiast, diving into experiences and wanting to start straight away without all the data gathering may find that part of the learning process to be frustrating and pointless. If you were itching at the thought of all the data collection in the last lesson, you may well have thought, 'What's the point of all this? I know what the problem is. The dog is just a food guarder. They need to be taught how to drop and leave it, maybe a little desensitisation and counterconditioning. I have just the thing to fix this problem!' then you are probably right there in the enthusiast, activist section. 'Let's get started!' might as well be your motto.

On the other hand, you may find that you enjoy data gathering and reflection, and you hate people forcing you to make rash decisions. You hate it when people put you on the spot and want a quick fix. Analysis is your forté and you enjoy reading around the subject, or watching videos of people trying it out. If your client presents with a problem, you might want to mull it over and pass it via your trusted colleagues and collaborators. Sometimes, being a reflective learner means you're cautious and you want to see the big picture, not just dive in tinkering straight away. People who want immediate solutions and answers may well frustrate you.

Theorists want a logical plan. No slapdash diving in and flying by the seat of your pants. They want step by step, rational, laid-out, logical, clear, tied-and-tested plans that have been studied and researched, with conclusive feedback. They don't just want to sit with a theory that the dog jumps up only on people who aren't used to dogs, but they want to test it. Theorists know all the whys and wherefores and they want to put it into action using solid models. If you're a theorist, you'll get frustrated by enthusiastic activist types running around like their hair is on fire, sometimes getting things right by instinct, sheer determination or luck. You'll also get frustrated by the reflective types who want to sit and ponder, without ever coming up with an action plan. If you're a theorist, solid action plans, goal-setting, timelines, deadlines and step-by-step guides are the aspects of work you truly relish. These logical thinkers find holes in all enthusiastic planning. They're the fault-finders, the critics and the people who say, 'well, that'll never work!'

Finally, pragmatists want to put the theory into practice. They enjoy carrying out those action plans, meeting deadlines, crossing off dates and goals achieved. They don't act hastily but at the same time, they want to carry things out - just not in the crazy way of an activist, acting on gut and instinct rather than solid information, good theory and clear action planning. They're the solution finders when logical theorists give ten ways something is bound to fail and they're likely to want to put things into practice having considered all the tensions, potential pitfalls, bear-traps and difficulties.

The trouble is that "like seeks out like" where thinking is involved. It's not unusual to meet a team filled with gung-ho enthusiastic activists who run out of steam for the final minutiae or a department full of cynical theorists who criticise all attempts to innovate and barely change at all. The same is true of our social media groups and the organisations we join, the colleagues we collect as critical friends. If we're desperate to get going, we don't want some old cynic of thirty years telling us how our plan is doomed to failure for X, Y and Z reasons, as well as probably U, V and W reasons as well, and that they'd tried it in 1976, but it was doomed back then as well. Nor do we want a floaty head-in-the-clouds reflector waffling on about their theories related to nerve damage, prenatal trauma and reactivity when all we want to do is get the dog through the park without barking at birds. We might find solace in the company of a pragmatist who's keen to put theory into practice, but theories and thinking may well be an anathema to us.

Similarly, if you enjoy theorising and thinking, you may find it deeply offensive, even disrespectful when other colleagues want to dive straight in or get started. You may think them glib and naive. If you find your hackles pricking whenever someone says they've tried something without even knowing what the problem is, then working with those enthusiasts in life may not be your cup of tea.

We create our own echo chambers both in real life and online. By doing so, we surround ourselves with people who think exactly the same way we do, if not for the entirety, for the major issues and our major values.

We also do this from an ethical perspective.

We seek out colleagues whose ethical standpoint on training reflects our own. If we're "positive-only" trainers, or "force-free trainers" we might steer away from "balanced" trainers or those who use shock. If we're balanced trainers or we use head halters or choke chains in our work, we may find ourselves shying away from what we consider to be the fluffy pink unicorn world of reward-based dog training. We may even find the "other" side to be extremely triggering. I remember watching a rather old-fashioned gentleman trainer who'd been in the business fifty years, a genuinely nice man who'd forgotten more about dogs than I know now. He didn't use aversives, but his language was occasionally dogged by rather sexist, even racist language, filled with cringe-worthy stereotypes and controversial generalisations. Yet to not listen to him would have meant missing out on inordinate amounts of wisdom buried in among the other stuff. We fall into polarised camps and thus we fail to see the tensions and drawbacks of our own narrow way of working. We may decide that we're never, ever going to set foot in the other camp. Of course, there are trainers who can't bear to hear of the use of choke chains and shock, never advocating their use and unable to listen to anyone who might use these tools. Likewise, there are dog trainers who find the use of food to be unethical and manipulative. Just because you can get a dog to sit for a biscuit makes it no less coercive in intent than using a push-sit in their view. The methods may vary, but the intent does not according to them.

When we never listen to other speakers or other people outside our own narrow paradigm, we miss out on their fault-finding about our methods. We also fail to see that in reality, they probably use those methods much less than they'd think.

"Balanced" dog trainers have a lot to teach "force-free" trainers about where food fails - and they're often right. They'll say that trying to use food with dogs who have high predatory drive is often no competition, that you're not using the right reinforcer, or even that if you want behaviour to be reduced then you need to use extinction protocols. All of these things are right, from a scientific point of view. Matching law, competing reinforcers, establishing operations and 80 years of learning theory all confirm these potential tensions of dog training. Only when you are then able to say, 'so you need to habituate and generalise using duration, difficulty and distance' or 'you need to make the recall so automatic that it's done before the dog's had time to process and you need a lot of cold trials', or even 'ok, but extinction protocols are stressful without differential reinforcement of the behaviours you do want', that's when you're ideally placed to help your clients. Your clients won't disagree with you or fail in training because they're not committed enough, but because they fall into regular and predictable bear-traps that we may be unable to see if we are operating solely within our own paradigm set.

"Balanced" trainers are going to give you all the arguments and problems your clients will give you. Likewise, if you're a "balanced" trainer and you never contemplate trialling less invasive or aversive methods, then you're never going to see that there are many ways that are more beneficial for your relationship, perhaps even easier. It's also why those of us coming from a Behaviourist or Skinnerian background need to listen to those from a medical background, an ethologist background, or a psychological background. If we stick within our own narrow paradigm, whatever that may be, we are unlikely to ever see the whole picture or to be able to see the faults within that model.

Dialogue with colleagues whose views do not support your own is not easy, especially if you feel angry or cynical about the way that they work. However, sticking solely within your own echo chamber means that you are unprepared for what real life will throw at you. Of course, you may then go on only to choose clients who think like you, but going back to earlier lessons, is that who you want to be?

There are many people in this life from whom you can learn. Listening to them all objectively without an instinctive dismissal of their clearly ludicrous, unethical, unscientific, impractical, potentially dangerous methods is not for the faint of heart, but it will help you open up your mind and training a little.

It will also help you truly empathise with your client.

The hardest thing you may do might be watching a video of some internet or TV celebrity dog trainer and finding the points you agree on, but if you can understand why your clients are going to gravitate towards their methods, then you are prepared to be able to discuss these objectively. For instance, watching one video of a celebrity TV dog trainer, known for causing polemics in the training world, his methods of desensitising a dog who is reactive to people who pass the car were not that bad. His timing was a little sloppy, but he made a good point about the client using the opposite hand to feed the dog away from the window.

Being able to have these discussions and then say, 'Well, instead of this video where his timing is a little sloppy, here's Patricia McConnell doing the same thing and her timing is really sharp. Let's take that advice about feeding the dog away from the window and import it into what she's doing…' and instead of alienating your client from the get-go, you're helping them cherry-pick the best of what their idols do and the best of what your idols do. After all, all boats rise with the tide. When you've practised the other, earlier steps of the lessons in this manual, you'll hopefully find it much easier to be open-minded without compromising your ethical standpoint. You'll also be able to address the very real problems that clients will undoubtedly face and can't simply be brushed off.

But in all, step out of your echo chamber and seek out the advice of your colleagues. If you're an enthusiast, find a willing logician to pair up with. If you're trapped in reflection and abstraction, lost in studies, find a partner who can show you what they look like in action. And be open to other voices in the dog training industry, even if it is only to prepare yourself for the 'Yes, buts…' that you will need to confront from your clients. Remember too that the detractors of the methods you despise will also have cherry-picked what they show you in order to demonise "the other side" and to convert you to their way of thinking, if not harden your views. It's all very well to find five times they completely messed up, but you need to take into account the ninety-five times they didn't. That said, it's also important to know when to say 'this triggers feelings in me I don't like, so I'm stepping away from it at the moment' - nobody said you need to sit through ten hours of a course by someone you consider to be unethical or that you need to join up the largest Facebook group you can find of people training differently than you do. That's just cruel and unusual masochistic punishment.

Be open to others, but not so much you find yourself more judgemental of their methods, and listen to others but not so much you find yourself angry, upset or annoyed for days after. Doing so will keep you much more grounded and much more open. That in itself will be good for business, unless you're able to operate in a niche bubble where every client arrives with views which perfectly mirror your own. This is equally true if you work in a larger team. Not everyone will share your same ideas and methodology, and that's fine. In fact, it's more than fine, because if we are not learning from their methodology then it challenges us to justify our own.

Remember, it's not just beginners who can profit from the professional opinion of a colleague: we all can. Even if you're just discussing a case a week, having a critical friend to help peer review your processes can really help. Not only that, in those cases where you may not see the progress you expect or where the outcome is poor, having colleagues to support you is essential. Collaboration is a two-way street as well. This is especially true the more successful you are. It's not about giving back at that point, it's about having trusted colleagues who can help spread your work further and support you in your own growth.

You may also benefit from having a wider team of trusted kennels, groomers, veterinarians, nutritionists, dog walkers, other trainers, behaviour consultants and holistic practitioners who you can call on to take cases when you can't. Coming back to your effective triage in Lesson 6, other colleagues who you can refer out to are an absolute blessing. They may not agree with your ideology on everything, but having them as part of your trusted inner circle will really help when you need it. That's also true of other trainers and consultants whose work complements your own. You may be specialising in family problems with dogs, but if your colleague is specialised in separation-related behaviours and fearfulness, it's always useful to be able to recommend clients to them. The worst thing we can do - even if we are busily researching and collaborating behind the scenes to educate ourselves as we go - is to take on cases that are beyond our capabilities. There is no shame in passing these clients on to someone with more experience in that field. Naivety won't just ruin your reputation before you start your career, it also has potential fallout for your clients and their dogs. Nobody is well served by a naive but well-meaning trainer.

Working with humans and animals on behaviour modification is not anodyne, and we need to know that we can improve the situation rather than worsening it.

As you become the expert in your field, remember once or twice to step outside your comfort zone. If you're the Agility Queen or the Dog Parkour King, check out a shelter programme from time to time and remember what it feels like to be a novice-expert again. Not only will you learn about things beyond your expertise, but you'll also be able to export what you know to another group of people who might well have never seen things through your eyes before. Just to prove that point, a group of trainers from a local club who regularly use choke chains and shock collars decided one year to volunteer at a local shelter where the shelter only permitted positive reinforcement methods of training and working with dogs. They had to step right out of their comfort zone. One of them was very highly ranked internationally in protection sports. Working without their usual methods with dogs who very much needed them to put those tools aside taught them a whole new skill set.

Not only that, they had hundreds of ideas about how to work with the shepherds, collies and gundogs who struggled to cope in the shelter, bringing in mantrailing, scent detection and associates who trained dogs for customs and excise detection work.

It's awfully brave to go naked and vulnerable into a completely new world, especially if you're revered within your own field, but it's a profoundly humbling and educational experience. Collaboration with peers - those whose views mirror your own, and those who think differently than you do - is vital. Listening to colleagues from a variety of different disciplines also helps you bring a more holistic approach to your work.

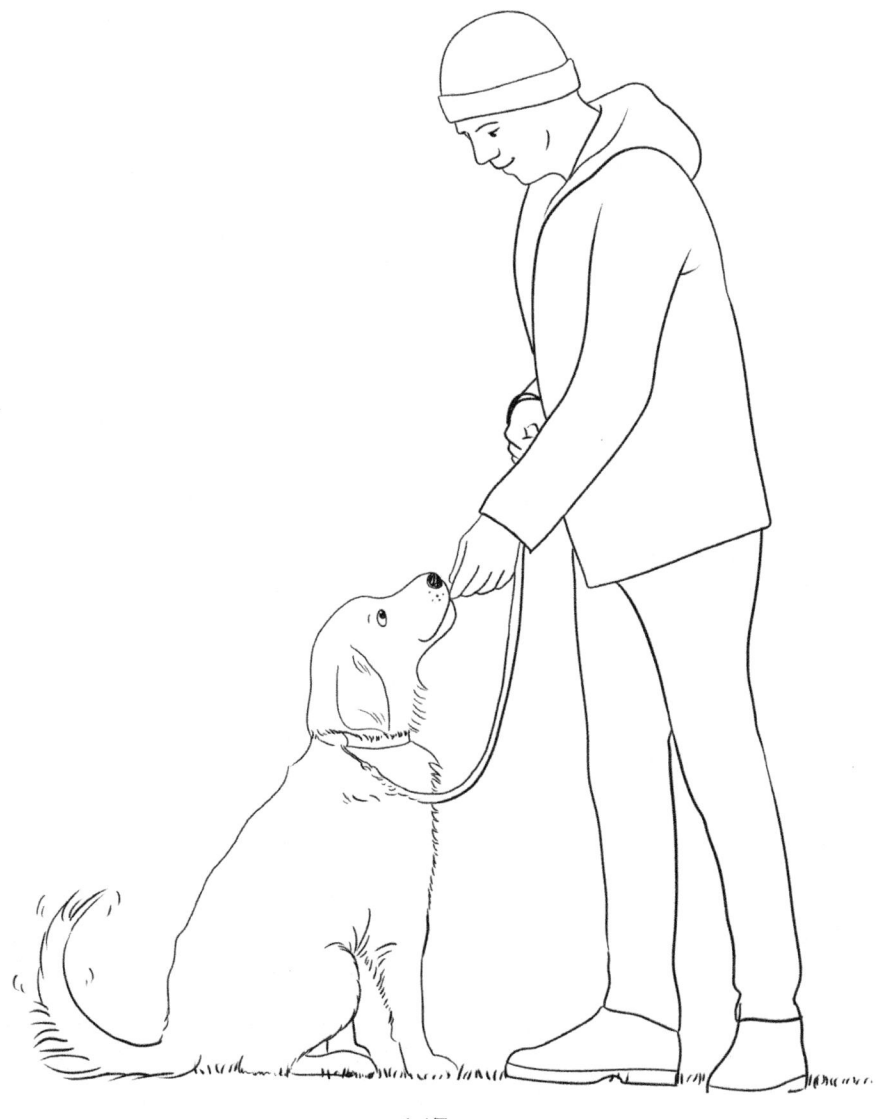

15. Learn to match solutions to problems

In the world of dog training, someone somewhere is selling the ideal package to meet the needs of your clients. Someone, somewhere is charging £10 for a great book, £60 for an online course, $40 for DVD or €200 for a blended learning package that is not only much better than everything out there on the market, but also may potentially be hundreds if not thousands of pounds cheaper than your service. Someone, somewhere has written the perfect puppy package that a dog guardian could buy online. Someone, somewhere has written the best guidance for resource guarding that anyone could possibly access. Someone, somewhere might well have a great free social media group or a wonderful YouTube channel with free content that any dog guardian could access.

So why don't people want this?

Just like physical health, if you wanted to get a DVD for $15 or pay for a daily app that gives you a different 20-minute daily HIIT workout, you could pay that.

So why do people sign up for gyms and personal trainers?

Some like to work with others. Remember, collaboration sometimes means learning from what others are doing. Many people benefit from group dynamics, be it envying the Spin instructor's amazing washboard abs to needing a high-five from a group of joyful friends after Zumba. Some people benefit from the habit-supporting qualities of peer group membership. Camaraderie, team work, group support and positive peer pressure are key reasons why people sign up to classes. It may also be the cheapest method to get a good education despite it not being particularly personalised or without having very much contact time with the trainer.

Others like to work alone, or their particular needs do not suit group situations. Their timetable, logistics, workload, lifestyle or capacity might not be suited to group situations. They may also not yet be at the level where they're capable of joining a team. Or, on the other hand, they may well be in need of something that goes beyond what the group can offer. After all, you're not going to sign up for tennis club if you've never played a match in your life; neither are you going to do so if the tennis club people are lovely but you've been playing professionally since you were twenty. Some people understand that the outlay is more but they want something specific to their needs.

Your clients are not with you because they're happy to work through a package on the internet. They could have done that without you. They are not looking for you to hold their hand through a package that somebody else has prepared and you're delivering.

Understanding your client's needs is vital, not just to help you get leverage.

Some clients will come to you in crisis. You may very well be needed to help them firefight and manage the crisis. Their territorially aggressive dog may well be perfectly cut out to follow a pre-prepared package you picked up two years ago following a course by an industry expert, but if your client needs you to recommend good fence panels and show them how to install rolling bars on top, then you should never, ever overlook the crisis.

That also means beginning with the problem that is causing the most difficulty and pain for your client.

That may not have been where you wanted to start, but it's what your client needs. You also may need to work on something they value before they're ready to truly sign up for what you want to propose in the long term. Quick fixes may be the very opposite of what you like to deliver, but if your client needs something that will take the pressure off - if only a little - it makes all the difference. A quick win is a win for you, the client and the dog.

For instance, one client signed up for reactive rover classes because her dog was barking at cyclists and joggers. Although it wasn't what she asked for, the trainer could see that the dog was actually getting more and more worked up because their collar was uncomfortable. Although the trainer never made it a big deal to tackle walking equipment on the first day, she knew she needed to in this case.

Switching to a comfortable harness took the edge off just a little and the guardian was much more able to work with the dog. It was a quick win that came from careful observation of the problem.

Finding quick wins means listening carefully to what your clients are saying. That includes listening to the dog. When you can identify what's causing them the most distress, then that is something you can work on. This doesn't mean you shouldn't tackle the difficult problems or that you should underestimate your client, but as you'll learn in Lessons 17, 18 and 19, sometimes our life circumstances mean that we can't cope with making the big changes that we ought to just yet. Stress makes us much less able to cope and it also makes us more pessimistic. If your client is telling you they cannot cope with a simple activity like learning a simple routine, then it's vital not to get frustrated or angry with them. It's not that they are unwilling - they are paying for your time - it's that they can't yet see a way to do this. Pitching your help at the right level is important here.

On the other hand, you're also the expert. You know the kind of things that will make a difference in the long term. If you only stay within the client's safe remit, then you may never really change their relationship with their companion. Likewise, if you only deal with the small conflagrations they need to put out when firefighting, you may never get to the huge great blazing bonfires of significant issues that the clients really need to tackle. Some trainers may help clients take small step after small step, yet never really help them put them together efficiently to help them cope in the real world or build on their successes.

Picking the right problems and situations to work on with your clients is half the battle, especially in one-to-one sessions. We need to ask ourselves what the important problems are to the client, and what the truly important problems are. If there's a mismatch, then we need to be able to compromise, perhaps starting with a small win before tackling the complex and thorny problem that would make a real difference. We also need to think about our clients' capacity, motivation and ability. If they don't have the skill to carry out a complex training programme, or they don't have the dedication, we need to bear this in mind. We also need to be able to find the quick wins, the low-hanging fruit that can be easily picked, and consider the small building blocks to much more challenging training.

When we work on our clients' problems, this should act as a stimulus to get them moving and get them involved. That also means at times having the ability to fade out discussion about problems that won't make much of a difference in our clients' lives. Sometimes, this means digging into those blind spots and getting to what is really on their mind, if we can. Other times, that means accepting resistance or dissonance for the time being. At times like this, it's helpful to give permission to your client to say what's really bothering them or what's really happening. Even a very simple statement can help. The trainer could say something like: 'It's really important that I help you pick what will make the most difference for you. Now I know some clients are embarrassed about explaining what's really going on or admitting what's really troubling them, but I'm here to help, not to judge. If you think I've got it perfect with my dogs, then I need to let you know that they're just dogs and I'm just a person… and I'll do my very best to help you get what you need, but I can only do that if I'm truly helping you out.'

Ultimately, clients come to you rather than watching free videos on YouTube, because they want a coach. They want someone to act as a spotter would do in the gym. Spotters don't push you to lift more weight than you would safely, just help you out if you're outside your comfort zone. They're there for assistance. Your job is also a cheerleader - more on that in Lesson 16. But you're more than a spotter or cheerleader - any old Joe from the street can do that.

You're there as a specialist and expert problem solver who can help create a bespoke solution to match their specific problem.

That requires you to be able to see what the problem really is, to be able to take a good look at the client, their lifestyle, their capacity, their individual environment, their personal situation, their shadow side, their blind spots, their intentions, and the amount of energy, time and money they can expend. Then your role is to find a solution that best fits their needs. There are so many trainers who are convinced the only way to manage a certain type of behaviour is to do it "their" way that they must haemorrhage all clients who aren't ethically aligned with them.

Imagine, for instance, that your programme to help guardians with destructive dogs is to rely on crates, x-pens and baby gates. Yet, living in a big, open-plan house, baby gates aren't feasible. Their dog is 45kg and can easily knock an x-pen over, and crating has the consequence of making the dog howl and cry all the time, no matter how long you try to desensitise the dog to it. You spend weeks trying to train the dog to get in the crate, creating a problem that the client didn't even know existed. You've added to the problem rather than reducing it. Perhaps the client is ethically opposed to doors, crates and shutting the dog away. What solutions can you offer in such a circumstance if your repertoire only includes things that they can't or won't do? Not only that, they then run the risk of walking away to a trainer who uses shock and not only have you disappointed the client, you've also compromised the dog's welfare.

Being able to find a solution to the client's exact problem means working with them to discuss what options and opportunities they have. It also means truly understanding the problem. Imagine, for instance, that video reveals the dog is bored and frustrated when home alone, but that the guardians are only gone for a couple of hours. Getting a dog walker for an hour and giving the dog a whole load of appropriate things to chew while making sure all other chewables are out of the way may equally solve their problem. If they don't have funds for a dog walker, they might have an annex and be happy to host students in return for occasional dog sitting. Their elderly next-door-neighbour might relish the opportunity for an occasional guest. There may be a friend who's happy to dog-sit while the dog is being supervised more minimally as they learn what to chew and what not to. Scheduling the day differently so that the dog has lots of destructive enrichment and some physical exercise before the guardians go out and gradually increasing absence might be your strategies. You might find that they're best placed to teach the dog how to cope on their own and do some settles, mat work and independence-building activities.

There are often hundreds of reasonable and ethical solutions to any one problem.

But if your toolkit only has a hammer in it, you'll pretty soon find out that a hammer is not useful when you need to twist in a screw.

Not only is it important to have a full toolkit of all kinds of potential solutions, but to become a kind of living, walking index of solutions that would be appropriate depending on circumstance and cost. It's also important to know which tool is right for the job and what kind of job you're looking at in the first place. This comes back to your need to specialise, to some degree, and your ability to collaborate with others, but also on your ability to provide a bespoke service for your client.

So many trainers fail to find solutions that really match the client's problem that our contracts can be destined to fail from the start. We need to find the right problem to work on with the right tool. That means we need to take a thoughtful and collaborative approach.

16. Bring hope

When your clients arrive with you, they will often arrive when things are at their worst. They may have had sleepless nights. Along with the negativity bias that you learned about in Lesson 12, there are many reasons why your clients may feel hopeless. What they are looking for is not just a coach but also someone who can show them the possibilities that lie before them and help them take advantage of any unused opportunities. They will have little idea of how the future could look; if they knew how to achieve that future, they'd have done it already. Our clients are stuck when they arrive, and have no idea how to make changes. They're lacking a sense of direction.

One vital step before you start to take action is to imagine the future, to find that direction and to bring those possibilities to light. When we start to take action before we really know what we're working towards, it's like setting off on a journey without a map, without a destination and without real intention. If progress is that journey, taking action without it is like going and getting your bicycle, your car, your bus or your train and setting off not really knowing if the direction in which you are going is the direction in which you want to go.

Of course, sometimes that is a lovely thing in itself. Travelling with no destination in mind can take you to places you had no idea where you wanted to go. You can find the most amazing, off-track layovers that you had no idea would be as good as they are. The same is no doubt true of dog training. We see so often the people who start off with basic obedience and find a real passion for agility or for heelwork to music. Along the route, if we're enjoying our travels, we may very well find our niche. Life with dogs can be like that. We might start with heelwork to music, realise that scentwork and detection is more our dog's thing and end up being part of a volunteer team of sniffer dogs to find lost dementia patients or as part of a mountain rescue team for hikers.

But when our clients arrive with a problem situation, they are in no place to set out without knowing exactly where they are going. Training their dog for the sake of training is an exercise in frustration and futility. Setting clear outcomes is going to be an integral part of what we need to do before we take action - that means bringing a sense of hopefulness.

And what is hope, if it is not thinking about our goals and dreams?

Hope gives us determination. Hope puts fuel in the tank so we can get where we need to go. This is why, if we're working with pessimistic clients whose reserves of hope are low, we're going to need to make sure we take small steps at first. Hope is certainly a renewable energy source, topped up by achievement. Each goal achieved tops up our hope reserves and gives us more for the next journey. Only when we've got a few achievements under our belt will we dare to dream bigger and realise just how far we can go. But seeing the tiniest of steps can also diminish hope in the first place. Imagine working with the client in the previous lessons whose dog cannot cope for even sixty seconds without her. Seeing that today you will be celebrating success if you can leave your dog for sixty-four seconds instead is debilitating and depressing. That's why we need the big goals, not just the micro-goals. It's much easier to show clients a progress chart which starts with an additional four seconds of absence and ends with four hours' absence at the end of sixty days than it is for them just to see that tiny first step.

Goal-setting, then, brings us the will to improve and feeds our motivation. It's integral to the process of hope. Hope also gives us a sense of agency: we feel like we can make changes, that there are things we can do to improve our situation. When we're hopeful, we also set more goals, make them more challenging and feel more success. It adds to our sense of resilience and gives us reasons to persist. If you don't help your clients be hopeful, you'll end up with clients who are more limited and pessimistic in their outlook, who don't have a desire to change and who don't feel the inner agency needed to really drive actions. Kindling and nurturing that small flame of hopefulness is vital.

To do this, we need to start with what is possible, helping our clients imagine what they could achieve. When we're missing out on optimism and confidence, it leaves us feeling a sense of inertia and powerlessness. It also keeps us in a place of uncertainty and ambiguity, because we have no idea what the future might look like with our companion and no way of knowing that it could ever be achieved. Inertia and powerlessness are debilitating and frustrating. We see this in clients who arrive having completely given up on the prospect of taking their dog for an on-lead walk without the dog pulling them into the bushes or dragging them into oncoming traffic. We see this in clients who wished only for a dog who enjoyed being a good companion, yet spends every absence destroying the furniture. These are aversive states in which our clients have been living, and for many, they may be feeling a sense of learned helplessness if all their efforts to change have been thwarted. Hopelessness also fills us with rigidity, as we cannot think creatively or flexibly.

Many of us will find it frustrating when clients arrive with incredibly complex problems having lived in misery for many months or even years - and then these same clients ask for a simple solution. It's invariably true that the clients who arrive with the most complex problems are the ones who demand the most simple solutions. There is a good reason for that. The more hopeless we feel, the less likely we are able to contend with the complex. When we hand over a seventy-point plan to our clients to help them deal with their long-ingrained problem situation, we should not be surprised that they drop out of training or that they find it too confusing or overwhelming to even do one single, simple thing.

The more overwhelmed we are, the more overwhelming everything else seems to be.

For example, one client who arrived at her wit's end with her 50kg dog who pulled on lead had 'tried everything'. Shocks, prongs, chokes, "Easy Walk" harness, head halters and reinforcement training had failed to curb her dog's tendency to pull. Even starting a very simple activity to walk off-lead with the dog and drop a treat every three paces was overwhelming. Her timing was poor. She fumbled the food. She'd stop when she dropped the food and fail to move on, so the dog was eating the food and running ahead. When we're overwhelmed, everything is complex. Having hope that this can change is vital. Her persistence was minimal and her frustration on a hair trigger. It can be hard to work with clients like this if we start to feel that they are incapable or deliberately seem not to be trying. What we need to remember is that we need to be able to give them a sense of hope. Rather than giving up, having a sense of hope can make us feel that we can keep going.

Generating possibilities is one way of generating hope. This is especially true for our clients who think there is only one right answer. One way we can do this is to help clients come with as many possibilities as they can. That might even include being silly and considering the ridiculous. Karen Pryor's excellent book Don't Shoot The Dog works on exactly that premise: sometimes there are many potential solutions that clients should consider. For a dog who needs a modification programme for separation-related behaviour, for instance, we may need our clients to suspend all absences. Helping clients generate ideas such as doggie day care, dog-sitters, hiring students from the local veterinarian college in need of some cash, swapping dog-sitting for an hour of cleaning, using the neighbours, asking if a local retired person wouldn't mind helping out, getting security for the car to take the dog on errands, seeing if the boss will allow them to take the dog to work, using the spare room to host a workaway traveller… These are all possibilities that clients could generate with a little prompting and can help them find solutions.

Trainer: I know you said you were going to find it impossible to make sure Toby isn't left for a couple of months… yet that's going to be integral to his progress. It might be that we can't start treatment just yet, but what kind of possibilities might there be to get in someone to help for an hour or so, or to be able to take Toby to them?

Client: None. It's just not possible. There's no way I'm going to be able to find anyone who could do it.

Trainer: A neighbour maybe?

Client: Well, there's an elderly lady next door. I barely know her. It would be really cheeky to ask her. I don't even know if she likes dogs.

Trainer: Okay, well I'll just put her on the list for now. Let's not be too fixated on the reasons why they can't or won't, but is there anyone else in the neighbourhood who you can think of?

Client: There's a family over the road. They work though.

Trainer: So they're all out all day?

Client: Their son's home sometimes. He's at the local college.

Trainer: Okay, that sounds like another possibility.

Client: And there's an old couple next-door-but-one. I don't know them, but she's house-bound I think. They have meals on wheels come round every day, and a nurse a couple of times.

As you can see, going from 'nobody to help', there are actually at least three possibilities that come up within 100m of the house. People who need help often hate asking for it, but the neighbour's son might enjoy a little extra pocket money and playing with the dog. Who knows - maybe the busy family has consistently refused to get a dog given their lifestyle and it may give him a way into a small dog-walking business that gets him through college? Perhaps the elderly couple would love to have a dog, but their health prohibits it?

You can also use one idea to stimulate others. The trainer does this in the conversation above. Obviously, there's not just one single neighbour. By the end of the discussion, the client had come up with twenty local neighbours who might be willing to dog-sit for an hour here and there, especially if paid.

You should also encourage clients to think of the wild possibilities. Ask them what they would do if they had a million pounds to solve the problem, especially if money is one reason they can't seem to find a way forward. Often solutions are cheaper than they think. For the couple who lost a kitchen door every other week, seeing that taking their dog to a daycare facility would cost less actually helped them see that they could save in one area in order to spend in others. If clients are unable to spend the time, ask them what they would do if they had 24 hours a day available to solve the problem. Again, few problems take 24 hours a day to solve. Another way to talk about time is to say, 'If you had six months to solve this, what would you do?'

These kinds of questions also open up your client into thinking about potential solutions.

Generating possibilities can also include limitless imagination and freedom. What would the situation look like if it was solved most perfectly? What changes could they make to the dog's life that might solve their problems? What do they need that they don't have now? For example, one client who really had very little money to help solve her dog's problem of jumping up on guests needed a solution for her large open-plan house to secure the dog when guests arrived who insisted on reinforcing jumping up rather than reinforcing the behaviour the guardian needed. Using a mat and a baby playpen she picked up from a free recycling site as well as a donation from a friend of a Kong and a lickimat helped her out enormously. While it may sound ludicrous, many dog shelters also get people leaving donated equipment that they can't use themselves and might be happy to loan. It doesn't matter if your client won't be able to do even 5% of the things they suggest. They won't need to approach sixty neighbours or have a million pounds to solve their dog's problem. It may be that, when it comes down to it, spending a small amount each day over a couple of months is all that is needed.

What is also helpful for you is to keep those lists for future reference. When you can occasionally steer your clients into divergent thinking simply because things other people have done, that can really help. Being able to explain how other people managed the same problem is a really great way of giving a bit of hope and some possibility.

Moving on, you can then narrow down on the changes that could make a difference. From seeing no hope or potential, the client who couldn't suspend all her absence catches up with her next-door-neighbour who is more than happy to come round and help once a day for an hour in return for some help in the garden. The client who couldn't see her way to stop her dogs barking at the window when she is out realises that instead of screening off her four curtainless French windows in the living room, all she needs to do is move the dogs' beds to the kitchen and put up a baby-gate instead. When we eliminate the improbable, the impossible and the impractical from our original list, we're then able to move into making choices.

17. Understand human habit forming

Without understanding how humans form habits, the best goal-setting and action planning is likely to come undone if you don't understand how humans form habits. We will need to use this knowledge to help you plan to support them through the challenging bits. Without a rudimentary understanding of why your clients will start off with the best intentions and then stumble at the first hurdle - even if that hurdle seems like the most simple and easy obstacle to overcome - you may be left with winning action plans that none of your clients ever implement.

Most of our behavioural habits are, just as they are with animals, an automatic thing. When we're used to doing things in a particular way, that's what we do without even thinking about it. It becomes part of our procedural memory which helps with performing specific types of tasks at an unconscious level. For instance, when you learned to drive, you probably had to think hard about everything working together - especially if you have to change gears. Even simple things like automatically checking the mirror before you pull out had to be performed in very deliberate ways as you were learning. As you become proficient, these pass into automaticity so that we perform them without thinking. To a certain degree, all behaviours, actions and skills like this can be performed automatically. Most of the day, we're doing things automatically and without really thinking about it. We don't have to make choices or decisions, we just behave without conscious thought. Some skills are fairly straightforward, involving simple actions and few body parts. Take, for instance, checking the kettle has water in it before switching it on. You probably have a quick cursory glance at the water level, or pick it up to see if it needs filling, and then you flick the switch. Other habits are so complex that it can take an enormous amount of effort to do them, like swimming, cycling and driving.

This is not the complex part of human habit-forming that you need to understand. Sure, it's helpful to know that you're going to have to work on drilling your client to make behaviours instinctive and unconscious, and that this is part of the learning cycle. So if you're working in class to teach a hand touch one week, you'll do as well to revisit it and practise it in class every other week as well until clients can do it automatically and fluently, just like their dogs. That's the simple part of habit-forming.

The complex part is understanding that where we're rebuilding new habits over old, we need to be conscious of where those are likely to fail. What is the best situation is to start with clients who've no experience whatsoever. Building habits right from the beginning, from the bottom up, is the easy bit.

Deconstructing old habits, putting them on an extinction schedule to fade them, and building replacement ones is the hard bit, just as it is with animals.

The problem is that when things have happened in the past that previously triggered us to do one behaviour, it can be very hard to do differently if we're not conscious and deliberate about it. In other words, when we come under stress and we're put into the exact same circumstances, new habits are likely to fail under stress and old habits re-emerge as the default behaviour. What that means is if our clients have had a way of dealing with behaviour in the past, such as barking, by yelling at the dog or punishing them, even if that was not effective at all and had driven them to our doors, the moment it gets stressful again, they're likely to go back to the behaviour they'd previously learned no matter how much they'd tried to build new behaviours. So even if their previous attempts to discipline their barking or jumping dog had failed, even if they'd been 100% successful with the new behaviour you'd been working on training both the human and the dog to do, the moment they slip into automatic behaviours, the old behaviour is likely to spontaneously recur. This is especially true if we default under stress. Old habits are surprisingly robust, and new habits are surprisingly delicate.

What we need to be aware of is that new behaviours are likely to be put to the test at some point. That is most likely to be when the going starts to get tough again. As trainers, we need to be especially conscious of this if our clients have responded in ways that are likely to be dangerous to them and we need to share this concern with our clients. For example, one dog had bitten his guardian following the removal of a sharp thorn from his hind leg. The guardian had held on to the dog and pulled. The dog had bitten the guardian. After that, the guardian had needed to apply topical antiseptic, and in doing so, the dog was naturally wary of her attempts to hold on to him. He growled repeatedly and would not let her approach, so she ended up restraining him with his collar. What happened was a complete breakdown of trust between the guardian and the dog. Because of her deep-seated beliefs that dogs should just tolerate manipulation, she was initially very resistant to cooperative care protocols. However, having seen initial success, following a simple muzzle training programme and starting to build up new cues for recall, she had two years of calm with the dog. She did not attempt to grab him and there were no further incidents of aggressive behaviour. Despite this very long period of calm, when out on a walk and the dog picked up a briar, she reached down instinctively and pulled it off. The dog bit her again. Both the client and her companion returned to their previously-learned behaviours. Not only that, when she called the trainer to say that 'training had failed' (despite two years of very successful handling, grooming and cooperative husbandry), she was very resistant to go back to the new habits she'd been practising for two years. Forceful behaviour was not the only thing to have returned: her belief that dogs should just tolerate force had also been recovered. Spontaneous recovery of behaviours we'd considered to be extinct is not just a problem in dog training.

It's for this reason that we need to work carefully with clients to make sure they understand that the dog's problem behaviours will return if they do not consciously practise what they are learning with you. What they need to know is that it is very likely they'll return to doing what they once did. Under stress, the guardian who previously chastised their barking dog without success is likely to recommence chastisement at some point. The guardian who previously let their dog jump all over the guests is likely to let them do it again at some point. The guardian who has solved counter-surfing by becoming vigilant at putting food away will eventually leave the butter dish out on the kitchen side. Addiction clinics are so conscious about the recovery of former behaviours that most of them include some kind of sponsor or support to help people through stressful times. This approach is not just for addiction, however. It's useful for any kind of habit change.

Only when habits are so ingrained that they are part of our instinctive behaviour can we truly know that we've cracked it. For instance, for a small spaniel who would often get up onto the guardian's table if chairs were left as a way of ascent, the guardian quickly took to pushing chairs under. It became so habitual that the family continued to push chairs under the table long after the dog's death.

One of the things that can help both the client and their dog is to eventually build up practice in the exact same circumstances where the behaviour is likely to fail. Just as we do with animals, where we make the circumstances easier, we decrease distractions and difficulty, we need to do the same again. For our clients who previously tried to frogmarch their reactive dog past other dogs, if we want them to be able to do a u-turn instinctively when faced with adversity in the future, we need to practise this until it is fully automatic. If we don't, or we only work with the client when the going is easy, then we run the risk that when it gets difficult again, they'll resort to their former, failing responses. So as part of your planning with your client, towards the end of your programme, make sure you build in some coaching time where you can work with them in more challenging circumstances. We really need to make sure our plans cater for the entire lifespan of the action plan. Just like people going to diet clubs don't just go, pick up all the information and walk away, so we need to rely on those regular check-ins. It's the same for all human habit-building, be that regular haircuts, going to church, going to the gym or even trying to overcome addiction.

Regular check-ins and coaching clients through the tricky bits is the vital part. For people who use support networks like Alcoholics Anonymous, the important thing is to have a sponsor. That's not someone who can babysit you and supervise you, but to help you when you are finding it challenging and also to help you should you fall off the wagon. Our clients need the same. They need to be able to call on us when they are finding it challenging and they also need to be able to check in with us straight after if they resort to previous methods of responding. For that reason, it's useful to make it plain in your literature, in your regular sessions and in your post-contract work that they should call you if the training plan seems to be tough to stick to, or if the dog's problem behaviour re-emerges. It's not the end of the world if they yell at the dog as they once used to if the dog counter-surfs, but it will become a problem if they keep doing it. What you want is for your client to recognise that they've had a temporary setback and to call or message you straight away, if for nothing other than a pep talk and a re-set.

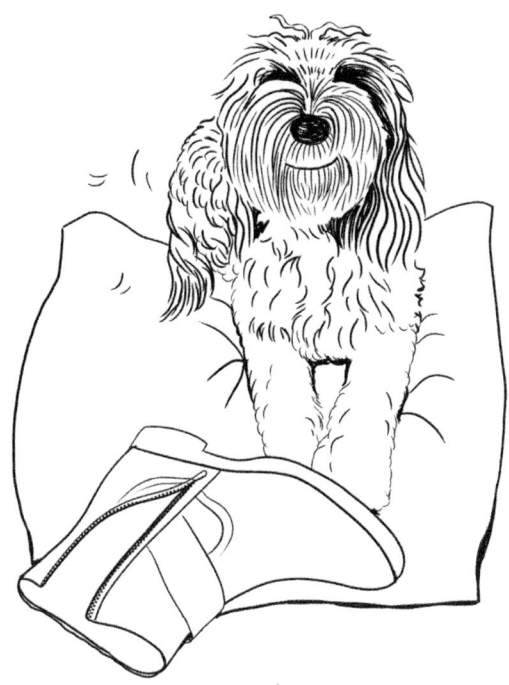

What also helps at this point is understanding the usefulness of small wins. This is another reason to pick off something that is important to the client and can be resolved easily, even if it is not your long-term goal.

Small wins set the foundations for much larger changes. Their influence is often completely out of proportion with what they achieve, since they cement your client's commitment to the process, their faith in you and renew their trust in their dog. They set in motion other small wins that grow into much larger habits. This again comes back to the times when we may feel like we should change everything. The dog's diet may be poor. They may be irregularly exercised. They may be in need of work on husbandry and cooperative handling. They may need enrichment adding to their lives. Their toys may be completely non-existent or inappropriate. A complete revision of the dog's activity timetable may be necessary. You may want to recommend a switch to a harness and a long line rather than a neck collar and a flexi-lead. You might want to request a vet check up. But when we ask our clients to change everything, don't be surprised to find that they change nothing.

Focusing on one small, simple, modest goal gives further momentum.

Remember change isn't just about what you tell clients to do or ask them to change. It also works through mentorship, where what you do also motivates clients to emulate you. It's important also to think of small wins as not being some kind of logical or linear stepping stone system. They can be scattered. You might have a small win with a little enrichment and a few training games. It might just be related to the installation of a baby gate and a silicone bone that can be stuck to the wall to occupy a jumping dog when guests come. Small changes are much more likely to become part of daily practice. The easier these small wins are, the more likely the client will stick with them. They will then snowball into bigger and more momentous changes.

At first, as habits form, you will need to understand that each and every small hurdle could potentially become a huge obstacle in your training. You may feel like you need to be able to keep many clients going and that means weekly appointments at a set time with little communication between. You may feel like you do not have time to acknowledge twenty clients daily, or check up on them. It may feel frustrating to engage in conversations and check-ins if you are not being paid for them.

For this reason, it's much better to charge more, have fewer clients and to lay out your expectations for contact. Saying that you expect daily check-ins with a quick video and some daily feedback for the first three weeks is one way to get around the problems that are likely to occur if you are overwhelmed with appointments. If you find that you are going from week to week without contact from clients, or, worse, that you do not expect them to contact you outside your designated helping hours, then you will find that if your appointment on a Monday is followed by a problem on Tuesday that your clients have six days to practise old behaviours instead of practising new ones. Ultimately, if you want your clients to be successful, charge more and build in the expectation that you will support them a lot as they move new training into the realm of unconscious habit.

This is especially true the longer the dog has been practising the problem behaviour, the longer the guardian has been responding in the way that they have and the more complex the behaviour. The guardian has been practising their response too; it is just as likely to be an ingrained response as the dog's problematic behaviour. Your client's success rests on your availability to be there for the relapse, so make sure you leave yourself time to be available and that you are compensated for it.

Another way to counteract disengagement at the first hurdle is to plan for it.

Planning for the worst-case scenario and working out what you will do in that case can really help. Imagine the client is working on a simple problem: the dog jumping up on guests. You may be working on a replacement behaviour, such as touching their shoulder to their guardian's legs that the dog can use to request attention in a polite way. By leaning gently into the legs of guests, it can function as a much more polite request. Before, the guardian had been letting the dog jump on guests, and guests had also been encouraging the dog because who doesn't love a really friendly golden retriever? But the golden retriever had knocked the grandmother over and broken her hip, so the guardians knew something had to change. You may feel like throwing many changes at the client. Change the food so the dog is less fuelled by poor-quality carbohydrates. Add some enrichment so there is less excitement resting on the visitors' arrival. Suspend all visitors until the dog has learned the new behaviour. Install baby gates and a tether just in case. Teach a mat game and put down snuffle-mats and Kongs to keep the dog busy. Take the dog to basic obedience classes. Any and all of these might have an impact. But if the client is a busy mum and visitors come in and out of the house from school end to bed time, that's going to make it really hard to keep up with the demands of running a household, working a full-time job, preparing meals, greeting visitors, supervising children, answering the phone, sorting out homework for the next day and dispatching older children to pick up the younger ones. It's likely that the guardian is going to take her eye off the ball at some point and that training will fail. What might be worthwhile here is a clear management timetable, with a dog walker coming to pick the dog up at 5pm until 6pm, giving mum time to prepare the evening meal without having to supervise the dog. Prepared chew toys and Kongs can then be set up in a safely-managed area away from the door so that mum can manage entrances, along with a sliding lock and a message on the door asking visitors to send a message to say they were at the door. If it just needs time for the new behaviours to embed, then make sure there are safety nets set up for those evenings when all the dog's triggers arrive together.

We know, too, that new habits fail under cognitive load. That's to say, the more we're occupied with something difficult, the less likely we are to stick to new habits. The more plates we're spinning, the harder it is to stick to new habits. Essentially, the more we're focused on something challenging that is taking up all our conscious thinking, the more likely it is that our newly-formed habits will fall at the first hurdle. Again, this comes back to making sure your clients don't have too much on their plate when they first start training. All it takes is for someone to ask a simple question and all training is likely to crumble.

Take the guardian who has been working with her dog on a 'Look at That!' cue to help her dog overcome reactivity around unfamiliar people. All it takes is for her to be thinking about what she needs to get ready for work the next day and a strange person to appear out of nowhere for her to go back to pulling on her dog's collar and shouting 'no!' as the dog lunges and barks. It's for this reason that it's often sensible to make sure clients have put their phones on silent and put them away, and that they are only working with one dog at a time. For clients in multi-dog households, management during training will be an important step for both the humans and the animals as they all learn new habits. The dynamics of trying to deal with a number of other situations and demands can easily make new habits crumble under pressure.

Be conscious that many clients will disengage mid-contract. They'll do just enough to alleviate the main problems caused by the behaviour, to make their lives tolerable, but they may not continue until they've become completely successful.

This is also human nature.

We diet until we feel comfortable. We might not ever meet our goals because as soon as we get to the point where our major problems are solved, we resort to old habits. The same is true for much behaviour change. It is going to be true of your clients' contracts with you. It's worthwhile acknowledging this with a formal break in the contract and a reminder that they are welcome to pick up for support in the future.

If you charge for a package, you may be much more relaxed about clients who disengage mid-way through the contract. They've clearly reached a point where they can live with whatever the dog is doing, and you may not feel like chasing them up especially if they've become a little evasive. Plenty of gyms do the same when they take a year's membership up front and never bother chasing the client past the failure of their January resolution.

The problem is that unlike huge gym chains, our clients are more conscious that they disengaged and will be less likely to get in touch with us again in the future should things go wrong. Shame and embarrassment may play into that. Talking about the difficulties of continued behaviour change, finishing midpoint contracts neatly and leaving them open-ended (even if that means reimbursing the client for some or all of the remaining sessions) leaves them much more likely to contact you again. Just as there are plenty of dieters who've worked round every club in town, there are plenty of dog guardians who've worked their way around every dog trainer in town. Not that we particularly want repeat business, as it would be nice if all interventions finished so fluently and positively that our clients never need to contact us again for training, losing clients because they are embarrassed to get in touch again is a more realistic picture.

Also, as we come to the end of contracts that conclude successfully, especially if the problem behaviours were deeply emotional in nature, you may find that your clients are a little reluctant to let you go. This is another aspect of human habit forming that we need to be aware of. We may well have been their crutch, their emotional support mechanism. We feel wobbly when the stabilisers come off and we don't feel brave enough to go it alone. This is especially true when situations have been complex. One thing that can be incredibly useful here is to stretch the time between consultations and half the time you spend with clients. For instance, if you have been working once a week, you can then move to fortnightly and then monthly. A review after two, three and six months can also help clients move to independence in their own habits. Likewise, if you had a 90-minute session the first time, then moving to 45 minutes, then to a 30 minute session can also help. You can also gradually reduce the way in which you contact clients, moving from intensive face-to-face support into online or phone support and then support via email and social media messaging.

18. Understand why change is difficult

Not only are new habits hard to form, especially when they're sitting on the foundations of old behaviours, change for many species is a huge threat. That is as true for humans as it is for other species. What you learned in Lesson 12 about learned helplessness is a part of this. When we've been living in a problem situation for a long time and all our attempts to change it have been thwarted, not only do we not take the opportunity to change when it is presented, but we may also need guidance in order to take the first steps in the first place.

In the laboratory, animals put into new circumstances and new contexts when things change exhibit many stress signals and displacement behaviours. Change makes them more anxious. The familiar, no matter how aversive it is, is safer than the unfamiliar. It truly is a matter of better the devil you know. For example, prey species that have been given five days to adapt to a new environment before a predator is introduced have a much higher survival rate than those who've just been transferred. All kinds of threats emerge when we're in unfamiliar territory, and even the simplest challenge can send animals into "fight or flight" mode as the sympathetic nervous system fires up. Of course, our stress response is more complicated than that, and asking clients to teach their dog a simple 'wait!' behaviour before the door opens is not in the same league as a prey species threatened by a raptor, but the principles remain the same. We fear change and we want to protect the status quo.

Preserving the status quo is part of our in-built nature. In Changing Rooms, developed by Willis Towers Watson, an activity often played during leadership conferences, participants are asked to partner up with an unfamiliar delegate. Once with their partner, they are asked first to take a good look at their colleague and then to turn their backs on one another and change five things about their appearance in a thirty-second window. Despite how easy this activity sounds in theory, many participants are momentarily panicked by the time frame and by working with a stranger. They exhibit body language that shows their concern, but also the "freeze" behaviour we find as we become momentarily indecisive when faced with threat. Then there is a flurry of change. What happens during this time is that most people make superficial and easy changes, often involving taking something off rather than putting something on. They take glasses off, or jewellery. They take jackets or cardigans off. Few people break convention or do anything daring. The same is true every time this game is played as a demonstration of the difficulties of change. The first changes are always the hardest. They invariably involve removing things.

When the time is up and delegates have to turn back to their partner to identify the changes their partner has made, many are unable to even see what their partner has done despite having studied them carefully only a minute or so before. This is a fairly universal bias, that we are unable to see what other people are doing simply because we're so fixated on our own behaviour and change. Most people then begin to start "fixing" things and putting them back to how they were. When the course leader asks participants to repeat the exercise and make five more changes, something very interesting happens in the second round. Here, participants start to pick things up. They may pick up their bag and put it on. They may put their coat on. They may put pens behind their ears or pick up binders and folders. They also start looking around and improvising. Even in a very short window of time, people start borrowing ideas from the other delegates they can see around them. This round is marked by far fewer stress behaviours and much less hesitation. Delegates know what they are doing now, and start to relax. The second changes are more profound, creative and innovative but they are also preceded by huge sighs and resistance.

After this second round, when the course leader asks each delegate to turn back to their partner and identify the changes the other has made, participants are much more aware of the changes made. They're also moving into scanning the environment. Usually, there is some laughter as someone will have done something unusual or silly, like putting their shoes on the wrong feet or using waste paper baskets as shoes. This time, they're also ready for the fact the game might not be over even though they've not yet received further instruction. There is much less change back to their original state, even if they're wearing shoes on the wrong feet.

Finally, the course leader can ask delegates to do the same activity again, making it clear that this will be the final time. This is where participants tend to get really creative. They start to adapt to what they've seen around them. Humans are, after all, great at aping and mimicry. Not that they always copy what they've seen, but also that some will also use that to generate further changes. If someone has swapped shoes to different feet in the last round, they might make a silent deal with a person opposite them from another partnership and switch shoes with them. Occasionally, shirts come off and cups get turned into impromptu hats. Paperclips get turned into earrings. Change becomes creative. The relief is often palpable even though this has not been the most stressful of experiences. Largely, this is to do with the fact that the end is in sight and it has been kind of fun. Sure, delegates have had to talk to and scrutinise an unfamiliar person. They've also had to change minor things about their appearance. But this unpleasant experiment in change is nothing compared to the huge changes we are asked to make in the real world.

What is also interesting is what happens immediately after the exercise finishes. People revert almost immediately, undoing all the changes they've made. This is not unusual: it's a contrived exercise and most people were pretty happy with the way they looked before the activity. The same is true with many habits though. As soon as the pressure is off, we revert to previous behaviours, especially if they weren't that uncomfortable. For someone to keep the changes, those changes really have to be something quite powerful and beneficial. In other words, tweaking with things that your client finds trivial or unimportant will be doomed to failure the moment your contract ends. If we want clients to stick with new behaviours, we don't just have to build new habits, but show them that what they're taking on is worthwhile and important. They have to feel that too.

Another curious thing happens during the exercise. Most people have limits placed on them by individual values or cultural norms. Nobody gets naked. Very, very few people remove wedding rings. The course leader could have asked for a hundred changes and it's unlikely these values will change. What this reminds us is that there are shadow-side issues that are fixed points on our moral compasses - values that never waver when we're asked to change. We need to be aware of what these values are when we engage with a client, and this is why it's important to go back to understanding cultural factors and shadow-side issues. It may be that our client has an unwavering belief that dogs should just "be" obedient and that food is spoiling them. It may be that they have a fixed view about neck collars and short, flat leads. So many problems with dogs jumping up would be resolved if we'd just bend down to greet them, but humans can be stuck in thinking that means to do so would be out of the question. These fixed values are those our client is going to struggle to change, and they're also the first thing that the client will undo when we end the contract.

What we learn from this exercise is that we're quicker to take things off than take things on. It's easier to dump the unproductive than it is to take on something new. Also, we benefit hugely from seeing other people's creative attempts to cope. Peer learning is far from being a negative experience. This is why small, private, problem-specific social media groups of your own clients can be helpful. We should add a caveat that these should be supervised, since all it takes is a small adaptation in the wrong direction from one client to send all the others the same way if it seems to be successful.

Change is challenging. It takes us way beyond our physical and emotional comfort zones. It asks us to become vulnerable and to place ourselves in danger. That's as true of asking clients to teach a 'drop' without force as it is asking them to go into a foreign battlefield.

The status quo is seductive, no matter how bad it is. We've all heard the analogy of the frog in boiling water. Place the frog in boiling water and they would quickly hop out. Put them in cold water and gradually turn the temperature up, and the frogs will stay in the water until they boil to death. The analogy is false of course: the frog will jump out regardless. But as we see from Martin Seligman's experiments about learned helplessness, both humans and dogs are likely to tolerate aversives for a lot longer than we might predict if they've been thwarted in every attempt they've made to change their situation previously.

What we need to understand, though, is that humans are very good at cherry-picking one or two small adaptations that improve their quality of life without really making any substantial change.

They're more likely to want to cope in a situation that mostly resembles the one they have already rather than benefit from a vastly improved situation in a life that differs enormously from their own.

Again, coming back to the importance of those foundational changes, that means we need to make them count. Keystone changes that make the most amount of difference for the smallest amount of effort are vital. We may not be able to deliver the magic bullet our clients are searching for, that easily-swallowed panacea for all their problems, but if we fail to listen to their need for something simple with powerful consequences, then we run the risk that they'll continue to tolerate whatever situation in which they find themselves, no matter how easy it would be to change it.

When we understand why people resist change and how to work with them to take the first steps, really embedding the changes they make, as well as supporting them beyond their contract with us, that's when we can make the most difference for our clients and their companions.

19. Appreciate the fallout of stress

It's not just that new habits are hard to form or that change is difficult that may cause tensions in our working relationship with our clients. It's also the fact that stress makes humans behave in irrational if predictable ways.

Stress can work positively, of course. It makes us take action. It motivates us. Positive stress can make us determined to change things and resolve issues. Our bodies were not born for homeostasis, to stay in "rest or digest" mode indefinitely. Stress is necessary for even the most basic desires.

But to live in a state of chronic stress is debilitating. Many of our clients who arrive with dogs who're behaving in complicated or disruptive ways could have been living in a state of stress for many months or years. Imagine the effects of living with a dog who barks throughout the night, or a dog you can't leave because they're destructive or they self-mutilate. Imagine the daily grind on the soul of living with a dog who barks at every noise or who behaves in ways that you have tried hard to comprehend. It tries our patience and our resilience. Sometimes, moments of acute stress can be fraught with complex emotions. If we think about the dog who ran out into a road and whose recall was poor, or the guardian whose escaping dog was lost and on the run for days, or even the times following a bite, these kinds of situations really test every fibre of our being.

You've read already about learned helplessness, but stress also affects our decision-making ability. Complex situations may lead us to make instinctive choices that we wouldn't have made under other circumstances. When we're stressed, we're more fearful. That affects our likelihood to invest in change. It also means that we see every solution as a possible threat.

When we're stressed, we're also more risk-averse, meaning we're less likely to take chances or to just see how things go. It means we might need more persuading and reasoning than we'd need under normal circumstances. We also become less rational when we're stressed; the way in which we think means we're less able to rationalise. Our own biases and shadow-side issues can paralyse us. When we're stressed, we're also more impulsive. It's no wonder people end up behaving in ways that disgust them when they reflect upon it later. When clients say things like, 'I just wasn't thinking!' or they're unable to see why they behaved as they did, we need to make sure we're not adding fuel to that self-judgemental fire.

Living with chronic stress also makes us less patient, more sensitive to threat and more aggressive. Following a fraught six months of a behaviour protocol, a hair-second resurgence of guarding behaviours meant one guardian felt she could no longer trust her rescue dog. Even though she'd seen success, she had reached in to grab a dropped chicken bone from her dog and the dog had growled at her. On a whim, she took the dog to the veterinarian and demanded a behavioural euthanasia. Afterwards, she wrote a hard letter to the rescue association, blaming them for releasing a dog who, in her view, had significant issues. Her letter was accusatory and filled with hostility. The association president was worried that the guardian would file charges and had consulted with both the behaviour consultant and the veterinarian who had euthanised the dog. Both felt that the guardian's behaviour was completely understandable in the initial incident and the letter that had been written, if unjustified. She finished the letter with bitter recriminations about damaged dogs, without acknowledging there had been no recurrence of the food guarding for six months.

So why write such a mean-spirited letter?

Largely because she herself was hurting. She'd been living in a state of chronic stress and even though the dog had proved to be trustworthy during those six months, a person living in chronic stress is unable to rationalise easily. Had she contacted the behaviour consultant that she'd worked with to resolve the behaviour, they would have perhaps been able to rationalise with the guardian, and remind her how far the dog had come. A reduction of regular biting to one single growl in six months over a valued resource is enormous progress. Some might say this is a complete resolution. Yet when we are stressed, we are unable to rationalise clearly in the same way.

Acute stress is the same. Most rescue associations have stories of dogs returned after a single event, even years after the adoption.

Everything we have explored so far in terms of negativity biases and blind spots come to dominate our thinking when we are suffering from chronic or acute stress. Chronic stress also makes us more irritable and more hostile. Redirected anger is understandable, even if it is not excusable. That's evident in the letter the rescue received. Underneath her anger lay all her unvoiced self-reproaches, her own feelings of failure and her own grief about a dog that, although she had not bonded with, she had still made enormous progress with. Of course it is easier to blame the dog and anyone else involved in the dog's life than it is to blame ourselves - and blaming ourselves is no more useful than blaming others. Would it really have improved the situation if the guardian had written a letter filled with abject self-hatred and loathing, filled with self-recrimination, blaming herself for having failed the dog so completely? It might have had a more sympathetic response from the association, for sure. Does that mean her outward direction of anger does not deserve an equally sympathetic response?

Stress also makes us more selfish. When the going gets tough, we think of ourselves. Altruism, compassion and empathy are thin on the ground during crises. That also affects our relationship with our animals. We're less likely to understand them and their motivations when we are stressed. It also affects our moral decision making, meaning that we are likely to do things that we would not normally do.

Whenever people are living in chronic stress, it's more likely we'll see these outbursts. You'll learn about when you should take these seriously and when you should let these go in Lessons 20 and 21. For now, it's enough to know that chronic stress is often behind a lot of the anger and irritability we may see from our clients. That can go three ways: towards the animal, towards themselves, or towards us.

We should understand that angry outbursts reduce stress in themselves, temporarily at least. Consider the ways in which there are upturns in domestic violence when there are other social and cultural stressors. All it takes is a lost football match and domestic violence spikes. During economic downturns, animal abuse, spousal abuse and child abuse all increase. Societal pressures, cultural pressures and economic pressures all put us under stress and make it more likely that we will act out.

Remember: you are not a counsellor. You are not a therapist. You are not someone's anger management mentor and nor are you their punching bag. It's perfectly acceptable to disengage kindly and with care if you think there are external stressors that are affecting the relationship that will hinder progress. It's likely that during your career, you will be asked to work in situations where there are tensions between the humans involved in the dog's life, and that you may need to step away because you are not a marriage guidance counsellor or a priest or a family therapist.

It's easy to feel frustrated with the elderly lady who calls for help with her young puppy, without knowing that her family bought her the puppy because they figured that she was lonely and needed something to do. What the client did not want was a puppy. She wanted to see her family more. Now she has a puppy and a family who don't understand or can't meet her needs.

It's easy to feel like there's little you can do if the couple are at war, and one wants to use the Koehler method to train their dog and the other wants to follow Emily Larlham. The dog in this situation is a manifestation of how at odds the couple's values are. You can't solve their marital problems by fixing their dog.

And it's easy to get frustrated with the mum who hasn't time to train her spaniel not to steal from her children's dinner plates, a woman unable to keep the counters clear and keep on top of household tasks when her husband expects her to hold down a job, raise three children, train a dog and have dinner on the table for 7pm all by herself.

In such intractable situations where any impact you will have on the dog will be limited by deep, unresolved shadow-side issues that are likely to derail the whole process, the best you may be able to do is support them in managing the situation for the moment, perhaps rehoming the dog, even offering them the phone numbers of some really good therapists who could help.
Of course, you may need to make sure that the dog's welfare needs

are met, and even at times those of the family themselves, but if the stresses in the situation are caused by things beyond your skills and capacity, it's not for you to deal with them. All that will happen is that you'll shoulder some of those stresses and you'll be the one carrying them instead.

The simple way to deal with your client's stresses is to work out those with which you can help and also to be aware of the ways in which chronic and acute stress change how we behave. You can also evaluate the likelihood of your training making a difference to the client's daily experiences. If you feel that your client would be better placed to wait if certain life factors will change in the future, then it's more than reasonable to say so, especially if you can put in some support mechanisms to help them cope in the meanwhile.

20. Learn when to take negative feedback seriously

Bearing in mind all you have explored so far, it's pretty easy to blame clients when you get bad feedback or they disengage. It's easy to tell ourselves they weren't that invested, that the problems weren't that serious or that they had all kinds of unresolved shadow-side issues. We can say they were overly negative or that they were unable to follow even the simplest of instructions. We might reason with ourselves and say that they're just in a bad place right now and that they're suffering from stress, so they were just acting out of frustration or anger when they left us hurtful feedback or they told us we haven't made a difference for their dog.

How do we know then whether or not they're right if they directly criticise us?

The first thing is to acknowledge the specific issue that they're raising and where its roots lie. Unfortunately, dog training is an unregulated industry in many countries and many accreditation organisations are also responsible for delivering the course materials, so they are unverified and many would-be dog trainers have little way of knowing whether or not they are leaving with a "good" qualification that equips them to work effectively with dogs. The best courses are those which build up to external accreditation or certification, simply because they're more likely to be robust. Sadly, there are many education providers out there who provide courses that do not equip people for real-life dog problems. They may teach a course that's entirely theoretical, where you do not have to submit verified case studies and references. They may teach a course that's entirely practical, where your understanding of learning is never really put to the test. The more robust the testing, the more scary it should feel. There are also many course providers out there who do not teach you how to help humans, or how to plan classes.

Not only that, where there are, that doesn't mean you will also end up with the skills you need. It's not uncommon for people on CV to look like they are more than capable. Anyone who is responsible for recruitment will tell you that a First from a top university does not necessarily equip you to do the job any more than a Third from a low-ranked college. Some of the most natural and gifted dog trainers are the ones without formal qualifications; some of the worst dog trainers can have more badges and accreditation than you'd think possible simply because they're either good at passing tests or they've paid the right money to pick up accreditation.

It's not uncommon for us to hear about the Dunning-Kruger effect - that bias where people with little ability think they are more talented than they are. Most industries are awash with people who are either genuinely unaware of how few skills they have or who overrate the meagre skills that they actually have. In the field of pet photography, for example, there are people who are using point-and-shoot automatic cameras (and nothing wrong with those!) who sometimes post photos alongside the industry masters, whose depth-of-field, use of colour and understanding of composition and lighting show that they have been students for many, many years. The hubris of people posting what are often worse than family photos and charging money for them shows how easy it can be to steal a living. Happily, it's not always like that, and most dog trainers - alongside all other pet professionals - are much more likely to think they are imposters who don't know as much as they need to.

When our clients level criticism at us, then, we need to ask if that is fair, and we need to be honest with ourselves. Like anything in life, however, the more sensitive we are to that criticism, the more likely it is that it was unwarranted. However, if your response is one of burning self-righteousness, based on years of successful case resolutions, weeks and weeks' worth of professional development and supervised practice in the field and your clients are generally more than happy to recommend you to others, then you can say that it's probably unwarranted. Nevertheless, we do need to ask ourselves whether what they say is true and whether we took them on as a client without really knowing whether we could solve their problem. Many dog problems do deserve a specialist. Sometimes that may be a veterinary behaviourist. Sometimes that may be an aggression specialist. Sometimes that may be a specialist in fears and phobias. The problem is that when we are newly graduated and filled with enthusiasm, or we're activists who want to get out and get involved, we can take on cases that are bigger than we should be dealing with. Of course we can help them win a title with their Aussie shepherd at the national agility trials! Of course we can help them teach their dog to detect their child's seizures! Of course we can help them close the book on their dog's separation-related behaviour! Much of this comes back to Lesson 2 - not being afraid to specialise. When you specialise, that gives you time to keep up with the field, perhaps even keep ahead of it. When you are a generalist, then that can leave you floundering a little with the latest research and skills. Specialists turn cases away all the time. Generalists are more likely to take on cases that they have much less experience in.

During my first year of teaching, I worked with an incredibly gifted deputy head teacher who was also an incredibly gifted Economics and Law teacher too. He was in charge of time-tabling. He gave me not only English classes, but also some French, R.E and History. His view was that a good teacher can teach anything. Great as that man was, I believe he was also wrong. You have to also have a passion for your subject and a deep knowledge of it. Without it, you never have the command you need. From that point on, over the next fifteen years, I was on over two hundred staff interview panels. I watched thousands of lessons in my role as an advisor. What success always came down to was a passion for teaching and also a passion for their specialism. When both come together, it's a profound experience. I also watched English teachers deliver lessons at interview, upon which their future livelihood depended, teaching that less and fewer are interchangeable. I watched English teachers deliver lessons to 13-year-olds that were addressing curriculum targets for 6-year-olds. These weren't new teachers just out of training, but teachers with many years' experience. As someone who has been one of less than fifty assessment specialists of her rank, I have seen individuals rise through the ranks on YouTube and TikTok as so-called industry experts when what they have to say is risible.

I say these things not out of a place of cynicism and anger. Such is life, that there will always be people stealing a living and getting away with it. Good luck to them. In reality, what they have to say is probably at least 90% on the ball. Yet they seem like charlatans to those who really, really know.

The easiest test to measure this by is to ask yourself who you most respect in your industry and how you'd truly feel if they were to observe you. For the truth be told, for the occasional lesson I watched with the occasional less-than-adequate teacher, I watched hundreds if not thousands of amazing teachers. I enjoyed all their classes. I enjoyed participating. I loved seeing their students grasp things they'd never understood before. The most amazing had a third class honours from a university that usually ranks in the lower hundred on the UK university league tables. She had been teaching less than a term. I appointed her over five teachers who had been teaching longer than this teacher had been alive. She was sharp on her knowledge and even sharper on her teaching. The other interview candidates were either furious or upset. Their feelings aside, she was already ten times better than they were. What she had was a passion for teaching and a keen desire to make sure students found learning irresistible. I found working with her and mentoring her to be an inspirational breath of fresh air. At the very least, if we met the leaders in our industry, would we make them feel as excited about us as we feel about working with them? Just because you're a so-called expert in the field doesn't mean you're automatically tired and cynical of anything new and dynamic. What would your idols think of you? I hope at least they'd be the kind of people who'd be excited to work with you and your clients too.

I don't think we should all strive to be the same as our industry's leaders. I think there is a real need for the powerhouses of the industry who just keep their heads down and get on with it. But if those industry leaders were to look at what we were doing, would they look at our work with the same eye as a professional pet photographer looks at all those family snapshots, feeling a just little speechless that someone is genuinely buying those blurry, badly composed photos with hands and feet chopped off and bad Photoshop cloning?

What would their feedback be?

And what feedback would our idols give to us?

When we receive criticism, we really do have to ask ourselves if this disgruntled client has a point. Ideological disagreements are one thing, but accusations that we haven't helped are another. As you saw in the last lesson, there are times when clients will lash out and their anger is really with the whole world, including themselves. But there are also times when we need to ask ourselves seriously whether they have a point to make. Only the incredibly thick-skinned are impervious to feedback. Feedback is so important in our development. If your clients are afraid to give you feedback, then that's also something to think about.

Take for instance two local dog schools. One has 600 reviews on Google, despite being a one-person operation. Taking into account that most people who leave public feedback are either overwhelming fans or people with an axe to grind, looking at the feedback, we can see easily that he's clearly an experienced, helpful guy who has managed to give a lot of people what they wanted.

The other is a similar-sized school and has been in operation many years longer. He has 27 reviews. People don't give him feedback despite him having the same number of clients. The first piece of feedback says, "Too much aggression. Believes he knows everything about dogs and clearly knows nothing about humans." Knowing this trainer, I'd say that feedback is spot on. Of course, this person is never going to change their approach and people will continue to pay them to damage their dogs. In fact, his feedback also includes two reviews he wrote himself and one that his wife wrote. He even had the temerity to use his own name when leaving them. His clients either don't think he values feedback or don't want to leave any. Why don't they want to share their experiences?

Of course, you are reading this book and you are interested in improving your clients' experience of you, but it's important to always bear in mind what they have to say - and not just when they tell you how great you are. It's also important to know your own strengths and weaknesses. That need for feedback goes for your business head, your marketing head and your sales head as well as your trainer head. If you feel less confident working with humans, what are you doing to address this? If you feel less confident preparing publicity for your social media streams, what are you doing to address this?

So many pet professionals only take courses in the key aspect of their business without realising that other aspects of their work are letting them down. Once you know you have the best knowledge and skills in your area for your chosen specialism, make sure that your other skills are as sharp as they can be. Finally, don't be afraid to outsource what you can if you really know your skills aren't up to it. Nothing looks better than being able to outsource your graphics, your website and even your secretarial tasks to competent, capable people. Surround yourself with talent that complements your own and don't be afraid to accept your weaknesses. While you may be able to outsource a good number of your tasks, there are two core skills you will need to make sure that you're on top of. The first is easy: training. The second is one that is often overlooked: working with people. It's ironic that many professional bodies who certify or accredit members may require proof of ongoing professional development in animal training, yet do not include people skills within the courses they recognise or award CEUs to.

Make sure that you spend at least as much time annually on both sides of the dog training equation. It's important that you aren't just skilling up your training, but you're skilling up in terms of how you work with people too. And if that all seems like it's too much to stomach, go back to Lesson 2 and revise who you want to be as a professional. There are many, many exceptional trainers who do nothing but train dogs or who sell amazing training courses that involve no interaction from them at all. Perhaps you also dream of selling monetised courses that involve little from you. Bear in mind that if you do that, you'll really have to be at the top of your game, technically speaking. I don't mean technical training. I mean online presence, content creation and marketing. It's a crowded market and many of the great professionals who are rocking it are already outsourcing the technical, business, marketing or sales side. After all, if people have a choice between something that looks slick, well-polished and professional, and something that looks home-made, "quirky" and ordinary for the same price, you know where clients will be putting their money. This also depends on feedback as well, so overcome your embarrassment and start specifically asking your clients to give it. Testimonials, reviews, stars on Google and on social media sites do help your clients get a measure of whether they want to work with you or not. Don't be too afraid to ask for feedback.

Above all, ask for feedback and ask every client. Listen to it with an objective mind and ask if both their praise and their criticism are merited. If you find yourself frequently saying, 'It's them, not me!' or 'If only they'd done what I told them to!' then those are the times to take a step back and ask if you are as good at working with people as you think. If your cases frequently end without successful resolution, you should also ask yourself if you have the skills needed to truly help. Working with others in a helping capacity is not anodyne. We can't just sit back and brush off all criticism if we've failed to make a difference and that failure rests on us, not the client. In Lesson 22, you'll learn about the art of giving good feedback. That applies also to your own self-appraisal.

21. Learn to let unqualified negative feedback go

As you've seen, there are many reasons why we should take client feedback seriously and not just dismiss it, even if we think it was little more than a clash of values and a mismatch between our values and theirs, or if we think that they are not well-placed to make changes right now. There are also many reasons why clients' feedback may not be justified or appropriate. Caught up as it is with shadow-side issues, there are many reasons why we may have to let feedback go.

Many of us get hung up on negative feedback, whether it is warranted or not, whether it is justified or not. Even if we're the type of person to share any unjustified feedback with our friends just because what they said was so ridiculous, we're still internalising it. One trainer shares all negative feedback left via social media and it works well to show the absurdity of it. Her friends remind her that it's untrue. She gets to have a laugh at the absurdity of it and relieve some tension and hopefully puts it behind her. Even so, it clearly sticks with her even if she does nothing more than remind herself how ridiculous it is. We all know how easy it is for people to leave critical comments from behind an anonymous profile or even to do it in person. Worse still are the single stars or lowest recommendations that are left anonymously when you know full well they have been left by a business rival. Luckily, they're the kind of negative feedback we can quite easily ignore or overrule - it's the personal feedback from people that have truly been our clients that hurts, especially when that feedback is very pointed or when you have invested a lot of time and effort into helping them. Sometimes it seems like the more you invest, the worse their feedback becomes.

Negative feedback hits home particularly hard when we're dealing with our own sense of inadequacy. First, we have to rule out that we've been taking on cases that we're not particularly skilled with, instead of passing them on. On the whole, that's very unlikely. We also have to rule out that we might need to brush up on how we work effectively with our clients. After that, if we still feel some nagging doubt that the client was justified even though there is no evidence for it, that feeling of being an imposter is certainly something that we need to deal with.

Mostly, these feelings happen despite your outward success.

If 599 clients say you are doing a sterling job, and you can happily point to ten resolved cases of exactly the same type, then the problem is not likely to be you. Nevertheless, we can still take it personally and if we're feeling inadequate despite our success, then we need to stop and take some time to unpick those feelings.

If you feel full of self-doubt in the first place, that's when criticism hits hard. Of course the clowns who blithely sail through life thinking that they're doing a wonderful job aren't affected by negative feedback. That is of no consequence or significance to them. Oh, that it would but dent their armour of self-belief a little! But the people who are most likely to be adversely affected by feedback are going to be the people who are consumed with self-doubt to start with. It's not even something that we can confuse with lacking confidence or regular failure: often the people who are unduly impacted by other people's unwarranted negative feedback can be confident, successful people whose cases are largely resolved. It may have some correlation with perfectionism: those who feel the need to reach some unobtainable perfect goal are often those who are likely to be more sensitive to unjustified criticism from others.

One of the really important things to do here is recognise your own undermining self-talk. If you're catastrophising, you've got this. You know how to stop clients doing it. You know how to stop conversations descending and freefalling into a spiral of negative talk. Now do the same for yourself. Remind yourself of your successes. It's vital that you do this regularly, even if it's nothing more than keeping a brief list of the last 12 months' successfully resolved cases to hand.

Recognise negative thoughts as they arise, label them for what they are and remind yourself that it's your own critic talking, not the voice of anyone else. Remind yourself that you need to be kind to yourself. Sometimes, it can be really helpful to reframe the things you are saying and imagine if you were saying them to your best friend or your partner. Nobody would tolerate a nit-picking, fault-finding super-critic as a friend, especially not one who reminded them of all their failings. That's not a friend. That's a mean bully. No, a good friend would support us, outline exactly what we did to help, blow off any unjustified criticism and be wise enough to say, 'well, maybe…' if they truly thought there was something we could have considered.

Another thing that's really important is to open up dialogue with other colleagues. Sharing war stories with trusted colleagues is another way to stop the creeping self-doubt that goes with feelings of inadequacy. You can also nip it in the bud by running it past your colleagues in the first place. Having a critical friend check through your action plans, your advice and your assessment is a good way to stop needing to second guess yourself. You might never get to meet the trainer that you most admire in the industry, but you will meet lots of hard-working, talented professionals whose opinions are just as valid. Knowing that your colleagues would take similar approaches can help when you're feeling uncertain about your own abilities, and knowing that they too feel unsure about their own abilities is a key aspect to overcoming feelings of inadequacy.

It's also important in this age of social media to have a real understanding of what training and behaviour work looks like. People are very good at positive self-editing these days on a professional level. Who wants to hear about the times when they failed, right? And it wouldn't exactly be a resounding endorsement. Their Instagram feeds could be filled with their photos of agility success. Their Facebook feeds can be filled with videos of them working on turns for obedience. Their YouTube channels might be filled with wonderful videos of their amazing successes at heelwork to music. Remember: even the most graceful swan is doing a hell of a lot of messy paddling and maneuvering beneath the surface.

Unless you have colleagues around you who are happy to share their war stories in a more intimate setting, of course you're going to end up feeling like you are inadequate compared to carefully curated social media feeds. This is some of the issue with working in isolation: you think only you make mistakes. That feeling is worsened when everyone else's social media feeds look like they're all aces.

It's different when you work together daily: you see the times your colleagues mess up and you see the times people fail as well as their successes. That kind of trusted environment is wonderful. In shelter work, for example, in a big and busy shelter, you get to see the times your colleagues got outfoxed by a dog who's escaped from them and made a run for it; you know when they mess up and that it's not just you. You're not working in isolation. But for the majority of dog walkers, trainers and behaviour consultants, we're working in isolation and don't get to see the reality. That's worse still if you're in "expert" mode and you are constantly on show in front of a group of clients. When you fail in public, all your clients get to see that.

Understanding the nature of your work is important. If you always work solo and with a single client at a time, volunteering a little of your time in a shelter or rescue is one way to find colleagues. It helps keep it real. If you've seen the best-known trainer in your area, famed for her competition ring style and her firm-handed obedience, getting a nip from a kennelled dog that she was far too confident with or being unable to stop the dog pulling without her usual choke chains and aversive methods, you get to see people at their most vulnerable too. And if you get to see the most empathic and cool-headed trainers sometimes failing to make the progress they'd hoped for, that's just as useful.

You can't see others' reality if you only ever work alone.

And yes, reality means failing. It's another reason to remain as authentic as possible, for sure, so that people around you don't put you on a pedestal, but doing it with a safe group where you are permitted to be vulnerable and you trust the integrity and sanctity of that working space, that is another way to ensure you get to see all kinds of successes.

In science, there is something known as the publication bias. This is the tendency of academic journals to only publish studies in which there was a clear outcome. Many, many studies where nothing was found never get published. We do the same in our own lives and with our own histories, where we never publish our 'null' results, where we failed, where no change happened or where progress was slower than we'd anticipated. A trusted group of colleagues is one place to start sharing your own stories.

Working collaboratively or alongside colleagues is another way to get over your feelings of inadequacy if you are usually doing group sessions where you are required to be the expert. Become a student again yourself and find yourself in their shoes. By going to other colleagues' workshops, you'll get to see not only their strengths, being able to learn from them, but also where things don't go to plan. What you'll come to realise is that nobody is perfect. If they put themselves out there when they're working with dogs, surrounded by clients and with 101 tasks on their mind, you'll inevitably see them fail. The point of this is not to enjoy a sense of schadenfreude, that inward pleasure we feel when our enemies get their just deserts, but to remind ourselves that we're all human. None of us are perfect.

If you only ever go to see pet professional coaches who only work with humans, switch it up and make sure you see some working with animals. Anyone who doesn't regularly put out at least some unedited live content with the animals they're working with - and I don't mean carefully curated and refilmed twenty times to seem "real" - are people who aren't really giving you their authentic self. Don't compare yourself to them: you'll inevitably fall short.

A final point is to share your errors in public, live. That's not to say all of them, or the time you got jumped all over by someone's bichons. You don't need footage of you being dragged through a cow field on your backside by a rottweiler intent on going for a swim in the river on the other side, but it does mean showing your vulnerabilities as well as your strengths.

Start with YouTube or Facebook Lives, and start simple, just as you'd coach your clients. Start with the small five-minute sessions without animals, where you've got something of a script. Build up to longer sessions with dogs where you're working without a script at all. The more we contribute to this myth of perfectionism with our own carefully curated content, the more likely we are to feel inadequate.

Be honest, too. Be prepared to say you don't know, or that you need to ask. Having tricky cases where you say to clients, 'Do you know, I've seen something like this before, but this is rare for me and I want to run it by my colleagues or get them in on a Zoom call with us, is that okay?' is not a failure. It's a sign of strength. It also shows your client that you will do what's right for them and their companion. Share your training and your professional development. It's not a sign that you didn't know or that you're weak if you're undertaking further learning. It's a sign that the so-called "natural genius" doesn't exist.

Another myth that contributes to our feelings of inadequacy is that some people are just "good" at training - that they never had to learn. Conquering this myth by sharing your learning journey is a sign that you didn't get here by luck, you got here by learning. This seems to be something of a shameful confession to some - that you weren't born great.

When others think we are "just" naturally talented, we tend to believe the myth ourselves, only we doubt our talents and we see our faults. Reminding yourself of every step in your learning journey is to reveal your foundations, your inner workings, your hard work and your dedication. Of course, you can have undertaken all these things and still be a complete charlatan, but it's a more reliable measure of your success to see your learning than it is to think you're just naturally talented. After all, nobody can quibble with 300 hours of research that went into your qualification, or the 100 hours of professional development you've undertaken during the year. Not even you can quibble with that. But you can quibble with this intangible notion of talent. No wonder we feel inadequate if people think we're "just good with dogs" and we're in full knowledge of the whole facts, not just the ones they get to see. We're less likely to feel inadequate when we've undertaken thousands of hours of research, learning, discussion and observation in the ten years it's taken us to get to this point.

As you come through the other side and you're happy that you're not as inadequate as you first felt, it also becomes your obligation to coach others through the same process. All industries are improved by the sharing of experts and mentors. Acting as a mentor for others is part and parcel of dealing with unqualified and unjustified negative feedback from others, because you get to show others how to cope with it too.

When you have a strong sense of who you are and you trust in your knowledge and skills, then you're primed to let unqualified negative feedback go. When you remember how long your journey has been and you have documented every single step that you've taken to make it hard work rather than simply "luck" or "talent", then you are also better placed to fight off unjustified criticism. Having a small group of trusted colleagues - even those who don't think as you do - is a way to externally calibrate your sense of self from time to time.

After all, we're all confident in our abilities until the day we listen to the little voice that says, 'But what if you're not as good as you say you are?'. That's where we're going to need other people - people you trust - to remind you that you are. That's not to say you're going to go running around desperately in need of others' approval, but that you know how to use it from time to time to correlate their views with your own. It's important that these are the opinions of those whose feedback you value, too. If the only person who tells you daily how great they think you are and how proud they are of you is your grandmother, then you need to open up dialogue with colleagues. It's not that your grandmother is wrong, but if you know yourself that she's been saying this for everything you've ever done, from the collage made of pasta to your Masters degree, then her scale is not a reliable scale against which to calibrate yourself.

Having doubts when people say mean things to you is normal. Having doubts when people don't say mean things to you is normal. Letting them linger or affect you for more time than they should is where it becomes a problem. Recognise those feelings, acknowledge them and reason with them. When you can't reason with them, run them by a colleague who can.

22. Learn how to give good feedback and be a cheerleader

If only life was as easy as marking good human behaviour with a clicker! Sadly, many people go through life unable to give good feedback. That's as true for senior managers in a large multinational as it is for a business manager with a team of two people. Worse still, we're actually really bad at giving ourselves feedback too. When we work with people to train their dogs, we could do with the same precision, a clicker and some cake. However, given the uproar that invariably occurs when humans use Skinnerian principles with other humans, despite the fact that our behaviour is invariably shaped by Skinnerian principles, there are perhaps understandably far fewer trainers in business who use marker training with their human clients. It's a shame, because our feedback would be much improved by applying some basic principles we use when training animals. You can also find out more by exploring TAGteach, which focuses on feedback skills with human clients and how we give instructions.

Feedback generally can be divided into positive feedback and negative feedback. It can also be divided into specific feedback and general feedback.

Contrary to what we might think, negative feedback can be very helpful. Equally, positive feedback can be next to useless. You can plot positive and negative feedback against a continuum for specificity and generality to see which type of feedback you tend towards.

Let's look at some examples.

Saying, 'Well done!' is positive but fairly general. The target of this feedback might not know exactly what they've done well. If they've just done five or six things in a row, which bit was well done? Imagine sending in a piece of artwork to the Royal Academy summer show, and you receive it back with a 'Well done!' or 'Great stuff!'

Sure, that's lovely. It feeds our ego and makes us feel quite warm inside. We all need to be told we're doing a great job and it's nice to hear it. But it doesn't help us move forward. It also leads to widespread generalisation and superstition about variability. If I'm not sure exactly what was well done, I'll be more likely to try to emulate everything I did that I thought pleased you in the first place. Generalised, positive feedback is a killer of variety, and as you know, without variety, there is nothing to shape and little evolution. If I got a 'Well done!' one year and I want another the next, I'm going to largely duplicate what I did the year before because I don't know what you liked. It leads to anxiety because we can't predict if it was the light, the quality of brushstrokes, the composition, the use of textures, the ingenuity or inventiveness. That's not to say you should stop telling your clients how wonderful they are and what a great job they're doing, just to know that whilst it might come as an ego boost, it's also a feedback technique that fuels future anxiety.

Generalised negative feedback is equally unhelpful. 'Better luck next time!' is perhaps a very simple way to tell an artist that their work has not been accepted, but it's as unhelpful as generalised positive feedback. The recipient of the feedback has no idea precisely what they need to work on in future or what to keep. Was it all bad? Was anything worth saving? We also tend not to give this type of feedback to clients, yet we're frequently engaged with doing it to ourselves. 'That was terrible!' we might tell ourselves. 'Worst walk ever!' we might say. Generalised negative feedback also leads to uncertainty because we don't know what the person liked or did not, but unlike generalised positive feedback which tends to lend itself to a narrowing of variety and variation in an attempt to duplicate the exact same feedback, generalised negative feedback ends up with us throwing everything out and trying everything completely differently. Generalised feedback, be it positive or negative, kills variety. It gives the learner nothing to shape.

Specific negative feedback can mitigate a lot of the damage done by generalised feedback. Once, my department was subject to a very thorough and exhaustive work scrutiny from an incredibly well-respected outside consultant. He, no doubt with an instinctive knowledge of our gaps, asked a very pointed question about one area that we'd neglected. 'I suppose I'll see that tomorrow,' he said. I admitted right there and then that we'd overlooked that one area. He didn't even need to say, 'Such-and-such is missing…'. I went home that night, drew up a plan, talked it through with him the next day and he came back to see its implementation two months down the line. That tiny, well-placed, sensitive and kind remark meant the difference between really, really good departmental functioning and outstanding functioning. Specific negative feedback is not the end of the universe, particularly when it's accurate. Of course, you know this from Lesson 20. Knowing when negative feedback is something you need to address is a skill in itself. Recognising your response to negative feedback and managing your reaction are two further skills we all need.

When it comes to specific positive feedback, in fact, there are very few adults who are really good at doing this for other adults. We're really bad at being precise about the good stuff and we tend to fall into generalisations. 'That's nice… that worked'. What was nice? What worked? It's really important to be specific so that, just like animals who have a good understanding of clicker precision, humans know precisely what to replicate in future. 'Your timing was perfect' is good feedback. 'That was perfect' is not.

Specific feedback also uses a key skill of mirroring or describing what the client did exactly to explain what worked. Describe what they did well: 'You got past that cat without a problem then. Your pace was excellent and you kept the dog moving.'

This kind of feedback is the most useful in order to move forward.

We should also think about the balance of positive and negative feedback we're giving. Some people, especially those at the beginning of a long and stressful journey out of a complicated situation, are going to need more positive feedback than they will when they've mastered a skill. Take the client who struggled to even pick up a very simple taught skill even though you demonstrated it ten times. We know how stress impacts performance. This is not a time to tell them that their marker timing was excellent, but their body posture, treat delivery, position and recovery were dreadful. Shape what you want to see and be abundant with the specific, positive feedback at the beginning.

On the other hand, if you're working with a highly-skilled obedience champion who's come to you for some precision work on turns, then they don't need you to butter them up and tell them their timing and treat delivery were just lovely. They don't need to be told that they're good. Their medals and 93 out of 100 scores tell them that already. They want to know what to do to get 95 or 97 next time. If you're looking to sharpen your feedback skills, it's also really useful to go and shadow expert athletic or sports coaches. Precision feedback for enhanced performance is literally their bread and butter.

It's not just a matter of specific or general, negative or positive. We also should think about oral and written feedback. Oral feedback can be quickly forgotten, although it tends to be more memorable if it's negative than if it's positive. Using oral feedback might be all you need to do with the obedience champion looking for precision. We also have many ways to immortalise our feedback in writing, and when we do so, it's useful to remember that if you commit negative feedback to writing, even on social media in a private message, it's more likely to stick and your client is more likely to fixate upon it. Written feedback is ideal for celebrating success.

Though it's nonsensical to send a text message instead of giving oral feedback in the moment, if your client is dealing with change, with stress or they're in need of a little boost in motivation and determination, summarising their best bits in a written message or email to send at the end of the day can really help galvanise their success for the future. Especially if you're trying to build confidence or skills on virtually nothing, specific and positive feedback is often beneficial when you write it down and celebrate it. It's very easy to pick up the work atmosphere in a company by looking at performance records. If they're filled with written warnings and sanctions and records have nothing positive in writing, it's very easy to see straight away that the working atmosphere will be depressing. Especially as you move towards the goal of managing, leading or employing other adults in your own profession, be mindful that you should celebrate successes in writing, record notes of negative feedback but give it orally if possible, and that all feedback, just as it is with our animals, should be timely.

It beggars belief that in this day and age, employers or experts say things like, 'I need to talk to you about…' and then issue a time for discussion over 24 hours later. One technique picked up by exploitative managers in the 1970s was to issue bad news on a Friday evening when people were just about to pack up to go home, knowing full well that when the workers returned on Monday morning, most of the anger or disbelief would have been mitigated by the weekend. In many countries, it is the law that employees should receive warnings within 24 hours of their infraction coming to light. The same should be true of feedback, whether it is both positive or negative. This is as true for your clients as it is for any of your employees. The best feedback happens at the time of the behaviour. You know this already. You're animal trainers.

We should also learn to be good cheerleaders. What this means is that we should be happy to celebrate our client's successes and to give them a motivational boost when they need one. No matter how they're doing, the aim of a cheerleader is to unreservedly and unconditionally support their team in public. That's the same for us. It's as true of other professionals, especially our trusted colleagues, as it is for our clients. A good cheerleader visibly and unconditionally shakes their pom poms on our behalf.

Cheerleaders are there for encouragement and motivation. We're there to say 'I'm proud of you!'. That's especially true when it's the right moment. It sounds kind of silly, right? Adults needing other adults to tell them they're proud of them? We don't stop needing acknowledgement just because we're an adult, however. That's especially true when you're an expert or in a position of influence. Appreciation from experts who pick up the pom poms to cheer for us is one of the best ways to really motivate someone and encourage them. As an expert, as a person with power over others, your words matter. Don't think that it's unnecessary or glib: true appreciation and a heart-felt, genuine 'I'm proud of you' shouldn't come across as patronising or silly. Feedback is also, generally speaking, something we do when clients finish a task. It's a consequence. You might deliver it at exactly the right moment, like a marker word or clicker, but it's still a postcedent event. Cheerleading can come before they're about to do it or even at half-time before it's over. Encouraging others and motivating others affects their own motivating states. It's an antecedent event.

Good cheerleaders also do the postcedent bit, too. You can do this with oral feedback. Better still with written feedback. Even better with public feedback. If not to the world, at least in a small group like your class.

When you're great at encouragement, you're also able to say, 'You've got this. I trust you. You can do it.' That in itself is showing your faith and belief in them. When we can't find our own inner reserves, sometimes a little bit of cheerleading from those who are leading us through the process is worth more than its weight in gold.

And blunderbuss that stuff. Pepper it everywhere. Cheerleading shouldn't be reserved for the very best, hitting them like a well-timed and well-aimed sniper. It's powerful enough that it should be fired widely at whoever comes within target range. When you think it, say it.

Be genuine and authentic in your cheerleading. Remember that even the silly stuff might raise a smile. Just as we can't choose what is reinforcing to the animals we work with, we can't choose what our clients will find reinforcing. It sounds ridiculous but a lot of us still have a residual love of gold stars and getting 10 out of 10 on our report cards. You don't just stop loving gold stars just because you're not 7 years old any more.

Finally, you don't need to be stingy with the cheerleading when it comes to your colleagues. Tell them how much they mean to you.

Encourage them. Tell them what you picked up from their workshop, what you loved about the way they explained things, about how the technique they showed you really made a difference to your client. Just as you do with your clients, do it when it matters, but also do it in writing and do it in public too.

Most people spend all their lives beating themselves up for various things. The least you can do is stop adding to the number of voices who are criticising them. Also, cheerlead yourself. You won't be the first dog trainer in the world who's clicked and rewarded yourself, I promise! If you don't laugh as you do it, you're in need of some major intervention. You don't need to stick it all over Instagram, but make sure you write a note to yourself that you can rely on in future moments of self-doubt and moments where you feel inadequate.

23. Secure Commitment

Despite how much our clients may be paying for our services, this does not necessarily mean they have fully committed to the goals we set. When we work with clients rather than imposing goals and training processes upon them, this is one step in the right direction. However, it is never usually enough in itself. Working on the right problem for them and setting the right goals with them, we take the second step towards ensuring they are with us. Identifying and managing the shadow-side issues and blind spots also takes us a step further towards the achievement of those goals.

All of these stages simply ensure clients are signed up, so to speak. Back to the gym membership analogy, what we've done is signed them up and made sure they're signed up to the right programme for them, not the programme we think they need. We may have got them through the doors a few times, but we haven't necessarily secured their true commitment to real, long-lasting change. We may very well have done our very best cheerleading and encouragement every time they turn up and have cleared the path of obstacles, but securing commitment means that the change is driven from within the client and that they take full responsibility for the journey.

Initial commitment, be that signing up for a gym membership or signing a contract to work with our dog's problem behaviours, is different from long-term commitment. Getting through the door and taking the first tentative steps is not the same as having the commitment to carry out a three- or six-month training plan. It's not the same as completely changing our views and attitudes about how we live with our animals. Training a dog to accept vaccinations or nail clipping is not the same as committing to a lifestyle of consent, cooperative husbandry and grooming.

Several things help us truly secure commitment from our clients.

The first is from a rational and logical point of view. A simple cost-benefit analysis is easy for some of these tasks. For instance, purely from a financial point of view, if I am able to clip my dog's nails myself, then it saves me paying a groomer to do them. It also saves the cost of taking time off work or the cost of transport to the clinic or salon to have nails clipped. That time is then time I can use to do something more fun.

Some cost-benefit analyses are not financial, but emotional. The cost of training my dog to accept care and working with them on minimal restraint grooming and handling, and the cost of desensitising and counter-conditioning them to vet visits is beneficial not from a financial point of view but an emotional one. I am less stressed. The dog is less stressed. The vet is less stressed. Other dogs in the clinic are less stressed. The veterinary ancillary staff are less stressed. From a personal point of view, I will have swapped feeling embarrassed and ashamed of my dog, underpinned with self-pity and also a feeling that I have let my dog down, and I will have replaced that with a feeling of pride. I'll also feel relaxed and positive.

Sometimes, we have no concept of just how valuable skills will turn out to be. Despite some initial resistance and fear in the vet surgery as a result of a veterinarian who used force to restrain dogs, my own dog suffered a number of seizures over a two-year period that required frequent vet visits, blood draws, suppositories and injections. Knowing that he had overcome a level of fear that meant he'd involuntarily urinated on the vet table aged four to become a dog who was markedly less uncomfortable even when having a blood draw or surrounded by a number of staff meant I was much calmer and so were the staff. It's impossible to know just how valuable skills will become in the future. A cost-benefit analysis is likely to be pessimistic in terms of value rather than optimistic, since we find it so hard to conceptualise all the possible reasons we should need our dog to be comfortable doing this or that, and the benefits that we'll reap from seeds sown years before.

It is useful, however, from a practical point of view, to discuss the long-term benefits of the changes you are seeking to create.

It's also important to set appealing goals. Taking the example of minimal-restraint handling and cooperative care, the appeal of not having to wrestle a stressed dog in the vet surgery is clear. Nobody wants to have to wrestle a scared, muzzled 40kg German shepherd who needs four people to restrain him. That's especially true when we know that, in the long term, healthcare needs are likely to increase rather than decrease. Few animals get better as they get older.

To some degree, appealing goals are generally easy to set with our clients since they usually arrive with an unwanted behaviour and the cessation of such behaviour is highly valuable. Yet we should remember not all stakeholders in the problem will feel the same. To take the example of a dog who jumps up at greeting, that may be frustrating and embarrassing for the guardian but they may have guests who love the attention and make it really hard to put jumping on an extinction protocol even if you replace it with another behaviour, such as leaning gently against the visitors' legs to solicit attention.

Where goals are rewarding, however, in general they tend to be goals that our clients can commit to. That's why it's so important that these are their goals. To take the example of a dog who jumps up at greeting once more, if you have clients who love this kind of behaviour but you find it irritating and wish their dog wouldn't do it, if you set this as a goal for them, they're unlikely to commit to it even if you think it's inappropriate or coming from a place of stress and chaos. Asking your clients to visualise and describe how they want things to be in the future can certainly help you find the long-term goals that are important to them.

When we work with clients, we also have to accept that we are the experts and this alters our relationship with them and affects their goal-setting. If clients are asking, 'Well, what do you think the dog should do?', this is to some degree the client passing on responsibility for describing how their dog should behave in the future. These are not their goals but ours. Likewise if we really find our clients are ignoring a problem that is actually fundamental, even if we ask them to work on it and explain why they should, then we will find their commitment to the goal fades.

Consider, for example, the clients whose dog had attempted to bite a small child. If they have no concept that this will end badly if they keep allowing the same scenario to repeat, then not only are they unlikely to work towards goals but the dog is also likely to escalate in intensity.

Clients who don't see the potential long-term consequences of continuing to let their dog behave in ways that will end badly are ones where you might need to spend some time working on blind spots and shadow-side issues. For example, the client who perpetually lets their dog off lead around others but the dog is running up to others and is, all things considered, massively inappropriate and very unable to cope, standing in threatening poses, forcing other on-lead dogs to accept invasive inguinal or anal sniffing, putting their paws over the other dog and attempting to mount them. This is eventually a dog who will get into trouble and end up getting into a fight. It's also a dog on a clear trajectory since the behaviour is worsening not improving. The client's belief that things will improve or that it's not that serious will get in the way of goal-setting and also with securing commitment. The goal of walking nicely on lead and suspending all interactions until the dog has undertaken a thorough remedial socialisation package will not be their goal but yours. They are unlikely to commit to it. No matter how much you present them with the Doomsday scenario, showing what is very likely to happen with a series of gruesome footage from YouTube, they are unlikely to commit.

Compliance is the worst kind of commitment. You may see this in cases where the dog is subject to some kind of legal order. The courts may have forced the family to walk the dog on a lead or use a muzzle following a series of incidents. Non-compliance would result in the destruction of the dog. Compliance does not bode well for sustained change. The underlying attitude of the client will not change and the obligation is unlikely to have an impact in the long term.

Moving clients beyond compliance to a buy-in is some progress in terms of securing commitment. A buy-in happens when a solution is offered and the clients accept the importance of change, even if they did not generate the solution or goal themselves. 'Yes,' they might say, 'I accept that it's important my dog is on-lead all the time and that chasing cyclists is going to end much worse than it did last time,' and in such cases, you have a buy-in. A buy-in is simply agreement or acceptance, though it is a step up from compliance. Buy-ins usually end with clients looking for as many ways to opt out and find the exit clauses. Thus, they may be fixated on teaching the dog to work off lead around cyclists instead of fixated on the goal of teaching their dog to walk nicely on lead in all circumstances. Buy-ins also often end with clients looking for get-out clauses. For instance, a dog guardian might accept that, due to breed-specific legislation, their dog must be muzzled in public. However, even if they have bought in to this, they may spend a lot of time trying to circumvent the requirement, taking their dog unmuzzled to places they are less likely to get caught.

Your clients may buy in to the goal you have set, such as not running over and jumping up on strangers in public, but they may not buy in to your methods of behaviour change. This is another area where you need to secure commitment. If you don't, then don't be surprised to find them soliciting advice on random groups on Facebook or Reddit seeking different ways to achieve the same goal.

For instance, if you've imposed a DS/CC programme and are insisting on keeping the dog on lead in public, the guardian may well consider your goal to be an important one, especially since the dog caused a stranger to have a nosebleed after she ran up to them and muzzle punched them in a park, but they may not have signed up to the fact that this will take time to resolve and in the meantime the dog should not be allowed to practise. In fact, they may not have bought in where either your methods or your timeframe are concerned.

These are the kind of clients that may call you six days after your first session and say that someone on Facebook suggested that they tried training discs or that they should continue to let their dog off-lead and just tell people to ignore her. When you know that extinction bursts are likely to cause behaviour to escalate in the short term, or may turn into frustrated biting, this can be a blind spot you ignored that has gone on to cause much more potential damage in the long run than if you'd discussed different kinds of solutions earlier.

Maybe a client with a dog who jumps on people will return from their late-night foray into Amateur Hour on Facebook with the advice that they should use a choke chain and pull the dog off, saying 'no!' in a very loud voice, or blaming the people who get jumped on for permitting or even encouraging it. Perhaps they'll decide to take the advice of someone who tells them to pin their dog to the floor, alpha roll the dog, spit in its mouth and say 'no!' loudly and firmly, that sometimes you have to be 'cruel to be kind'. These are all actual pieces of "advice" this morning on a breed-specific group on a post that clearly states the original poster is already working with a trainer! The only person saying they should go back to the trainer and discuss got one like compared to the alpha role and spit, who had fifteen likes and not a single person debating this advice.

Not only does the client need to have ownership of the goal - it really does need to be their goal - but they also need to have ownership of the treatment process and also the timeframe. That's why it's vital to work through all possible solutions and discuss the probable and likely fall-out of each method. It seems ridiculous to have to run through why you should not use X, Y and Z method, or to do a cost-benefit analysis of each and every way in which they could solve the problem of their seven-month-old dog giving a dog-sitter two black eyes, especially when you have a very good training plan that fifteen other clients have used successfully, but this is a problem if you haven't secured commitment in terms of methods and timeframe.

You may also want to take a hard line on your clients using any other social media platform other than yours. You could put clear statements into your contract that you will terminate the contract and keep the remaining sum paid in advance if you see them soliciting advice on social media, but if you haven't secured commitment because they don't have true ownership of the solutions you're proposing or the timeline you've suggested, this is a common and well-known pitfall of the doctor-patient model and the expert model. Threats of terminating contracts, like all punishments, don't deal with the underlying motivation behind the behaviour - namely, that clients haven't truly committed to your solution or timescale.

Only client-centred approaches are truly going to work here, and yes, that's going to take you some time to work through blind spots and to work through all kinds of possible solutions to find the one that works for them.

The clear pit-falls of not securing commitment to your methods and timeframe are more than evident in posts all over social media, and all were exemplified in this single post. They're replicated every time someone posts a problem behaviour on any social media platform. The post will invariably come after some small obstacle. That may be 7pm when their willpower is low and they're feeling despondent about a 12-week training programme. It might come after they've failed to fully implement your instructions to the letter and some small setback has happened. Several people will also say they have the same problem. Someone will say it's innate in the breed, as if giving people black eyes is par for the course and it's some kind of kangaroo-type dog with specially selected traits to muzzle punch people in the nose. People will inevitably propose negative punishment without understanding the frustration and aggression that can be a consequence of this. Others will say, 'Oh, she's just a puppy... she'll grow out of it!' without understanding that the dog is in fact growing into the behaviours and it's escalating, because they have no understanding of reinforcement. Others will propose obedience, as if this is a cure-all for frustration. Some will blame the other person, as if the dog-sitter deserved to be given two black eyes by a dog who has a very clear history of doing this with other people, and one person actually blamed people who wear white t-shirts, as if this is a clear signal to the dog that muddy paws are a must. Or they blame the recipient saying that they said they're 'used to dogs' and blaming them for giving treats or greeting the dog, without understanding that ignoring (an extinction protocol) is actually likely to escalate behaviour in the immediate future, and, in the case of injurious jumping to get attention at greeting, the behaviour is likely to get a response eventually, no matter how much you ignore it. Extinction protocols with intense behaviours at high magnitude are the very devil to put into place. Others suggested using such a severe punishment that it was highly likely to leave a teenage dog with residual trauma and definite ambivalence about strangers. Some suggested flooding the dog with people and punishing the dog for reacting. One post erroneously pointed out that treat training makes it worse and didn't understand the attention dogs get for jumping up is the reinforcement. 'Tire her out' is other advice from people who don't understand that adrenaline is reinforcing in itself and a tired teenage dog is less likely to follow simple cues. People with similar dogs suggest avoiding other people, without realising this has potential fall-out that can be very severe. Punishments abound: "towel taps", choke chains, alpha rolls, spitting in the dog's mouth, yelling at the dog and being a "pack leader" are all proposed with no understanding of the consequences. Fifty-four responses and only two suggested using positive reinforcement of any sort and nobody suggested going back to the trainer. You absolutely do not want this lack of buy-in over your methods.

Avoiding these situations seems counter-intuitive. A simple problem of stopping a dog jumping on other people that would be best solved by better understanding of a teenage dog, a DS/CC schedule to expose the dog gradually to strangers and overcome the ambiguous feelings that are leading to the dog charging up and jumping on people, a well-taught replacement behaviour and a differential reinforcement of incompatible behaviour coupled with an extinction protocol would be perfect. Yet this is time-consuming and difficult to execute.

If you don't work with clients from the beginning to secure commitment to this because you've imposed a tricky and complicated plan, even if it is likely to be completely successful, don't be surprised if your clients are buying training discs and if you find out through the grapevine that not only did they disappear from your client list but they turned up on a colleague's after the dog had broken someone's nose.

To a large degree, this is not their failure. It's hard to admit, but it's ours.

It would be easy to spend a 60-minute session diving straight into training, setting up the dog with stooges, training the guardians to teach a replacement behaviour instead. You could finish the session pleased that they seemed to be compliant. And then at 11pm, you're tagged into a post on a local group where someone is recommending you as a trainer, not knowing that the person asking for help and wondering if a prong collar will work is already your client!

This is a clear failure of ours to take into account the client's needs, and a clear failure of ours to truly engage them with the time it takes to run through the costs and benefits of a variety of training methods exploring why they succeed or fail and to go with their choice. That's not to say we present them with all this terrible Amateur Hour advice from Facebook and dismiss each one turn by turn, but that we make sure the clients have truly bought into the proposed methods and timeframe, or, better, that they devised the time frame themselves and that they also chose methods that would work for them and they felt comfortable making. That comes with a commitment from us during the initial stages of implementation and a whole lot of hand-holding. This again is a time commitment from us to be available on social media, available for chats and available for troubleshooting. Commitment comes also because we're open, we're flexible and we are genuinely there for the client. Yes, this is time-consuming, and so you need to factor this in to your initial price and schedule. A true understanding of how hard things are, even if it seems as simple as saying, 'Well, we'll teach the dog to say "hi" by pressing their shoulder gently against people's legs and ignore them jumping up, but we'll make sure they've had lots of practice in a range of situations', is actually really, really hard to implement for most people. We might know that teaching a shoulder to leg touch is no more complicated than teaching a dog to sit, but to our clients, it may seem like teaching a tiger to have their teeth brushed.

Securing commitment, then, is not just about the client picking the right goal for them. It is also about them picking the right time-frame and methods for themselves. It's about setting up their environment for success. You know this. You do this all the time with animals. Weird as it seems, you're going to have to cut off their means to get reinforcement elsewhere by making it really easy to get reinforcement from you. You're going to have to shape and scaffold their efforts and make their learning attempts errorless before gradually re-introducing challenge.

Tempting as it seems to impose a cheap plan on what seems to be a ridiculously simple problem, this method will cost you clients in the long term. This means being absolutely transparent about your costs but also the services you offer. You can't do this cheaply and maintain a 100% success rate with clients. So put your prices up.

You can't be responsible for them working through all kinds of ridiculous methods before they get to you because you're literally the last thing they have yet to try. You can't be responsible if 50 people post on Facebook and say, 'This trainer changed my life and solved exactly this problem in 3 months!' and they ignore it. Accept that they will try all kinds of cheaper, quicker methods first and that you can't fight this by offering quick-fixes yourself at a cut-throat discount. All that will happen is your quick-fix and cut-throat discount will end the same way as the training discs and spitting in the dog's mouth: badly.

Now, you can do the same as the manufacturers of all kinds of quick-fixes and take the bad reputation and low success rates with the high volume of sales, or you can keep your pricey reputation and high success rates with a low volume of sales - sales that deliver a high degree of success for your client, be they canine or human.

What you can't do is both.

You can sell compliance packages if you like. 'Do this exactly to the letter and you will succeed'. It may be the best package around. There are many, many products like this on the market, from minimally aversive packages right through to hardcore punishments. All of them sell in relatively high volume at relatively low prices.

You can sell buy-in packages where you like, where these are shaped with your client because the client has little other choice.

Alternatively, you can work with total commitment that will certainly have taken you more time to put in place but is much, much more likely to succeed.

And, like pricing and sales, you can't do all of these options.

Ownership does not come cheap. It means that the client isn't following someone else's goals, timeframes and ideas. It means they aren't just saying this is an acceptable goal, timeframe and idea. It means they are saying, 'this is my goal, my timeframe and my idea.'

It is what they want to do.

Of course, you are allowed to have an opinion about the direction they are taking. The same as when we work with animals, we have to decide whether what's right for us is right for the client. Having strong ethical standards does not mean compromising them. It also does not mean leading the clients into the single choice you've already decided that's right. It does, however, mean navigating through shadow-side issues from time to time and tackling blind spots. It's important to do this when you're generating solutions.

Trainer: So what you really want to work on is the way your dog greets people?

Client: Yes. I don't want her running up to people in the park and jumping all over them. They've all been really nice about it, but it's really embarrassing.

Trainer: Absolutely. So if you could imagine the perfect scenario, what would it look like?

Client: Well, I want her to come back when I call her.

Trainer: So you think it's a problem more with recall than it is with jumping on people? Does she jump on people at home?

Client: Yes. She does it at home, too. And she gets nippy if people push her off.

Trainer: So it's not really a recall problem, maybe? Do you think you'd be able to call her away if you had guests at home and she'd stop?

Client: Well, that's what I want her to do.

Trainer: Do you think it might be easier if she didn't do it in the first place?

Client: I don't mind her saying "hi". I just don't like it when she jumps on people.

What you can see in this dialogue is the client isn't really sure what she wants. The trainer has to help her see a blind spot, that it's not recall that's the problem, but that it's the way the dog interacts with unfamiliar people in the home, too. You can see the trainer helping the client decide what they really want. When the client gets stuck and seems to be going down a route of letting the dog jump up and then recalling the dog, which will be difficult, then it's important to make that clear.

Trainer: Ok, so that might be a little tricky to get her to stop once she's started. It'll be much easier for you to teach her a nicer way to greet people, especially if she's not quite so excited to see them in the first place… but it sounds like you're saying you'd like her to say hello, but you don't want her to jump on people, and you want her to stop when you ask.

Client: Yes. That's exactly it.

Trainer: So what might it look like when she's greeting people?

Client: I want her just to be calmer and just sit.

Trainer: We totally could teach her to sit instead of jumping. But it's very hard when you're really excited to see someone and you're being asked to sit still. Would it be okay if she keeps four feet on the floor?

Client: Sure, yes. I mean, I don't need her to be completely still.

What we see here is a client who can't imagine what a dog not jumping up looks like. She's not got very many solutions to offer. The trainer can provide some options though. Don't shape these and present them in an order to get clients to make the "right" choice (according to you). Avoid giving the best first or last, or stopping when the client agrees on one. You don't need to present them with every single choice they could possibly make. Too much choice can be overwhelming when you're stressed or facing problem situations.

Trainer: So I'm just going to take you through five behaviours we could teach her to do instead of jumping. One behaviour we could teach instead might be a spin. It's quite natural for dogs to turn in a circle when they're excited, and that could be one thing we could teach her to do instead.

Client: I don't know. She's quite big and I think it'd be hard if she's in the hall.

Trainer: The second one might be to teach her a hand touch, where she uses her nose to touch the hand of the visitor.

Client: Ok. I quite like that one. But I don't think everyone likes a big dog's wet nose in their hand.

Trainer: To be fair, it's better than jumping on them, so there's that. A third thing we could teach her might be to lean on people's legs. People instinctively reach down to pet dogs who do this and it's quite a still behaviour.

Client: I guess so, yes. Unless they don't want dog hair on them.

Trainer: Again, better than muddy paw prints on their white t-shirts or a broken nose. Maybe we need to be able to ask guests, visitors or unfamiliar people first if they want to greet her?

Client: Yes, that would work. So I ask them if she can, and if they say yes, she goes to say 'hi' in a nice way?

Trainer: Yes. Absolutely.

Client: Ok. I like that. Well in that case, I like the leaning trick. That'd be nice.

Trainer: There are others, of course. You could teach her to sit and give a "high five" or just keep four feet on the floor when people pet her?

Client: I think the high five would just end up with her clawing people though.

Trainer: Ok. And just being a bit calmer? Just letting them pet her but needing to keep four feet on the ground?

Client: Yeah, I guess so. It's not as cute as leaning on people though.

What the trainer has done here is talk the client through options and pick her own. This is absolute ownership. The trainer has also set up some parameters to flesh out.

Trainer: So if we're imagining her in … how many months' time? … What will she be doing?

Client: I want her to wait by me, so I can ask, and then if the people say yes, I want her to go up and lean on them for petting. And I want her to stop when I say stop.

Trainer: And let's talk about timeframes. When do you need her to do this?

Client: Well it doesn't really matter how long it takes…

Trainer: That's true, but if you don't have a bit of a time on it, it'll end up on the "to do" list forever. What do you think is a reasonable timeframe for this?

Client: I don't know? A month?

Again, the client is a little stuck at this point, and it's important to help them think it through. Without any kind of deadline, it would just end up a task never done. The trainer helps the client set a deadline so that she can then work on action planning. What they do have, though, is a very clear goal. And if the client had asked for the behaviour to be learned by tomorrow, then that's another blind spot the trainer would have to unpick.

What you see here through imagining what it is exactly the client wants, the trainer can deliver it. It's a reasonable request. It's not the easiest request. Avoiding people for the rest of the dog's life would seem to be the easiest request. Yet how easy is it in reality to have a dog who never interacts with a single visitor or person in public? The trainer has also effectively steered the client into productive goals, rather than just stopping all jumping up behaviour. Yet at the same time, it remains very much the client's vision for their dog in the future.

It doesn't matter yet how this is achieved. Dog trainers tend to get fixated on how dogs learn things. Our method is not the important thing here - not yet. What we shouldn't be doing is running home to find fifty ways to teach a dog to do a shoulder-touch-to-legs and find that one "miracle" way of doing it quickly. What matters is the goal itself at this point, not how it is achieved.

First, secure commitment to a clear, objectively described goal. Then secure commitment to a timeframe. Eventually, when you move into action planning, you're also going to need to secure commitment to methods. You're still at the what and the when stage, not the how. These come later. Scaffolding an approach to teach the dog a new behaviour, talking the guardian through and supporting them in implementation, helping them manage the environment so that the dog isn't freelancing in their own time and destroying all the good work - these are all things to ensure plans become actions. They can only happen, however, when the client is committed to a goal.

24. Learn how to set realistic goals

Once you have secured commitment and ownership to a single goal and agreed an appropriate time frame, you can then start to help your clients map out their goals more specifically.

Although it is very old hat, the SMARTER acronym is useful for goal setting. While most people know what these things stand for, it's useful to run through them with your clients who may not have seen it before.

S is for SPECIFIC. Goals should not be something general or vague. They need to be clear and objective. Saying 'I want my dog to be calmer' is not specific. Saying, 'I want my dog to be able to greet guests without jumping up' is specific. Going back and revisiting Lesson 13 may be helpful.

M is for MEASURABLE. Goals should be quantifiable. Or, if nothing else, more easily quantifiable. Measuring calmness is not easy. You could do it perhaps with biological measurements such as heart rate and respirations per minute. Measuring whether a dog is not jumping up is much more easily quantifiable. This also requires us to take examples from Lesson 13 in creating a clear baseline. If we don't know what the dog is doing to start with, then we are not going to be able to measure and assess progress. Taking a baseline measurement is an essential part of the goal-setting process.

A is for ACHIEVABLE and AGREED. Coming back to compliance models, buy-in models and ownership models, goals should be more than agreed. They should be owned wherever possible. But they also should be achievable. Again, you may need to iron out the blind spots if your client thinks they can solve a 4-year aggression history with 3 hours of classes. It's largely up to you to help your clients get a picture of what is achievable. You've already covered the negativity bias in Lesson 12, but you will also learn about the optimism bias in Lesson 25. Navigating the narrow canal between pessimism and optimism is part of your work here. Goals, as you have learned, should be challenging enough. That said, they should not be too challenging. Achievable goals are all about finding the Goldilocks goal: not too hard, not too easy… just right.

R is for RELEVANT. These should be goals that will really address the client's needs. Teaching a solid recall may well have helped the client in the previous lesson with the dog who was jumping up in public and in private, but it wouldn't meet her goal of having a dog who can greet people politely. Again, this is where your judgement is vital. Is the problem that the client wants to tackle the relevant problem? Will it make a difference?

T is for TIME-SENSITIVE. As you learned in the previous lesson, having clients own the timeframe in which the action plan will be carried out will help them have ownership of their actions. However, too short a timeframe, or too long, and your client will either feel the frustration of not meeting their goals or they will feel the frustration of not seeing quick enough progress. There will be cases that you can tackle in one single contracting session. But there will also be cases that may need to take place over six months or even longer.

E is for EFFORT-SENSITIVE. In so many ways, those small wins at the beginning and those solid foundations are essential. They motivate us, they build momentum, they get us moving. From what you know about stress, you can see that unless you are sensitive to the amount of effort and exertion that your client needs to put in, they are likely to fail. If they are over-faced by what they are doing, then they are likely to fail. Remember there is a very good reason why things like training discs and shock collars sell well. They take no effort to buy or use. You may wish to change every single thing in your client's relationship with their dog, from their food to their activities, from their enrichment to their snooze times, from their training to their relationship, but if you overwhelm your client, they will undoubtedly opt out. Choose your battles. Make sure what you are helping them focus on is relevant to them and likely to make a difference. E is also for ETHICAL. We should always make sure the goals we set are the right ones and that we realise that behaviour modification is not a neutral process.

R is for RECORDED and REVIEWED. Paperwork may well be the bane of your life, but as you know, good systems help the smooth functioning of the rational side of things. Document what you are doing and make sure you build in periodic reviews.

When you have a clear SMARTER goal, then you can break it down into small steps. In general, remember the bulk of progress happens last in the timeframe and that progress is rarely linear. If your timeframe for meeting the goal is 6 months, then work out what you would expect to see at 3 months, at 6 weeks, at 3 weeks and after 10 days. If your timeframe is 3 months, work out your progress steps at 6 weeks, 3 weeks, 10 days and 5 days.

Break it into half, to quarters, to eighths and work it backwards, using time and difficulty to help you plan it into weeks. This is a plan for the lawn-mower-chasing beauceron. This depends on one person operating the machine and another conducting the work with the dog. For this dog, he had also connected the approach of the operator to the lawnmower and so he had to be desensitised to the operator moving towards the lawnmower. The plan actually started by writing in Week 12 as a 3-month goal. Then each week was planned backwards.

You can see that this plan may even need a few more weeks added. There were an additional 12 weeks of practice where the dog was off-lead with decreasing levels of supervision. It also built up to longer times and at closer proximity.

Helping clients plan a week-by-week outline that you review as you go gives your action planning measurability and momentum.

When you have done this, you can then do a day-by-day plan each week.

Week 1: Work on a long line and supervised in human-led activities like '1-2-3-Drop' or parallel walking using 'Find it!' and 'Let's go!' around the static lawnmower at 20m distance. Counter-condition the sound of the lawnmower being started from behind a screen.	Week 2: Work on a long line and supervised in human-led activities like '1-2-3-Drop' or parallel walking using 'Find it!' and 'Let's go!' around the static lawnmower at 10m distance. Counter-condition the sound of the lawnmower running for 5 seconds from behind a screen.	Week 3: Work on a long line and supervised in human-led activities like '1-2-3-Drop' or parallel walking using 'Find it!' and 'Let's go!' around the static lawnmower at 5m distance. Counter-condition the sound of the lawnmower running for 10 seconds from behind a screen.
Week 4: Work on a long line and supervised in human-led activities like '1-2-3-Drop' or parallel walking using 'Find it!' and 'Let's go!' as the operator makes a step towards the lawnmower from 10m away & repeat 10 times.	Week 5: Work on a long line and supervised in human-led activities like '1-2-3-Drop' or parallel walking using 'Find it!' and 'Let's go!' as the operator walks slowly to the lawnmower for a period of 10 seconds.	Week 6: Work on a long line and supervised in human-led activities like '1-2-3-Drop' or parallel walking using 'Find it!' and 'Let's go!' at a 30m distance from the operator on a stationary lawnmower for a period of 10 seconds.
Week 7: Work on a long line and supervised in human-led activities like '1-2-3-Drop' or parallel walking using 'Find it!' and 'Let's go!' at a 30m distance from the stationary but switched on lawnmower for a period of 10 seconds.	Week 8: Work on a long line and supervised in human-led activities like '1-2-3-Drop' or parallel walking using 'Find it!' and 'Let's go!' at a 30m distance from the slow-moving lawnmower for a period of 20 seconds.	Week 9: Work on a long line and supervised in human-led activities like '1-2-3-Drop' or parallel walking using 'Find it!' and 'Let's go!' at a 30m distance from the moving lawnmower for a period of 45 seconds.
Week 10: Work on a long line and supervised in human-led activities like '1-2-3-Drop' or parallel walking using 'Find it!' at a 20m distance from the moving lawnmower for a period of 90 seconds.	Week 11: Work on a dropped long line (trailing the dog but could be stepped on or grabbed) and supervised in activities like scatter feeding at a 20m distance from the moving lawnmower for a period of 2 minutes.	Week 12: Be off-lead but supervised at a 20m distance from the moving lawnmower for a period of 2 minutes.

Once you have weekly targets, make a day-by-day plan working backwards.

Day 7.

Work on a long line and supervised in human-led activities like Leslie McDevitt's Pattern Games or parallel walking using 'Find it!' and 'Let's go!' around the static lawnmower at 20m distance for 5 minutes.

Counter-condition the sound of the lawnmower being started from behind a screen at 5m.

Day 6.

Work on a long line and supervised in human-led activities like Pattern Games or parallel walking using 'Find it!' and 'Let's go!' around the static lawnmower at 25m distance for 3 minutes.

Counter-condition the sound of the lawnmower being started from behind a screen at 10m.

Day 5.

Work on a long line and supervised in human-led activities like Pattern Games or parallel walking using 'Find it!' and 'Let's go!' around the static lawnmower at 30m distance for 2 minutes.

Counter-condition the sound of the lawnmower being started from behind a screen at 15m.

Day 4.

Work on a long line and supervised in human-led activities like Pattern Games or parallel walking using 'Find it!' and 'Let's go!' around the static lawnmower at 35m distance for 90 seconds.

Counter-condition the sound of the lawnmower being started from behind a screen at 15m.

Day 3.

Work on a long line and supervised in human-led activities like Pattern Games or parallel walking using 'Find it!' and 'Let's go!' around the static lawnmower at 35m distance for 45 seconds.

Counter-condition the sound of the lawnmower being started from behind a screen at 20m.

Day 2.

Free work in sight of the static lawnmower at 35m distance for 30 minutes. Practise Pattern Games, parallel walking, u-turns, 'Find it!' and 'Let's go!' in isolation out of sight from the lawnmower.

Counter-condition the sound of a lawnmower being started from behind a screen at 20m.

Day 1.

Free work in sight of the static lawnmower at 35m distance for 15 minutes. Practise '1-2-3-Drop', practise parallel walking, u-turns, 'Find it!' and 'Let's go!' in isolation out of sight from the lawnmower.

Counter-condition the sound of a lawnmower being started from behind a screen at 30m.

When you have a day-by-day plan for your clients, you can then plan in your support. Day 1 will undoubtedly be a day where you will work together as you begin the action plan. You may ask for a video of Day 2 to be sent by social media or email. On Day 1, you can also work out the skills that you will need to show the client before the next session. You can also plan in the difficult leaps, where your client would benefit from your in-person support or virtual support during the actual session. A clear action plan seems like a lot of paperwork, but it gives you something to check against. Whatever field of change people work in, a clear and detailed action plan is a vital part of sustainable progress.

25. Understand and deflect the optimism bias

In Lesson 12, you explored how people have an instinctive negativity bias. You explored how humans talk themselves down, how they find it hard to see a route out of complicated situations, and how to work with clients who think and talk in self-defeating ways. The optimism bias isn't the polar opposite of this; however, it does affect our work with clients, particularly towards the end of contracts. It also affects our work with them in risk assessments and in managing the environment for their dogs.

The optimism bias is a cognitive bias that makes us think things are going to be less likely to happen to us. We think we're less likely to get bitten by a dog, that we're less likely to run into problems, that we're less likely to find our dogs involved in common situations that are often the inevitable outcome of escalating behaviour. The optimism bias means we believe we'll be less likely to be the victim. So if you're explaining to clients that around 40% of aversive training techniques are likely to end in the escalation of aggressive behaviours, your clients will inevitably believe that they're unlikely to be one of the people that this happens to. If you're explaining the risks of their off-lead dog running up to other dogs and getting attacked, your clients will inevitably believe that they're unlikely to be one of the people that this happens to, either. When we look to the future and conduct risk assessments or cost-benefit analyses, when we compare ourselves to the available statistics, the optimism bias makes us believe that it's unlikely to happen to us.

Where this is important is in planning with your clients for success. Sometimes, you know you are going to need a safe and predictable environment in which to practise behaviours. If you're working with a reactive, fearful or aggressive dog, you're going to need a predictable and safe space to do so. The optimism bias will affect how safe our clients consider the environment to be. One example might be that we insist on defensive handling techniques or that their dog is muzzled in public only to find that our clients are blithely carrying on as they were. The optimism bias makes us believe that accidents couldn't possibly happen to us.

Even if we know the statistics or we have anecdotes about the probability of accidents, of injury or of behavioural escalation, our clients may struggle to believe that they too could be one of the statistics. It affects not only how we assess situations but also how we take risks.

Having worked with aggressive dogs for a number of years, I now take incredibly few risks when working with them myself and I'm happy to say this has resulted in both my own safety and that of the dog. I am incredibly risk-averse. Where some trainers talk reasonably of two barriers between the dog and the human, I will often take three or four. When out in the real world putting skills to the test, I'll have checked the links on harnesses, the catches on leads, the buckles on muzzles, stress tested the muzzle material. My dogs will be working with a double lead, one on the harness and one on the collar. If transporting dogs with aggression problems, the dogs will be muzzled, on lead and in a transport crate. Having once been behind a van that spun off the motorway, where two dogs were then freed by the impact and luckily we managed to catch them before they got hit by trucks in driving rain, I imagine the same situation with aggressive dogs. Could some stranger catch a dog on a motorway in heavy spray and rain with lorries going at 110kpm? A dog who has a pathological fear of unfamiliar people? Could they do it safely? What if I'm rear-ended and taken to hospital? How would the police or fire services even manage to remove the dogs without danger? Experience is a cruel mistress.

Even if you have had these experiences and you are just as risk-averse, your clients may have trouble believing that if they don't work with their dog who enjoys charging up to other dogs when off lead, then their dog will get in a fight. They may have trouble believing that if they keep taking items from their guarding dog, then the dog will end up escalating behaviour. They may also have trouble believing that if they don't make sure the perimeter is absolutely secure, perhaps even with a double barrier, that their dog would ever bite a neighbour who came too close, or the neighbours' kids who just like to say hello.

These kinds of positive illusions seem to be a way of inoculating ourselves against negative events. After all, if we went around believing that all dogs could bite us and we could end up just another statistic, we'd probably end up with a pathological fear of dogs.

Optimistic biases may also help us regulate anxiety.

Evidence also shows that people in more individualistic cultures such as the USA and the UK are also more prone to optimism biases. We simply don't think it could happen to us.

This all affects how careful we think we are compared to the average, and also how capable we are compared to the average.

A third bias relating to optimism is our belief that we think we have more control over situations than the average person does. You can see how these might affect the risks dog guardians will take when implementing action plans. These may stem from our very egocentric natures and inability to think about how situations could have occurred for other people.

However, such unrealistic optimism in the face of risk is a warning to us: research suggests that people who think bad things are less likely to happen to them are actually more likely to have exactly that happen and also to put themselves in harm's way. We might deliberately put ourselves in harm's way just because we believe that something is less likely to happen to us.

It's a warning, then, if clients don't seem to be taking risks seriously, that they're less likely to do things to prevent accidents from happening.

Increased optimism is actually putting us at increased risk for negative outcomes.

It's horrible when this happens. No doubt other shelter trustees and senior staff will know of volunteers and junior staff members who consistently ignore warnings of risks. Yet these same people are less likely to take precautions and therefore more likely to end up at risk. Our in-built optimism bias makes it hard for us to consider that bad things will happen to us until it is far too late.

The bias towards such optimism is actually challenging to overcome. Sometimes, even in tackling the bias, we can harden our clients' beliefs that potentially hazardous situations could never happen to them.

There are other biases and fallacies that also affect how realistic our clients will be, including how much time tasks are likely to take and how much time they can dedicate to them. In other words, don't take it as gospel if your client says they can spend 30 minutes a day working on a task. In reality, plan for 5 minutes and if there's more, great. This also affects cost-benefit analysis. We're more likely to underestimate the costs and overestimate the benefits. Ironically, this is only true when we're involved in the implementation ourselves: outsiders tend to take the opposite tack, thinking tasks will take longer, costs will be higher and benefits will be lower. That means that you and your client are coming from very different angles simply because of who will be implementing the plan.

When you notice this particular blind spot with your clients, it's important to plan for contingencies, rather than tackle it head on. If you are incredibly risk averse, trying to get your clients to muzzle train their dog and always walk their dog on lead will be things that are likely to be doomed to failure. Firehosing them with negative literature and dog bite statistics is likely to only harden their belief that it won't happen to them. I'm sure I'm not the only one to think it largely ironic that many people catastrophise situations with their dogs that are unlikely to escalate, and are hugely optimistic in situations where the behaviour is very likely to escalate… the joys of human nature!

Clear and frank discussions about what clients think the negative consequences could be if they don't undertake a particular action are as equally valid in terms of securing commitment as thinking about the potential benefits. Asking clients what the worst that could happen would be is one way to help them plan for the worst. Encouraging clients to hope for the best and plan for the worst is one way to help them deal with their own optimism biases. We can also encourage them to be realistic about goal-setting and timeframes. When we see unmitigated and unbridled optimism, particularly when the dog is at high risk or the situation is potentially dangerous, it can be quite useful to go back to objectivity. Using a risk assessment with clients to objectively discuss the level of danger can also be helpful.

We need to be aware of human tendencies to be optimistic and to underestimate how long things will take, or overestimate how much they think they can achieve. When we see this and we tackle it as a blind spot, then we're more likely to ensure our clients meet goals successfully.

26. Understand how humans learn

As you move into implementing plans, a good understanding of how humans learn will be essential. Disengagement at this point because your clients don't understand your teaching approach would be a huge waste of energy on both sides of the client-trainer relationship.

When you have clear goals, this avoids some learning issues with your clients. One of the most frustrating aspects of learning for humans is not having clear, tangible goals with a clear purpose. Make sure you are clear with clients about what you are doing and why. For instance, in Lesson 24, you saw a clear goal-oriented outline of a dog working around moving machinery. One of the first tasks was using a variety of food toys and games over a 15-minute period at some distance from the machinery. It's important that when we include activities like this for our clients, we explain the purpose of doing this. In this case, we could tell our clients that we're aiming to create a relaxed and disinterested state around machinery so that it once again blends into the background rather than being something that the dog fixates on. It also allows us to gauge their body language and state of relaxation, to check that they can be distracted around the machine, since we will be doing a lot of work around the machine over the next twelve weeks.

We also need to understand that humans learn in multimodal ways. Some humans learn by watching, some by listening, some by doing and some by a blend of all three. It's not enough simply to show your clients and have them watch you; you will need to explain the processes you are teaching as you teach them. Some clients will also need you to let them do it with them and to shape their first attempts. One thing that is very useful in consolidating their learning is to let your clients "teach" the technique back to you, explaining the steps and processes. Nothing embeds learning like teaching it to others.

Dr. Anthony Gregorc is an American educator who developed another model of how humans learn, a Mind Styles model. In this model, he explores tendencies or trends for four different styles of learning. While this model, like all other models of how humans learn or learning preferences, is perhaps little more than an interesting way to consider how humans learn differently from each other, it does provide us some interesting food for thought.

One type of learner, whom he calls the Abstract Sequential, likes to learn in what we might think of as traditional research methods, reading in books and articles. You may find that some of your clients want to go away and research what you are teaching them. Indeed, you may find you have some clients who enjoy going away and reading everything there is to know on the subject. Coming back to other learning styles, this type of person enjoys the research aspects of a subject and wide reading and learning. They may enjoy the theoretical aspects of learning about their dog's behaviour but they may need time to go away and process what you have taught them in order to truly engage with it.

The second type of learner according to Gregorc is the Concrete Sequential learner. This type of learner is less abstract and more of a person who enjoys doing things, but they need a clear set of instructions and a step-by-step guide. They need order and chronology. Often highly practical, things need to be in order for them and they don't necessarily need to understand why they are doing a particular thing, but they do need to see the big picture. Think of this type of person as someone who needs the recipe, the clear instructions in a flatpack furniture box and frequently looks back to the picture on the front to see what it will look like in the end. Order, instructions, timeframes, chronology and step-by-step points are essential elements for this type of learner.

Gregorc's third type of learner is Concrete Random learning. These are the irritating learners who like to know why before they embark on doing it, and if they see you do something they don't understand, they are going to ask you why you're doing it. Many ape species are known copyists, mindlessly aping others and copying even the pointless steps they take. This is not true of the Concrete Random learner who will be the one who wants to know why you're doing it this way and not that. If you don't give this kind of learner the flexibility to work out problems for themselves, you will find very little commitment from them. They like to do things their own way, to solve problems and to find practical outcomes but they won't mindlessly follow if they don't understand the reasons for each action.

Abstract Random learners make up Gregorc's last type of learner. These learners are those who like to discuss as they go and who benefit from working as a group. Abstract Random learners do not do well with step-by-step guides or lots of reading. What they want to do is discuss it, and their relationship with you is the most important aspect of their learning. These learners like to share, to discuss and to get feedback.

While these models, not unlike other models of personality types or learning types, do not stand up to rigorous or robust testing, most likely because we learn in all these ways at various times and humans refuse to sit neatly in tidy boxes, it's important to bear in mind that how others learn - or like to learn - is perhaps not how you lead training. For instance, a client who likes to ask a lot of questions is going to do badly in a class with an authoritarian trainer who wants you to follow their instructions to the letter and never deviate. Yet, you will also find clients who need you to set out each step very clearly as you go.

You will find clients who want to do all the background reading and will happily absorb everything you give them before coming back to you for more sessions. You will find clients who like to send you detailed overviews and training plans every single week, with each step planned in and all contingencies covered. And thinking back to Lesson 14, where you explored the reasons why it's important to step outside your own echo chamber and also to understand different types of trainer who might complement your own way of working, you'll also find clients who are the same: the enthusiastic activist who wants to dive straight in without thinking things through thoroughly; the logical theorist who wants to do the reading yet needs to be prompted into actually making a change and doing something active; the practical action-taker who gets frustrated by complex theories but who wants to follow something tried and tested, not just respond with their gut. If we fail to understand that humans learn differently from each other, and that we all have our own unique fingerprint of what works for us, then we run the risk of isolating clients who can't learn in the ways we offer them. Being flexible and adaptable to different learners is important.

Humans also learn much more by trial and error, so it's important to be very mindful of the feedback loop. Some call this the plan-do-review or the performance-feedback-revision loop. Your feedback is vital here, and using specific positive feedback and specific negative feedback alongside occasional suggestions in a timely manner can make all the difference. For instance, in watching one client struggling to teach 'wait' in a way that wasn't encouraging her dog to superstitiously touch his nose to her hand, the trainer asked the client to slightly pull her hand back and sharpen her timing so that she marked when the dog's nose was just near enough. Instead of the fifteen frustrating tries where the dog was working by poking her hand and then pulling his head back, within two trials the dog had realised the treat was released when he kept his head still instead of trying to nose out the treat in his guardian's hand. Precise, timely, specific feedback like this can make learning much less frustrating all round.

Learning should also be punctuated and revisited. In other words, your clients need time to go away, to do something else and to internalise what they've learned, just as their animal companions will do. Revisiting and revising is an important part of learning, whatever your species. We need time to process what has happened, to make sense of it, and to let it take hold. All the same, it is a fine line between unnecessary repetition and useful revision. Having too much in the curriculum and being driven by tasks and goals can mean that we miss opportunities to allow our clients to really master something.

Just as access to novelty can be reinforcing to animals, and just as novel, surprising and emotionally strong stimuli are more salient, remembered for longer and in more detail than ordinary or routine stimuli, the same is true for humans. We all remember our unusual lessons from school: the day a dog got in the playground, the day a bee stung someone, dissections in biology, field trips and experiments, but the thousands of routine and mundane daily experiences are forgotten along with much of their content. The brain has an attentional bias for novelty, and this is something you can use to make your own classes memorable.

Novelty is not the only salient stimulus: variety is also a good way to make learning irresistible. Both within and between lessons, if you have a variety of learning experiences this will help it become more memorable. This means when we vary trainer-focused activities with independent activities, hands-on practicals with a little bit of theory, it all becomes much more 'sticky'. Like all learning, the Goldilocks approach of "Just Right" is necessary: too much variety and novelty is confusing and distracting. Multisensory, dramatic and interesting experiences will soon lose their value if they're used all the time. Most importantly, what we take from the Goldilocks story is that what was right for Goldilocks was not right at all for Mama Bear and Papa Bear. Our "Just Right" balance is unique.

Control is as powerful a reinforcer for humans, and where we have control over our learning and environment, we pay more attention, we learn faster, we have better recall and we have better self-control too. Control is moderated by the ascending reticular activating system (ARAS), which controls sleep-wake cycles, but does much more besides this. Overstimulation of the ARAS can lead to hyperactivity, hypervigilance and anxiety. The ARAS is involved in habituation but also in salience, as processes at this level help us decide what needs to be decided consciously and what does not. The ARAS is the part of the brain that shuts out all the external stimuli when you are truly immersed in a subject. But if you were immersed in your textbooks and then heard a gunshot, your ARAS would be the part of the brain that decides to switch attention. It's the function that helps us see the unusual in the usual, the familiar in the unfamiliar and to notice changes or alterations.

Understanding how humans learn also depends on understanding retention and recall. Generally speaking, it's simplest to think of short-term memory, long-term memory, procedural memory, episodic memory and semantic memory.

Much was learnt about short-term memory in the 1950s and 1960s. Psychologists found we have a number of different types of short-term memory, lasting about 20 seconds. Our short-term memory is useful for holding things in our head for a very brief period and generally works with 5-9 chunks of data. Rehearsal helps us move these memories from the short-term to the long-term, through oral repetition or visual processes. Some of us may remember images more easily than we remember sounds. Diagrams and pictures may be more salient to some than oral rehearsal. It helps explain why verb drills and the imperfect tense are remembered so easily after forty years without practice, or why we recall song lyrics and credit card numbers, phone numbers, price lists and how to label cell structure. It's yet another reason not to overwhelm our clients with too much information or too many things to do. Small chunks of information paired up with multisensory, dramatic, unusual or emotional events may make things much easier to recall. After all, there are thousands of song lyrics and the ones we commit to heart are the ones with emotional value. Earworms - those atrociously catchy songs - work on exactly these principles. It's also why, in the dog training world, short phrases like Jean Donaldson's 'Dogs Do What Works' are so memorable. Short-term memories become encoded as several different types of long-term memories under a variety of different conditions including salience, rehearsal, revision and their emotional quality. We may remember our parents' and grandparents' phone numbers after thirty years, but it's unlikely we remember many others unless they relied on patterns, unless they were meaningful or unless we'd rehearsed them a number of times.

Implicit or procedural memories can also help us. These are our automatic memories, the actions we do fluently without thinking. This is the kind of memory we want our clients to focus on, because this is our instinctive behaviour and action. Learning to walk, to run, to jump, to drive, to ride a bicycle, to do a cartwheel - all of these function on procedural memory. Think about cooking: at first, when you follow a new recipe, you need to follow the details, line up your ingredients, and go through the step-by-step guide. When you have mastered the recipe, it becomes almost implicit, instinctive and natural. Then you experiment, refine and adapt. Learning to train our dogs is just the same; how they learn also functions on the same principle. We benefit from our dogs' automatic procedural memory for recall. This has huge implications in dog sports of course: a dog who habitually doesn't touch the bottom of the A-frame will wire that behaviour into their procedural memory and lose points. It's why it's so important to take it slowly at the beginning and work on each component to fluidity rather than doing things too quickly. It's why we want our clients to practise to automaticity and why it's important to be there at the beginning as they are learning, not least to scaffold and support their first attempts so they don't later commit bad habits to their procedural memory which then become very hard to break. Humans also rely on procedural memory to run certain actions automatically. We can use this in class to make processes instinctive for our students too: when you instinctively stop if the dog pulls on the leash, if you habitually pick up treats alongside keys and poo bags, if you instinctively reinforce behaviours automatically. There are many benefits to having polished a behaviour to automaticity, not least that it leaves the brain free to do other things. The procedural memory is what saves us from colossal error when our brains are busy doing other things.

Emotional memory is highly implicated in fear-based learning, in respondent learning and single-event learning, rooted in the amygdala. Emotional memory is altered in panic disorders, phobias and other neuropsychiatric diseases. Where a stimulus evokes a very powerful fear response, it serves us well from an evolutionary perspective if it is encoded quickly and is easy to recall. The same is true of humans, and it may play a part in why some of your clients who have dogs with complicated behaviours may themselves need therapeutic intervention following traumatic events. We can use emotional memory positively though: making interactions fun and sometimes using silliness as part of your teaching makes it much more salient.

Episodic memories are stored in the hippocampus although episodic memory processes are supported by a much larger neural network. This type of memory relates to events: what happened, when, where and so on. It helps us remember times and places of events that have happened in the past. Episodic memory is what we use when we recall what the trainer taught us, the detailed information about the event itself. Recalling holidays, gatherings and dog training classes all involve episodic memory. In fact, animals also have the neural circuitry necessary for episodic memory; although this circuitry varies enormously across species, there is remarkable similarity in how the neural networks function. Since episodic memory can be strongly tied up with time and location it is as important for humans to learn to generalise as it is for their companions. This is why you want your clients to do lots of homework and send you evidence. Otherwise, they're as likely to become amazing at parallel walking skills when they're with you, but then forget everything they've ever learned the moment they step out of class.

Unlike episodic memory, semantic memory does not involve personal experience. Semantic memory involves sense-making of information, giving us our general knowledge about the world. If we didn't experience it ourselves, it's probably semantic memory. When we're learning new vocabulary and terminology, new theories and new ideas, it is our semantic memory that deals with it.

Recalling those semantic memories can be challenging. There are many ways that we can help embed new learning and ensure neural pathways become established superhighways rather than overgrown footpaths.

Ekwall and Shanker (1988) found that people can generally recall about:
- 10% of what they read
- 20% of what they hear
- 30% of what they see
- 50% of what they both see and hear
- 70% of what they say
- 90% of what they simultaneously say and do

Learning, then, if measured by what we can recall, is best done through practice and speaking. It's why often, our skills become best embedded when we start training. This also has implications for how we run our training classes, and for our clients. Active, multisensory, episodic, surprising teaching that allows learners the opportunity to experience and act rather than just to passively take in is much more salient than simply watching a YouTube video. It's the taking part that counts. This, after everything, is why your clients are paying you, rather than opting into a one-way information feed.

Whilst emotional learning can be very powerful, we should also be aware of stress on recall. Both chronic and acute stress make it harder to learn semantically. Threats - be they physical, psychological or emotional - are powerful inhibitors of memory. Having a class or one-to-one session where people feel safe, comfortable and relaxed is vital. The prospect of failure can also be a powerful inhibitor of memory and learning. Errorless learning is not just for animals. While we might accept mistakes and learn from them without too much psychological fallout, too much criticism and punishment jeopardises our learning.

Most learners benefit from support throughout the learning process.

You need to shape successive approximations of independence, not just expect it automatically. This means training should be carefully constructed so that learners become more and more independent. This will happen at a task-by-task level, but also over a period of time so that you gradually move your students to independence for each outcome, as well as over the entire programme.

Demonstration and modelling are two good ways to start the process. Whilst you may want to use a dog who has already mastered the skill being taught, be mindful that too advanced a demonstration can be off-putting to novices. If you start by using a professional golf player to model putting when you are working with people who can't yet play crazy golf, it can provide too much of a challenge. You can use live demonstrations and modelling, or videos from earlier, even videos of what it will look like. When learners have no concept of what they are learning, they have no idea if it's right or not. Always provide examples. Preferably provide examples that your learners can refer to out of your sessions. It's easy to share videos these days via private groups on social media, for example.

Analysis, explanation or discussion of the modelled example can also be really helpful. This helps your learners know what you're looking for. You can invite commentary from your clients but at the beginning, you might want to direct the commentary. You can also show and talk through your process. Sometimes, it is helpful to use video with commentary overlaid explaining why you chose to do it in that way.

Clear, simple written and oral instructions and steps can be really helpful, and it is useful if students can refer back to this. It is frustrating to have to explain, 'No, click THEN reach for your pocket,' if you are explaining this frequently to novices.

Guided work where the student takes over, but with support from the trainer, is the next step. You can use guided work in many ways. Of course, in one-to-ones, you will do lots of guided work as you will model and then hand it over to the client to try where you provide feedback in the moment, but in class, especially in a big class, guided work can be really useful too. You could, for example, select a small group of three whilst others go off to work independently. This group may be in need of extra support. They may have already mastered the class and benefit from moving ahead. They may have more challenges in working with their dogs, so you can use guided work within a whole-class scenario. You can also pass over the small group-within-the-group to someone who has already mastered the task or to an assistant, leaving you to circulate. Guided work in class situations stops people falling behind and being unable to cope, disengaging because they haven't mastered the early steps. It also stops clients disengaging because they're bored and they've moved on much further.

Paired work also helps scaffold the learning. This moves students more gradually towards independence whilst still having a partner there to check they have it right. This can also be useful in classes like Reactive Rover classes where techniques need to be learned and applied outside of the classroom context before dogs will be able to join a class together. This may also allow the trainer to do one-to-ones within the class setting.

Independent work also benefits from the 3Ds, just as it does with dogs. Easy to start, for a short duration and with minimal distraction. Some of your clients may be happy to go straight to independent work, which will enable you to work with those who need a hand.

Scaffolding also involves reviewing. Performing in front of a large group in class situations can be very stressful, so using peer reviews and partners is helpful. In general, the more novice someone is, the harder it is to review your own performance, and so a helping hand may be necessary.

Having all of these things in mind is vital when we engage with human learners. Sharpening your understanding of human learning and also of methods of teaching can really help you scaffold your clients' learning in the most productive way possible.

27. Get feedback

At the end of contracts, many trainers leave things relatively open with an invitation to come back if necessary. Sometimes classes finish with a small celebration and clients move on. How many times do we stop to get official feedback on the courses that we have provided and the contracts we have undertaken? Rather than the voluntary feedback of testimonials and social media reviews, how many times do you stop and audit, asking if your clients have truly achieved what they wanted to achieve, and whether you could have done anything differently to improve their experiences?

Feedback of this type should be in writing and should be specific to the service you provided. You can do this either on paper or using a virtual questionnaire service. Always list the objectives and expected outcomes of the course you offered and ask your clients to complete a Likert scale (1-5 or 1-7 from worst to best) to document their experiences.

For instance, if one of the skills on your puppy class agenda is that the puppy will have learned basic loose-lead skills, ask your clients whether or not their puppies can do this. If you wanted your clients to understand basic cooperative care principles, ask them to what extent they now feel comfortable doing this. If you were running a class on canine body language, you can ask clients how confident they feel in recognising certain behaviours; if you were running an individual one-to-one, say for instance to help their dog overcome their fear of strangers, you can list their goals as expected outcomes and ask them to what extent they and their companion have met the goal. Using intake forms and initial assessment data can help. If you undertook a functional analysis, including a final follow-up analysis as part of your process of disengaging can be helpful. If you have phased out support gradually, booking in a time 3 or 6 months after the final sessions of the contract can be a good point to review progress made and give clients a reason to keep working beyond the termination of the contract.

You should also give your clients space to comment on the processes and their own successes. You can also help them provide specific negative and positive feedback by asking for examples. While it's lovely to pick up a stack of feedback forms that say, 'Great!' or 'Wonderful!', 'Loved it!' or even 'Didn't meet my expectations', it's really important to elicit specifics if we want to use feedback for anything other than simply feeding (or destroying!) our egos. Many people hesitate to ask for feedback precisely for this reason. Our ego can really take a bruising if we're not robust, and it can fuel perfectionism and a feeling of inadequacy if you're poring over twenty intake forms and wondering why you got one single 4 out of 5 when all the others were 5 out of 5. Like everything in life, the more you do it, the better you get at learning what's important on feedback forms and what is not.

Think also about the type of questions you are asking. It's helpful to ask specifically for the one thing that could have been done differently rather than simply asking for a general thing like whether they have any feedback or thoughts.

Feedback is not the end of the matter. In the Performance-Feedback-Revision loop, we can use client feedback to improve our own delivery. Again, this will require us to decide whether feedback is qualified or not. Feedback gives us an opportunity to modify what we do. The more we get of it, the more we can sharpen our performance. If you think of top athletes, even top performers in dog sports, the actual performance may only have been minutes long, yet they may spend hours analysing video footage in minute detail. Such perfectionism isn't necessary if you aren't driven by competitive goals, but some reflection after performance is vital in a service-driven industry. After all, we're trying to improve our services for the client.

In industry, 360° feedback is a process by which feedback is collected from your bosses, your colleagues and your clients. We often focus on the client in our work, unless we are working for somebody else in a group setting. Usually, feedback from our bosses tends to be fairly formal and ritualised as an annual review or something along those lines. We also get feedback from our clients if we think to ask and we've done so in a way that allows them to really share their thoughts. What we don't necessarily do is get feedback from our contemporaries and our colleagues. This is absolutely true when we are working in isolation. It's another reason to go back to Lesson 14. Our colleagues' experiences of us, whether that's in shadowing us or in pairing up with us from time to time, is another valuable method of getting data that we can use to revise our performance. If you're really, really looking to make progress, having a mentor or a coach can be really instructive. This person doesn't have to be someone within the industry or even an expert, but it is definitely helpful if they are trained in coaching. After all, you don't have to be better than the top athletes to coach them to top performance. Many sports team managers were often average players themselves, and many of the best players are poor coaches once their professional playing days are behind them. Coaching is an art and it's useful to find someone who is good at it if you want to improve further.

360° analysis also includes self-appraisal, auditing and self-assessment. There are many great tools to help you do this. How often do you set time aside, no distractions, to consider your own business? Do you write down your past performance in terms of client numbers, hours delivered, action plans written, classes delivered, feedback percentages, followers on social media, people on your email list, number of participants on courses, even your financial income? Do you then use this to set yourself SMARTER targets for the year ahead? Do you spend as much time on growing your business and understanding how to grow your business as you do on your dog training skills?

Many career enthusiasts spend an inordinate amount of time and money on developing their skills within their actual career. We may, for example, spend thousands of pounds or dollars a year on professional development and learning how to be better at training dogs. Are we balanced in the development we seek out?

Do we spend as much time on business practicalities, on improving our marketing and social media skills, on working with people? If not, that's the same as working only on one muscle set in the gym. Sure, you may end up with enormous biceps and triceps, but make sure you schedule a leg day from time to time. Our businesses are the same as our bodies: if you don't exercise and work on one part of it, it will atrophy.

What is useful is to sit down and review your own business using a self-assessment business tool. Take a couple of hours out. Hire a hot-seat office for that time. Go to your local library or a coffee shop where you won't be disturbed. Sit down with your pad and paper and plan out your own business goals for the next year, bearing in mind the 5% - 10% challenge. If you sold twenty online support packages this year, plan to sell twenty two by the end of next year.

With those goals, do the same as you do with your clients. Half them. Then quarter. In three months' time, you'll need to have sold six online support packages. That's two a month. What are you doing then to meet these goals? As always, set your goals first and then decide how you're going to achieve them after. Don't take an arse-backward approach and decide to work on your social media without a specific goal in mind. Schedule reviews periodically and book them into your diary, fixing them in stone. Whether you're going to stop in 3 months and take a morning out to go and have a picnic by yourself while you review your progress so far, or whether you partner up with your business coach to talk it through, make sure you do exactly what you coach your clients to do: review.

Don't just let contracts and classes end without any kind of feedback. Don't drift from one year into the next without any aims for your business, and don't ignore the very useful feedback you can get from a whole host of people tangential to your business. Not only is it useful to help modify your trajectory, it's also reinforcing in itself.

28. Understand biases and the irrational ways people think

No matter how much you work on your helping skills and coaching skills, you'll still get the clients who defy logic. You'll get the ones who are so stuck, who are so helpless and so self-defeating that to help them move forwards seems impossible. You'll also get clients who seem to be so lost in irrational thought that you can't reason with them. Indeed, reasoning with them makes them worse, it seems.

Humans come with all kinds of biases that affect our experience. We love to think of ourselves as neat, rational decision-makers who would always make the smart choice. Yet what psychology teaches us over and over is that we're filled with hundreds of cognitive biases that play into those shadow-side issues and create enormous blind spots. No wonder Skinner's Behaviourism is now relegated to a mainly American specialism for dealing with people with problem behaviours. As part of my psychology degree in the 1990s, Skinner was barely a footnote, despite how familiar most animal trainers are with his name. Pavlov didn't even get a mention. People don't like to think of ourselves as input-output machines in the same way as Skinner showed pigeons to be. In fact, pigeons are way more complex than input-output machines, as we well know. Not only do they have navigational skills that defy our comprehension, but they also recognise a Monet is a Monet and a Picasso is a Picasso… life is more than a Skinner box.

Many of these biases can be frightening simply because they're irrational or they seem counterintuitive. They form part of that a-rational shadow side in making people perform in ways that defy what we might logically expect. But when we understand them, we recognise them and we can predict them, it helps us out in our work.

Take priming for example. Priming means all the daily drip-feed of information that your clients are exposed to before they even get to you. It matters if they've been more exposed to Cesar Millan than to Victoria Stilwell on TV. It matters if they've been exposed to positive reinforcement methods before they get to you, or if they've been exposed to punishment-based methods. It matters the more your clients have read about dominance and alphas, even the time they listened to some character on a TV show talk about how he had to act like the Alpha wolf.

We also have an anthropocentric bias which makes it incredibly tough for us to imagine the experiences of non-human animals. When we do try, we give them all of our traits as humans. We transfer our own feelings and thoughts about how human society functions onto dogs and describe them in terms of human societies. Yet when we talk about other humans, we tend to dehumanise them, too. Thus, we might be really bad at empathising with other people who 'just want to say hi to our dog' whilst at the same time convincing ourselves that our dog is a tinpot dictator intent on ruling over the household.

Confirmation biases are also rife in humans. We seek evidence to confirm our theories and dismiss evidence to the contrary. We pay more attention to things that confirm our biases rather than challenging them and we also tend to only test things that confirm our bias rather than testing the alternatives. For instance, I know I can tend to be very dismissive of "protective aggression" in dogs. I find it very hard to be convinced that a dog growled at or bit someone on the street because they were protecting their guardian, and I tend to believe it's more likely to be generalised stranger danger or dislike or fear of strangers in general. That's my biased belief. What is important is performing tests to rule out protective behaviour, such as giving the dog to another person to be walked (if that is possible with aggressive dogs, which it is not always) and seeing if the dog's behaviour is the same. Yet I know I'm very reluctant to test out this alternative hypothesis and hesitant to believe clients. I tell myself that it is their selfish and anthropocentric bias that can't conceive the dog could have reacted out of anything other than a desire to protect their human. We see these confirmation biases at work in our own caseload as well as with our clients. We need to be able to be able to recognise them and manage them. We can also see correlations and patterns where there are none. It's not unknown for trainers to diagnose a particular problem over and over again. If you find yourself diagnosing dominance aggression or status-related issues in most cases you work, then this may well be a confirmation bias too.

Worse still, we cherry pick evidence and theories that support our views and when people challenge those beliefs, we just become more entrenched in the view that we already hold. This is especially true for emotionally loaded content. It's also why you won't win an argument about punishment because simply by challenging it, you can cause the belief holder to become more entrenched in their views.

You can throw all the evidence you like at it and it will have the opposite effect to the one you intended.

Many inexperienced trainers often ask on social media for studies from other trainers on this or that, hoping to win over recalcitrant clients without truly understanding that to do so is to run the risk of firming up views rather than undermining them. This is especially true for emotive topics such as the use of punishment or dominance. The irony of cognitive dissonance is that the more we're confronted by "the reality", whatever that may be, the more painful it feels and the more angry, indignant, defensive and self-righteous we become. We're also conservative in the ways we revise our opinion. When we've held an opinion for so long and someone challenges it, even if they completely destroy our argument, we won't revise our opinion as much as we truly should. It takes time for us to soften or come round. This conservatism bias affects how little we might modify our opinion despite overwhelming contradictory evidence. There is also a curse of knowledge that affects us as trainers, where we find it impossible to believe just how little someone might know and we find it impossible to empathise with their experience. If you're used to seeing lip licks, displacement behaviours and shake offs, it can be hard to empathise with clients who aren't as attuned as you are. Similarly, if you're a great marker trainer, it can be really hard to get your head around just how bad some people's timing can be.

As trainers, we can also run the risk of relying heavily on packages we've invested in. Neuroeconomist Dan Ariely gives the example of a dentist who buys a CAD/CAM machine to make crowns for patients with hairline fractures in their teeth. Suddenly, they're doing hundreds of procedures compared to dentists who didn't invest and outsource crowns to other manufacturers. We prioritise what we've invested in, and sometimes this can mean that we rely on training materials, medications or packages, unconsciously promoting them because we see them as a solution to everything. The Frequency Illusion also contributes to this: once we see something once, we tend to start seeing it everywhere. You'll see this on social media too, with the same trainers recommending the same techniques and solutions time after time as a solution to more things than you thought humanly possible. I know I do it. I have several favourite books and protocols that I recommend far more than any others.

This process is not necessarily explicit but our own preferences definitely colour the recommendations we make to our clients, meaning that we're perhaps not as neutral in helping as we intend to be. We also have a bias to jump to the conclusions we expect when we look at data. If we're expecting to find it, then that's what we'll find. Another bias for us to keep in check.

Success in the past also reinforces the likelihood we'll proffer one training package or approach over another. It's why certain vets and behaviourists will rely on recommending medication where others use it as a last resort. Both are natural behaviours: we keep repeating our own successes even if it's not quite right for the client.

Our conflicts of interest are much more pervasive than we think they are. These conflicts of interest and confirmation biases deeply affect the problems we see as trainers. Consider, for example, the zeal with which diet is discussed in the canine community. Worse still, the more we talk about certain approaches or methods, the more we'll repeat it, as if the very fact that I'm telling you about something means that it must be good, which in turn affects my own beliefs. True objectivity is incredibly difficult to achieve and this can derail our relationship through our own biases, not our clients' biases. Another bias that affects us is our overconfidence and to overestimate our own judgement. Again, it's really important to seek out voices from beyond your echo chamber from time to time, just to keep these biases in check. The more esteem we're given, the more we're likely to be overconfident as well.

There are so many biases that affect our client's way of thinking - and our own. One we might frequently come against is the Zero Sum bias, where we think that if someone else is gaining, we are losing. This is the opposite of the idea of win-win solutions. How often do we come up against guardians who think that if their dog's life improves, because we are asking them to give their dog prime steak or lamb, then that must mean in some way that the guardian's life is diminished? This can be a tough bias when our clients believe their dog is dominant, because they already believe they are "losing" compared to their dog's "gain". Seeing things as win-lose rather than win-win is challenging for humans. Guardians can tend to see "negotiations" with their dog, or those negotiated settlements or compromises as being the dog's "victory". It's important in these cases to discuss what the client is getting out of it too. We're mean-spirited and hate to think of others getting one over on us, especially if we think that is "only" a dog. Any compromise seems to impinge on our children's liberties or our own selves if it seems to benefit the dog. This is why it can be tough to overcome people's biases about asking their children to refrain from certain behaviours such as grabbing the dog or getting in the dog's bed. The dog seems to "win" at the expense of the children's freedom of movement.

It works both ways.

If a dog has behaved aggressively towards members of the public, clients can become resentful of the liberty the dog has "lost" at the expense of other people's protection. Zero Sum thinking especially tends to affect our biases in relation to freedom and liberty, or finance. It's not uncommon to find people resentful of what their dog is costing them in terms of finance or freedom, simply because the dog seems to be winning. Working with a resentful client who was fixated on the cost of their "problem" rescue dog, they were fixated on how much the dog had cost them for the behavioural modification package and obsessed with the fact that a puppy would have been a better choice. When they put up the adoption fee and behaviour modification fee against the cost of a puppy from a good breeder, you can imagine their surprise that even if they'd had two years of behaviour support, it would still have been cheaper than a purpose-bred puppy in good health and from a good breeder.

We also see biases in planning, not least the negativity bias and the optimism bias. We can be very challenged to drop something that's not working if we'd planned for it. It can be very difficult to drop the plan if it's not working for us and we'll tend to stick with it much longer than we should. That's as true for us as it is with our clients. We have biases about time, thinking things will take us longer to implement if we're framing the event negatively than we do optimistically. We also have a bias towards wanting immediate gratification rather than delayed gratification. It may well be that we've lived for ten years with our barking dog, but we want them to stop immediately. It's inconceivable that it might take three months of work.

We can also run into our clients' biases (and face our own) relating to stereotypes and gender biases. Being a young woman (as many dog trainers tend to be) can be the seat of much resentment if you're successful compared to older men. It's not uncommon to face unspoken resentment because of your age, gender or race. Being a small, young woman, you may need to be mindful that if you are seeming to "control" the dog better than the guardian, they can see this as a real challenge. It also affects how they view our authority and our knowledge. The dog training industry is deep with these stereotypes. Look simply at one example: the proportion of top-performing YouTube dog training channels who are men compared to the proportion of women in the industry in general. We see this in all kinds of social media, where men are favoured over women, particularly if they look a certain way (the Halo Effect) whereas women's talents, prowess and skills are significantly underestimated. Remember the apocryphal Ginger Rogers' line when asked about how she felt dancing with Fred Astaire? 'Darling, I did everything he did, just backwards and in high heels'. To be a highly-achieving woman in the dog training world means facing up to people's implicit gender biases and belief systems, and being successful often means doing everything backwards and in high heels. In other words, you'll have to be more skilled and more proficient in more challenging circumstances and you'll also have to live with the fact that you may never get the true respect you deserve.

These biases play into our shadow-side behaviours, the a-rational ways in which we think and act, just as they do for our clients. They're not something we can't overcome, but the more they stay in the shadows and the more blind we are to their existence, the more they run the risk of derailing our work. Humans have many biases that stand in the way of progress, and taking the first step to managing them and even working with them is to understand them.

29. Set boundaries

We've all been there. The call at 8pm on a Friday night from a prospective client who says, 'This better work or I'll be putting my dog to sleep', or the clients who ask us 'Do you run doggie boot camps?' and want us to take the problem off their hands and return their dog without any unwanted behaviours.

If you've not been there yet, count yourself lucky!

We can all label this kind of behaviour as emotional blackmail. The hardest thing to do is recognise that, on the whole, they come from a place of desperation, not a place of manipulation. Of course there are people who ring you and try to pass off all responsibility for their poor choices and put them on to you. As a trustee in a shelter, I've received calls at 8am on a Sunday morning on my private number asking me personally to pick up a so-called "stray" cat colony that someone had been feeding for a year and who had, surprisingly to the caller, turned from a 3-cat colony into a starving 20-cat colony, all full of diseases, ticks and fleas. The 'or else I'll have to…' calls still come from a place of desperation, even if you are really angry at these people's repeated attempts to get you to do something NOW even if they've not done anything about it for months, even years.

Recognising this is desperation not emotional blackmail is important. Yes, it may be their fault. Yes, they may be the most thoughtless individuals you've come across in days, weeks, months or years. Would it be any better if they broke down in tears and wept for three hours about how stupid they'd been? Is that what it would take for you to help them?

If so, accepting that 'or else…' calls are exactly the same as 'I've been so stupid…' calls are coming from the same place - an appeal for your help - can be a really tough thing to stomach especially because one is bound to get your back up and the other is much more likely to get your response and help. If you'd help people who admit their frailties but you wouldn't help people who haven't managed to phrase it right, then that's our problem, as well as theirs.

Deal with the calls that seem like emotional blackmail in exactly the same way you would deal with calls from clients fully immersed in their own self-pity, shame and guilt. Both are asking for the same thing. Your help. Both are an admission of failure, even if one seems to be intent on passing the buck. Sure, the angry, belligerent blame-shifters are much uglier and less pleasant to deal with. That's a given. But it doesn't do us any favours to prolong their misery if we would help, just if they turned that anger, belligerence and blame inwards.

That doesn't mean you have to be a complete mug or doormat. Nor does it mean you have to be trampled all over because you're a helpful person. It does mean to say that you have to take responsibility for the things that relate to you, and to have clear boundaries. Part of this comes back to good triage and charging properly. When people ring you up in a real emergency, you should have the ability to help them if you can - regardless of whether they point the blame at you or themselves. That's only true if this is a genuine emergency that needs to be dealt with right now.

Most situations aren't that real emergency that needs to be dealt with right now. Most things don't need our intervention at that immediate moment in time, especially if they've been like that for a while. This is where it's vital to have clear boundaries. If the problem didn't happen overnight, it won't be solved overnight and nothing you can do will make a difference in the next twenty-four hours. What these potential clients need is a lifeline and a timeline. A small hope that action will take place, and soon. Good triage will help you with that. It's absolutely vital to direct that triage process quickly so you don't end up without any boundaries at all. So for the potential client who rings you on your private landline at 8am on a Sunday morning, having been given your number by a so-called friend, then it's fine to say 'I'm happy to help. I can see you feel really desperate right now. I'm free tomorrow at 1.30 for a chat if that's okay? In the meantime, let me take your email address and send you my intake form so you can fill that in before then'.

You've already started them on the course to hopefulness and action. You're already giving them something to do to change things immediately. Throwing out lifelines often costs less in terms of time and energy than getting into a discussion about why we can't or won't help.

Triage helps you direct all these potential clients in the right way. It's vital for boundary-setting.

For the potential client who rings you at 11pm because her dog is in the middle of attacking her other dog, you'd be able to refer to your triage, give defensive handling over the phone there and then and recommend management strategies to help them cope until you can get someone else there who can help them. Really, these clients should be so few and far between, where your immediate intervention is required, that you can give them the time it needs. For the potential client who rings you at 11pm because their dog bit a neighbour two weeks ago, then directing them to your website and intake form also gives them a lifeline. Letting them know you've set the wheels in motion gives them something to do. It doesn't cost you much time at all to send them a list of five go-to YouTube videos, a pamphlet and a few articles to read if you've set them up already for those "non-emergencies" who seem to have decided that a problem that's been brewing for ten years is suddenly something you need to deal with straight away. It will probably cost you much less time than being confrontational (even if they deserve it!). If you're the kind of person who dwells on conversations for hours after or you need a chat with a colleague to recalibrate and calm down, then you might as well have said, 'No problem… Let me give you a number for someone who can help…' right from the start. I guarantee you won't spend as much time brooding on it afterwards.

When you're faced with desperation in whatever form, what you need is to end the moment quickly and give yourself both space to assess, unless it truly is one of those really urgent situations you do have to deal with right now. Dealing with people in crisis is one thing, but dealing with people who have worked themselves up into thinking it's a crisis when it isn't is another thing entirely. You can shrug it off, call them toxic, get angry at them for attempting to make you responsible for situations they created, or you can acknowledge that you're just the last call and the last action in a series of actions that have probably been going on until they got to you.

You may find a number of different types of pressured behaviour. The first are those who might threaten you or your reputation if you don't comply with their demands. You know, 'If you don't help, it's curtains for the dog'. The second type are those who threaten themselves if you don't comply: 'If you don't help, I don't think I can keep going on anymore'. They're expecting us to help because we're afraid of potential damage to our reputation, or because we're afraid of what they will do to their animal. They're expecting us to help because we feel obliged to, perhaps because we're animal lovers. They're expecting us to help because we know we'd feel guilty if we didn't. People who try to manipulate us may press any one of these buttons. These buttons are especially easy to press if you're feeling inadequate in the first place.

The thing about pressure is that it escalates the more resistance you put up. The more you confront or face them down, the less you give way, the more pressure they'll put up. Diffusing this quickly with a: 'Sure, I'm happy to help. This is my website and these are my prices. Can you fill in an intake form and we'll get back to you with an appointment time' can be one way to do this. You may of course face challenges over your prices and your terms. It's up to you whether or not you want to offer a payment support system; indeed, you might not be in a position to be able to. You don't have to feel guilty for being expensive. Likewise, though, you don't need to be completely intractable. Finding a balance between being reasonable and being completely inflexible is not easy. Having packages that work for people of all different kinds of income is one way to help them. Whether you've got a cheap DVD or online training course, a book recommendation or YouTube channel for free, it is important to recognise that just because they don't have funds doesn't mean you should cut them off completely. If you find yourself cutting people off and getting their backs up, regularly involved in emotionally-charged situations over your charges, it's worthwhile looking at your triage system again and being able to direct them to appropriate methods of support. After all, there are people who turn up in A&E departments of hospitals who demand immediate treatment when they need an aspirin and a sticking plaster, and frustrating as it is that they can't assess their own needs appropriately, if they're not dealt with, they're the type of people who explode after 4 hours of waiting. Most of this is caused from frustration: giving them something active to do is the first step. Pressure and frustration are both liable to build and escalate, not diffuse.

It's very easy to dismiss all people who make unreasonable requests at unreasonable times as being narcissists, blackmailers or even psychopaths. The truth is that most of that comes from desperation. If you find yourself constantly dealing with people you consider to be narcissists, blackmailers and psychopaths, then it might be time to take a look at what it is that you're doing to attract these people and to set your own boundaries. Perhaps it's just in the way that you are framing their behaviour rather than the fact they are truly horrible people.

Sadly, if you find yourself saying that people who use lines like 'it's you, or else…' are abusive, that you shouldn't waste your time with them, that you should call their bluff, that it's coercive, lousy behaviour, that they're weaponising your guilt, that it's manipulative… It's time to go back to the hypothesis of generosity in Lesson 9 and ask, 'What is the most generous hypothesis I can make about this person's behaviour with me?'.

Often the answer is that they are absolutely desperate and are looking for help. That's all.

Simple as it is.

Some of the wisest words I ever heard were: 'Blackmail is a duet, not a solo performance'.

We need to be able to ask ourselves why this is pressing our buttons. Having been at the receiving end of several 'Take this dog now, or else!' calls as part of my shelter work, I can say a number of things. Firstly, the majority of times this happens or dogs get returned on Sunday mornings, it's actually reasonable and understandable, even if the people were completely and utterly stupid, even if they made ridiculous, illogical choices. Yes, sometimes people have ridiculous and unreasonable expectations of dogs. Yes, people leave dogs tied up outside the gates. Once, an anonymous person left a dog and her seven puppies boxed up outside the shelter on Christmas morning - the only day we are well and truly shut. Those puppies got out and were running all over the neighbourhood by the time we were notified, and it took a lot of effort from staff and volunteers on their one day off to go round them up. But underneath that stupid, stupid action is shame. To be too ashamed to come when the shelter is open, to be unable to face handing them over in person, that takes a lot of shame. That's not cruelty or a deliberately manipulative person who thought, 'how can I ruin the Christmases of twenty good people?' That's someone who was too ashamed of what they had done to bring the dogs in when they knew the shelter was open but they cared enough to leave them near the shelter and not on a motorway. Another time, a woman threw six puppies off a bridge in town - four of them saved by a boy who swam into the river to get them and then brought them to our shelter. Yes, the woman was caught and prosecuted. Of course, there were angry people who were furious that two puppies had died and the other four had suffered. But these were the actions of a desperate woman who thought she had no way out. When I hear people's stories, I don't hear the stories of monsters. I hear people who made bad choices, who did the wrong thing. I don't hear stories of people who've set aside a portion of their day to annoy me, but stories of people who can't think beyond themselves for hundreds if not thousands of reasons.

Then I remember, who am I to judge? I didn't properly socialise my puppy because I had no concept of what I was doing and ended up with a nine-year-old dog who's taken a lot of work but turned out alright in the end. Who am I to judge when for years, I kissed my cocker on the nose only to realise those lip licks showed her discomfort and I'm lucky I didn't get bitten on the face? I once took an 11-year-old yorkie home for the weekend in foster care because he looked so cold and sad in the shelter. He had prostate problems and he woke up at 3am and peed on my bed. He screamed every time I touched him and got in fights with all my other dogs, who were walking on eggshells around this pint-sized dog. After 48 hours, I was exhausted and despairing, knowing I couldn't see him through to his vet appointment the next day. I advertised the hell out of that dog, all behaviours and medical needs disclosed, because if I'd have had to have another 24 hours, I'd have been forced to return him to the shelter. Another foster had such incredible separation anxiety that I couldn't leave him, but I was working full time and couldn't take him with me so I had to return him to the shelter. Other times, I've been able to cope with fosters who had separation-related behaviours, but I already had three fosters at that time who already had complex needs. I had to take him back to the shelter not because I'm an unfeeling, stone cold bitch, but because I literally couldn't cope any longer. And finally, I live with a dog who I deliberately adopted because she had complex predatory and aggressive behaviours yet she had bonded to me and I couldn't imagine a single other person she could live with right at that moment. I live daily with the knowledge that one day I may have to choose behavioural euthanasia if my circumstances change or if the vet who is responsible for her behavioural assessments decides that it would be best in terms of the safety of the community. I often say, 'There but for the grace of God…' knowing full well that only a pay cheque, a turn of health, a life circumstance, bad luck or a behaviour that I just can't address at the time stands in the way of making tough decisions. It's only luck that separates me from a potential client who calls saying, 'If you can't sort this, then it's curtains for Rex.'

Sometimes, "sorting it" means passing the guardian to another trainer because I can't help. Sometimes, I really don't have the time and have to pass it on. It doesn't mean dealing with it myself, nor does it mean compromising my own standards or prices, or accepting rude behaviour. Sometimes, when tackling blind spots, it's clear that the guardian (or future guardian, in the case of potential adoptions) is never going to see what is right for the dog, and that has consequences too. Having a thick skin isn't something you're born with: it's a skill you develop through time and practice. Being able to see off unreasonable demands, see those who are desperate from the very few who are completely blinded or irrational, that's a skill. Again, a support network can be great for those moments. Between our independent shelter network, we have a private group to draw attention to individuals who have contacted one of the shelters. You won't be surprised that a very, very small number of people are turned away from one and go on to cause exactly the same problems at a neighbouring organisation. LIkewise with local trainers: we too have an informal support group that is a trusted environment to share situations that emerge. It won't surprise you to know that the same names go between trainers creating the exact same problems. But these people are very few and far between.

Having good triage, having a very good sense of your own capabilities and capacities, having a network of support from your other colleagues and knowing that the vast majority of unreasonable behaviour actually comes from an appeal for help is essential. Accepting that there are very few people who really shouldn't have animals and who are problematic for everyone else is also important. When we deal with investigations at our shelter, it won't surprise you to know that the one or two who cause real problems (like the time we turned up to a guy brandishing a shotgun!) are already known to social services, to municipal authorities, to the police and even to psychiatric services.

Even then, there are so many factors that contribute that when you really know what has been going on, it's not hard to find at least some empathy.

Understanding compassion fatigue, recognising its symptoms and how to offset it are all things that can help.

Having boundaries and knowing how to manage compassion fatigue is important, but it doesn't mean trying to work in all situations that you are asked to. Luckily, most people who reach out to you will want help of some kind. That first contact assures you of that. They are looking for solutions. However, that does mean managing their desperation at times, but also managing their optimism that situations won't worsen or bad things won't happen to them.

Clients who invariably message on social media, especially out of office hours, might send you inappropriate friend requests and you need to have thought about how you will deal with this eventuality. If this happens regularly, you might want to send out a statement about how and when to get in touch. It's not so much that you will have problems with your own boundaries, but that you may need to shape your client's boundary-setting a little also. Vets will often have an out-of-hours messaging service with a statement on it that can be quite useful to mimic. Asking clients to quickly describe the problem on voicemail if the problem is urgent, and that you will get back to them as soon as possible is one way to avoid the out-of-hours situation. The same thing can be used for email and social media, where automated messages are a gift to help you triage effectively. Of course we will listen to these, even if they come in at 11pm, but that does not mean we need to respond to them then.

I only respond in office hours other than automated messages unless the situation is critical, in the same way that veterinarians or doctors' surgeries also do. I set aside the first half-hour of the morning to work through things that came in overnight and to respond to clients who updated me out of office hours. I have different automated messages for when I am out working and I use these in the same way to filter through emergencies.

Make sure, too, that you clearly delineate work time and holiday time.

In holiday time, I have one of my trusted colleagues as a reference point, and they pick up my urgent work. I do the same for them when they are away. It's things like these that stop you sinking under and being swamped. You might even want to engage professional administrative services to help. The better you get, and the more your reputation for excellence grows, the more contact you are likely to get from desperate people whose messy lives run the risk of making yours messy too.

The most messy for me was a client whose dog would bark throughout the night. When the dog had a very bad night, I did too, because the client would send me very long and distressed messages at 2am telling me all about it. In many ways, her behaviour exactly mirrored the dog's appeal for help and the dog's own anxieties. Reinforcing what you want (appropriate messaging at appropriate times) and putting other behaviour (like texting at 2am) on an extinction protocol works just the same as they do with animals: if you start responding at 2am, you're likely to see more. This extreme example works in just the same way if you start responding to messages during your leisure time too.

Messy clients and complex situations make it even more vital to have very clear boundaries.

Some clients will need you to spell out that you do not accept friend requests on social media, that you don't respond to chit-chat and to shape their behaviour with professional behaviour of your own. Dog trainers are not alone: all professions are suffering from 24-hour availability and the fudging of clearly delineated work times and leisure times. For your own sanity, though, make sure you are strict about your boundaries. In the end, what you are doing is reinforcing respectful and business-like professional behaviour.

30. Keep learning about people and never stop

So many of us continue to develop our professional knowledge and expertise in order to work with dogs. We sign up to training conference after training conference. If we're lucky, someone at that conference will speak for an hour or so over the weekend about how to work with clients. Usually, those sessions are really well attended and get amazing feedback. It's clear that we're all interested in knowing how to get the best out of our clients. Yet there we are, sitting at a conference where most of the material will be about training dogs better, not working with their guardians.

Make it your own SMARTER goal to build on your training about humans. After all, it's at least 50% of the work that we do. In some cases, what our dog training knowledge contributes to the situation is small in comparison to what our human knowledge needs to contribute. Right now, for example, I have a client who engaged with me via social media who has completed her initial intake session. This was followed by my request for a time in the next twenty-four hours for an hour to go through the intake plan. The client then updated me to say that her dog-reactive new rescue has just bitten a person on the street. Despite my demands for more haste and a request to engage by phone or video messaging within the next eight hours, she has now postponed the interview for ten days because of family activities and she wants to go straight into a face-to-face in a public space (during a pandemic, I should add).

In my view, this situation is critical.

The dog is continually being put into situations with which she cannot cope and her guardian is glib about the continued escalation and stalling to start. Not only that, she's willing to put me in harm's way, as well as other members of the public. I wouldn't be the first dog trainer to get bitten by a dog on the first visit because the guardian hadn't taken the dog's behaviour seriously. Instead of putting up walls and washing my hands of this client, telling myself she is clearly not invested enough and convincing myself that her dog - now a serious risk to the public - is her responsibility, it's important for me to run through why she might be doing this. What the client needs to know - and doesn't understand - is that her dog's behaviour is escalating. I have to run through a hypothesis of generosity about why she is stalling. Perhaps she is worried about fees as some people stall until the next pay day. Perhaps she has unaired shadow-side issues and believes I won't understand her dog until I see her in person. Perhaps she has a busy holiday period planned and now is the wrong time. If that's the case, and the dog is likely to come into contact with a large number of people, it's absolutely vital that I express these feelings. Asking for a brief phone call as soon as is convenient to the client might assuage some of those problems and if not, then it's not enough just to wash my hands until or if the client re-engages when things have got worse.

And what happened when I raised this reluctance with the client? She explained she hates the telephone. She is partially deaf. That certainly explains why she was so quick to fill in the written email form and so reluctant to move further unless in person. It wasn't that she was being deliberately evasive or dismissive, just that she was embarrassed of her disability. That wasn't even on my list of potential things I should have been generous about!

Cases like these remind us why I need to keep learning and keep practising about how to work with people. The dog side is easy: managing the environment, a variation on a DS/CC programme around dogs and humans in public, a crash course in body language and defensive handling for the guardian, and a bit of re-education about why flexi-leads and choke chains are a poor combination. Reactive or aggressive dogs in public is practically my bread and butter, and what the client will get will be a variation on materials I have delivered many times over the last few years. Truth be told, bar small adaptations, the majority of my programme for reactive and aggressive dogs hasn't changed very much in five years. Yet I go on course after course to understand this behaviour better.

But what am I doing to help myself progress with the human side of the equation?

Am I dedicating as much (if not more) time to the human side as I am to the dog side?

Am I dedicating as much time to understanding my own responses as I spend understanding the responses of the dogs I work with?

What training courses have I got lined up for professional development in this area? Have I a mentor signed up to help my progress? Are my bookshelves as full of books about working with humans as they are with working with dogs?

If nothing else, this should be a balance. Of course, if you are running agility courses or working with clients to pursue mastery at competition in obedience or protection sports, this will be less important for you. Even so, a good sports coaching course is a valuable asset in any case.

The more you are working with humans in awkward, complicated or critical situations, the more vital it will be to keep learning about humans and to keep your library as full of books about people as it is about dogs. Instead of despairing, realise that you, too, just like your client, are in a situation in which you need help, and work through it in the ways you know so very well already. Learn more, practise more, review more, adapt more. Then, you can sit back and watch as your reputation grows and your business flourishes. After that, you'll need to get better at turning people in other directions, and that in itself is a huge learning curve for many of us as we learn we need to trust our colleagues even more than we do.

Concluding statement

Hopefully, these lessons have helped you work through some simple ways to improve your work with your clients. Whatever your specialism, it's undoubtedly going to be the people that will cause you the biggest headaches and nightmares. Even if you have expertise beyond measure with dogs, there'll be that one client who'll stubbornly refuse to make as much change as you think they should. They'll bring you their messy and disorganised scenarios; they'll fluff the simple stuff; they'll be seething with hostility or unresolved issues that you simply can't begin to get your head around. I'd like to hope that at least some of these lessons will help you reduce the times your clients disengage and they'll help you coach your clients better. Working the human side of your business should be just that little bit easier.

As you end, I hope you now have some understanding of why your human clients are so messy, irrational, difficult, lazy, disengaged, contradictory, surly, stroppy, argumentative or challenging, and why you can be so stubborn, opinionated, touchy, defensive or vulnerable to their barbed comments, slights, slings and arrows.

When we manage the shadow side, even harnessing it to our advantage, we can go miles and make more progress than we could have ever imagined.

Our clients find that one trainer that sorts out their dog once and for all, despite having seen five equally worthy competitors. Their dogs live better lives and we can make more of an impact where it truly matters. How we work with humans also affects our success and profitability, and that helps ward off those niggling doubts that eat away at our self-confidence and self-belief. Maximal client engagement is good for the soul. And, should it all fail, understanding our clients and ourselves better will at least help us cope with the emotional fallout.

Good luck in your journey, and remember: humans are not as challenging as they seem!

Further reading

Ariely, D. 2008. Predictably Irrational: The Hidden Forces that Shape Our Decisions. HarperCollins

Ariely, D. 2012. The (Honest) Truth About Dishonesty. HarperCollins

Block, P. 2003. The Answer To How Is Yes. Berrett-Koehler

Blough, J. A. 2016. To Save A Starfish: A Compassion-Fatigue Workbook for the Animal Welfare Warrior. Deepwater

Bungay-Stanier, M. 2016. The Coaching Habit. Box of Crayons.
Brown, B. 2015. Rising Strong. Vermilion

Cockman, P., Evans, B. and Reynolds, P. 1998 (2nd ed.). Consulting for real people: a client-centred approach for change agents and leaders. New York: McGraw-Hill.

Cooper, J. O., Heron, T and Heward, W. 2007. Applied Behavior Analysis

Duhigg, C. 2012. The Power of Habit. Random House

Egan, G. 2002. The Skilled Helper: A Problem-Management and Opportunity-Development Approach to Helping (7th ed.) Brooks Cole.

Gilbert, P. 2009. The Compassionate Mind: A New Approach to Life's Challenges. Constable.

Pink, D. H. 2010. Drive: The Surprising Truth About What Motivates Us. Canongate.

Sapolsky, R. 2017. Behave: The Biology of Humans at Our Best and Worst. Vintage.

VanFleet, R. 2013. The Human Half of Dog Training: Collaborating with Clients to Get Results. Dogwise.

Whitmore, J. 2017. Coaching for Performance. Nicholas Brealey Publishing.

About me

In a former life, I was not a trustee in a large open-intake animal shelter in France as I have been for almost a decade. I worked in schools having completed a BA in English Literature and Psychology. The 21-year-old me had no idea if she wanted to write or study people back then, either, it seems.

What I really wanted to do was understand why children struggled in schools. That meant two years in the classroom as a minimum before post-grad studies. I cut my teeth on disinterested teenagers in the

North of England, and there, I fell in love. My finest accolade was driving 30 hormonal 16-year-olds through Shakespeare and Byron, Wordsworth and Dickens towards a compulsory qualification that few of them really wanted to take. Most of them came to have a grudging respect for literature, if nothing else.

What I realised (in the first week) is that primary school students are often like cats: none of them want to do the same thing at the same time. Some want to sleep. Some want to eat at really, really inappropriate times. At least three or four will need the toilet right after they just came back in from break time or recreation.

What I realised (in the second week) was that I quite liked teenagers, and by four years in, I was utterly in love with seeing teenagers learn. Teenagers are often like a sled pack of huskies. They're wilful, spend all their time trying to escape if you don't keep their sharp minds busy, you'll spend all your time trying to find ways to engage them, knowing also that all attempts to thwart them will fail, and when you finally get them all pulling in the same direction, it's both joyful and terrifying in equal measures. I don't think there's a finer accomplishment in my life than seeing a bunch of teenagers really get poetry or Shakespeare. So I never did get around to following my early dreams of becoming an educational psychologist.

Some years later, I left the classroom and spent four years as a consultant, where I completed my postgraduate qualifications in organisational change management, despite being told by a former boss that I was not a "people" person. She was wrong. I'm very much a "people" person and I remain as curious about how we function as I was when I was 21. Although I did not fully understand consultancy at the time, this usually involved being pulled into schools by headteachers and used as a weapon to beat their teachers with. And if I thought teaching 30 hormonal 16-year-olds was a white-knuckle ride of sorts, teaching teachers can often remind you why adults are not always more rational than teenagers. I still work in education where I work mainly with students with dyslexia and other learning obstacles. I'm also hugely involved at a national level in the assessment of English and literacy skills in England. Human learning is still a passion of mine. I'm not done with it yet.

Now, through various twists of lifestyle and random acts of fate, I find myself years into a behavioural career with a different species: dogs. I work mainly on aggression cases through vet referral and do a lot of in-shelter support as well as outreach for various rescues and associations in the community. I live with a recalcitrant malinois who reminds me very much of a girl I once taught in a school I'd just moved to. She'd been sent to me for discipline as she'd thrown a hammer at another teacher. She looked at me with scorn and said, 'So you're the new one?' as if she'd made short work of the last. Understanding that her behaviour was rooted in the belief she'd be excluded and could then take the week off to go to a music festival helped me find what really made her tick. She stayed in school, finished her education and is now a wonderful parent to an amazing young lady who gives her just as much trouble as she herself caused. My recalcitrant malinois may never finish her education, but we're past her proverbial hammer-throwing days. I also live with my handsome-as-heck Groenendael cross, who is ever the gentleman. My young firestarter has put paid to my previous habits of borderline animal hoarding, but she is worth it. I think. She reminds me that we're all yearning to be understood and to find the people who make the world safe for us so that we don't have to resort to violence. She reminds me that if I can come to adore a dog who grabbed my ponytail and pulled it for five minutes, as she did the first time I met her, then humans are - on the whole - likely to be a whole lot more docile.

I am still as obsessed with learning about dogs as I am about people. I graduated with an Advanced Diploma in Canine Behaviour (Level 6) and wait each term with anticipation for each Fenzi Dog Sports Academy calendar to be revealed. I have also completed (and loved!) Professor Susan Friedman's Living and Learning with Animals which I think should be an industry fundamental. There are many amazing trainers, behaviour consultants and certified applied animal behaviourists who have influenced and continue to influence my work and I am a proud member of the International Association of Animal Behavior Consultants (Certified Shelter Dog Behavior). I am also a tutor for The DoGenius where I get to geek out about my favourite stuff: behaviour, ethology, psychology, neuroscience, people, dogs.

You can find my blogs at www.woofliketomeet.com where I write about dog training, dog behaviour and supporting rehomed and rescue dogs.

Feedback is always welcome - just make sure it is specific, if you don't mind.